The Curtis-Culligan Story

The Curtis-Culligan Story

From Cyrus to Horace to Joe

by Matthew J. Culligan

CROWN PUBLISHERS, INC., NEW YORK

To Pat Weaver, a COMMUNICATOR,
and my son, Kerry,
who is determined to be one

"It is not the critic who counts, not the man who points out how the strong man stumbled or where the doer of deeds could have done them better. The credit belongs to the man who is actually in the arena; whose face is marred by blood, dust and sweat; who strives valiantly; who errs and comes short again and again; who knows the great enthusiasms, the great devotions, and spends himself in a worthy cause; who, at the best, knows the triumph of high achievement; and who, at the worst, if he fails, at least fails while daring greatly, so that his place shall never be with those cold and timid souls who know neither victory nor defeat."

Theodore Roosevelt

Preface

I am considered to be a controversial figure. This is not by design, though I never ran from controversy if it were a concomitant of what I wanted to accomplish.

The presidency of Curtis Publishing Company was offered to me when, by consensus, the company was ninety days from bankruptcy. Other business leaders, some more qualified, refused the challenge.

The actual board of directors meeting at which I was appointed was marred by disagreement. One director, quite opposed to my nomination, resigned from the board because of it. My battle to save Curtis from bankruptcy and dismemberment was fought in a goldfish bowl. The final battle against character assassination and charges of mismanagement was starkly portrayed in the public press in an unprecedented and still incomprehensible press orgy.

Here is my story of this widely publicized episode in my business career. I invite you, the reader, to sit beside me in the president's chair of one of the world's greatest corporations, and see the view from the top.

Matthew J. Culligan
New York
May, 1969

Prologue

Three years of uncharacteristic indecision ended in mid-December of 1968 with my decision to publish this book. Authors, agents, editors, even lordly publishers came at me in full cry, immediately after I left Curtis in 1965, with interesting offers. One publisher offered me an advance of $35,000 for such a book, but as a friend advised me *not* to write it. There was still, at that time, the hint of scandal hovering over Curtis, the result of the attempted character assassination that went on below the surface of the public controversy.

There were no heroes in the Curtis drama, and few villains. The survival of Curtis was still very much in doubt. The publicity attending the attack on me had diminished advertiser confidence in Curtis, and Curtis magazines lost at least $11 million in advertising revenues in the fall of 1964, as a result of the controversy.

On the very practical side, Curtis owed me about $500,000—two years' salary, amounting to $300,000, and ten years of deferred income, amounting to an additional $200,000. If Curtis failed, I would become one of a long list of creditors, and perhaps get just a fraction of what I was owed, in a Chapter Eleven (voluntary) Bankruptcy.

Some very admirable, honest people did some not-so-admirable and dishonest things under the grinding pressure of the bitter final battle. An exposure of these incidents would have further weakened advertiser confidence in Curtis, and might well have brought on a flood of legal actions on behalf of shareholders against management and the board of directors.

The strongest deterrent was my own distaste for disgruntled losers who used magazines, articles, and books for revenge, or purely dollar gain, doing injury to companies and industries that had supported them and their families well over many years. At forty-seven years of age, I anticipated at least another fifteen years in the communications industry. "Kiss and tell" businessmen are not popular with the Establishment, the solid influential circle of leaders who set the ethical tone for United States business. Any book by me about Curtis, while the controversy raged, would not have been constructive.

I decided to grit my teeth, take my lumps, wait out my enforced sabbatical, get a new job, gain a new success story, make a capital formation, leave the business world, and go into public service. This seemed readily possible. General Ted Clifton, Military Aide to President Kennedy and later to President Johnson, had approached me about the possibility of joining either the State Department or the Central Intelligence Agency.

The matter of a book might never have been reconsidered had I not had my first serious illness in March of 1967. By then I was reemployed, as president of the Mutual Broadcasting System, enjoying life, working veiy hard, on a diet, drinking several quarts of grapefruit juice a day, smoking heavily, traveling to three to five cities a week, punishing myself physically. I took the Mutual job for 10 percent of the stock of the company, mainly because network radio was the only national communications medium in which I could work without violating the noncompetitive clause in my final agreement with Curtis Publishing. Calm on the surface, I was still brooding at times over the treatment I had received in the final days at Curtis. Also, not knowing all the details was somewhat frustrating. At that time, all the elements simply did not add up.

Even my few weekend hours of relaxation at golf were ruined by one of the leaders of the attack on me at Curtis. Jesse Ballew, former publisher of *The Saturday Evening Post,* was also a member of my country club, Apawamis, in Rye, New York. In the middle of a beautiful, sunny day, birds chirping, drives soaring, putts dropping, all's well with the world, I'd see Ballew on another fairway (never in the rough, damn him), and I'd boil. My regular opponent at golf, Ken Bilby of RCA, would immediately try to double all bets, knowing that after I'd taken one look at Ballew, my golf swing would go spastic.

All these forces were working on my insides (my duodenum, to be precise), and one fine day, in the lobby of La Fonda del Sol restaurant (great advertising for a Spanish restaurant), I collapsed and regurgitated a stream of blood. Rushed to Lenox Hill Hospital, I was told I had a bleeding ulcer, the acid had eaten into a vein, and I had lost a third of my blood supply.

The hand of fate was involved in this illness. The attack came at the ideal time of day, in the most convenient place—a few steps from my own office building. Within minutes after I collapsed, my assistant, the faithful "Smoky," and my associate and friend, Jim Fuchs, were at my side. Smoky called the surgeon, who arranged for the hospital. Jim got a wheelchair and two nurses, and cleared a path to the Radio City Medical Center for emergency treatment. A fine doctor there correctly diagnosed the problem, rushed me to the hospital, where, in an intensive care unit, I was filled with drugs, tubes, nostrums, and was on my way to recovery in short order. My doctors—a surgeon and an internist—were skillful and very engaging. The internist particularly spent considerable time with me, once it was decided that surgery was not necessary. As the surgeon put it, with mock regret, "I have had to sheath my knife."

The internist asked me about my life style, my work, my worries. He had many questions about Curtis. His prognosis was encouraging. He felt my ulcer had been brought about by the atypical combination of dieting, excessive intake of grapefruit juice, heavy smoking, a dreadful work schedule, and a delayed reaction to all the grief at Curtis plus the subconscious stress of resentment at the people in and around Curtis who had been responsible for my difficulties there.

According to the internist, my decision to remain silent through the entire battle might have been a very good business decision, but it was the worst possible choice from the standpoint of my health. He recognized that it was too late to do anything about it, but he did suggest I count my blessings, warning me that if I had kept bleeding for another half hour or so, I would have had a heart arrest from a lack of blood for my heart to work on. That shocker was softened, however, by his admiration for my recuperative powers. Remarkably, despite the great loss of blood, I never needed a transfusion. My system replenished my blood supply from its own resources.

The internist had other words of considerable comfort. He said he had never had a patient with an ulcer before fifty who later died of a heart attack, and explained that the same conditions that could lead to an ulcer in a middle-aged man (I winced at that description of myself) would probably have brought on a heart attack in an older one. An ulcer, particularly a bleeding one, was a splendid warning. He told me not to drink for at least a year and to forget about dieting until the ulcer was completely healed.

As for the most serious matter, stress, he advised me to "get the Curtis thing out of your system." When I asked him how to do that, he had no suggestions. Then I told him about the offers to publish a book, and he agreed that it might be the ideal therapy.

Conditions have changed drastically at Curtis, but the issue of its survival is still in doubt. *The Saturday Evening Post* is dead, killed by a combination of absentee owners, excessive bureaucracy, inept managers, flocculent directors, encysted editors, some venal lawyers, predatory corporate raiders, and destructive competitors—though Martin Ackerman came roaring in with ringing assurances that the *Post* would not fold, among other boasts.

A dreadful, new public controversy has broken out among Ackerman, the Curtis-Bok family, the Curtis Council of Unions, and the preferred stockholders.

Three of the principals in the original drama have died. I would not have published this book if they were still alive. They unwittingly contributed to the near-disaster of Curtis during the fifteen years between 1947 and 1962. However, I would not have caused them unhappiness during their declining years.

J. M. Clifford, whom I brought out of near-retirement and made executive vice-president of Curtis, and who later became president by default, has been removed. Serge Semenenko retired from The First National Bank of Boston with his record intact. He is now chairman of the board of Chemway Corporation, of which he is a major stockholder. He honored me by inviting me to serve on his board of directors.

I hope my motives in writing and publishing this book will be considered tolerantly. It is not written in the heat of passion for self-justification and revenge. Moreover, there is one further, more obscure reason for writing it—the awesome staying power of the printed word in the press. There are people in the business world, very important to me, whose only knowledge of Curtis came from press accounts, particularly those in *The New York Times* and *Time.* Many of these influential leaders know me personally, respect me for past accomplishments, but they have a net impression that I *did* mismanage Curtis in some ways because *The New York Times* and *Time* trumpeted the charges of mismanagement and muted the vindication. When the Investigating Committee of Curtis, two senior directors and two lawyers, officially found the mismanagement charges to be without foundation, this fact was fleetingly and incompletely reported in the deep recesses of *The New York Times,* and never reported in *Time.* In fact, one full year after the Investigating Committee dismissed the charges of mismanagement, *Time* printed the statement: "The Culligan-Blair regime was a textbook example of mismanagement."

Thus, a tendency remains to downgrade me as a business executive though according me full honors as a marketing executive. Even today, some of my acquaintances introduce me to their friends and associates with the description, "best marketing man in America," or, as Senator Bill Benton put it, "the best media salesman in America." (He was amused that I disagreed with him and rated Roy Larsen of *Time* as the best.)

Two of the most dramatic events in the history of business and publishing in the last two decades erupted during my time at Curtis. They were so startling that they became public property in the entire English-speaking world. Only I know both stories. They will be told fully in this book.

The first, the ghastly Butts-Bryant libel case, will undoubtedly be hotly debated for years. It became a case of the "landmark" variety in law. The second is the story of the Timmins ore strike, which uncovered copper, zinc, and silver, as well as greed, avarice, and passion of a major order.

Researchers, writers, historians, and other seekers of the truth will be digging into records, newspaper and magazine morgues, reading everything available about Curtis for decades. A true picture cannot possibly be made from the material now available. And some of those willing to be interviewed will undoubtedly try to rewrite the record of their own connections with Curtis during its decline. A few of the principals involved with Curtis have much to account for to their own consciences and perhaps to irate Curtis stockholders.

Mary Curtis Zimbalist, the most attractive person in the entire Curtis situation, is now, I am told, infirm. She is a grand and interesting lady. One of the few material mementos of my Curtis experience is a note from her, slipped under the table to me during the first serious controversy. It said: "Dear Joe, you have friends"—it was signed "Mary." Unfortunately, her words did not include her son, Cary Bok, the part-time Achilles' heel of Curtis.

In this book I seek to answer two questions thoroughly, definitively, and dispassionately. First, what happened to Curtis between 1945 and 1962 that brought it to the brink of bankruptcy? Second, did I save Curtis from dismemberment and bankruptcy—how and at what cost?

Curtis had some special problems that, for a business story, aroused extraordinary public interest and curiosity. However, many of the Curtis problems, both inside and outside the firm, are not uncommon ones in industry and in social, military, and political organizations. The critical difference is that in other such areas these problems are dealt with and resolved circumspectly within board and conference rooms, executives' offices, and corporate lawyers' offices. Curtis became a public spectacle because of the unique compulsion of Clay Blair, one of the leading characters in the drama, and his skillful, cynical use of the press as a weapon, plus the lamentable habit of the press of making headlines out of charges.

I have a suggestion for responsible newspaper and magazine editors and publishers who read this book: Make it a policy to report the results of the investigations of charges in the same location in the publication and in the same amount of space as given to the charges themselves. Such a policy might spare some other businessman the truly agonizing experience of trial by press.

Agony notwithstanding, I do not regret my decision to take .the Curtis assignment.

1

The series of events that eventually led me to the Curtis Publishing Company started with a chance encounter in a little bar on Fifty-second Street in New York City. It was known as Jimmy Ryan's. It featured "New Orleans Gut Bucket" and "Chicago Barrel House" jazz music.

One of the superb drummers of our times, Zutty Singleton, headed up a small group of great musicians. Don Frye played piano during intermissions. On weekends, jam sessions with Pee Wee Russell, Jay C. Higgenbotham, Wild Bill Davison, Sidney Bechet, Red Allen, Wilbur De Paris, and Art Hodes were routine. I stopped in one late afternoon in midsummer of 1945 while still in military uniform—on terminal leave after retirement from the U.S. Army and busily making up for lost time with good food, better drinks, and wonderful girls. I met an older man at the bar who introduced himself as Glover Young. We drank together, talked a great deal, and when we parted he invited me to call him about a job when I was finally out of uniform. I accepted the invitation, landed a job with his help, though not in his company, and became acquainted for the first time with the Curtis Publishing Company—as a competitor.

My newfound friend was in the publishing business, but he admitted that his company, which published small specialty magazines, would limit my opportunities. He generously sent me to see a close friend, Harry Chamberlaine, advertising manager of *Good Housekeeping.* Glover Young was a thoroughly delightful person whose numerous good qualities had gained him countless friends. Our fateful meeting at Ryan's bar set me on a course that now enables me to say, and sincerely, "I've had more fun than anybody."

Very little that happened to me before World War II was significant, it seems to me now, except a childhood tragedy that touched me deeply at the time. When I was nine years old, my best friend, Neal Folsom, and I climbed to the forbidden reservoir in the park at Washington Heights in the upper part of New York's

15

Manhattan one freezing morning. The water was covered with what appeared to be a solid sheet of ice. Neal and I tried to cross the ice. It broke under us, submerging both of us in the deadly cold water. Somehow I got out; Neal didn't. He drowned. I wondered then, later, and occasionally now, how and why I survived. My emergence from this tragedy and similar deliverances from later ones have given me a spooky feeling that either I am the luckiest of the lucky Irish or I have been spared for something down the road, maybe to be hanged.

I attended a very good Catholic school, the All Hallows Institute, near Yankee Stadium. At graduation in 1939, entering college seemed foolish, since the draft threatened. Through family friends I learned of a good opportunity to make a little money, learn something new, and have some fun while awaiting the call to military service. My brother, Ernest, kept me advised. He was aide to General Lewis Hershey, head of the Selective Service Administration. The opportunity for me was to compete for a position at the New York World's Fair. The American-Standard Corporation planned an enormous exhibit there, and needed a team of guides to lecture on equipment in heating, air conditioning, and construction—and glad-hand visitors from all over the United States, Canada and Latin America. The competition was intense, but I was one of the ten chosen from a horde of applicants. We all received a crash course in thermodynamics engineering, vocal presentation, and human relations before being installed in the huge, semi-open exhibit which featured one wall of radiators and pipes!

I made my first meaningful spending money, had a hilarious social life, learned about girls (or thought I had), and for the first time started using my Irish blarney for profit. I also met people by the thousands as a guide at the Fair, took a real interest in many of them, and sensed that I had a talent for persuasion.

When advised that I could get a deferment because my brother and sister were already in the service, I applied for a program called the Volunteer Officer Candidate Program. This plan enabled qualified men who had family deferments to volunteer for service with a chance to gain commissions. I applied, took the necessary tests, was accepted, and arrived at Fort Dix ready, I thought, for anything.

During my first day at Dix I had an experience that shaped my life thereafter. All the recruits—and a sorry mess we were—

were lined up before a grizzled noncommissioned officer. He asked if there were any PMS men in the group. Four men stepped forward. The noncom told us to divide into four groups, each under a PMS, and "police the area"—that is, pick up cigarette butts and any other trash. I asked one of the group, "What the hell is a PMS?" and learned that it meant anyone who had had any previous military service. This qualified the lucky man to escape the more disgusting duties around the area and mess hall.

The next day when we were again lined up, a different noncom called for PMSs. I stepped forward. I was assigned a group of dogfaces to supervise, and so had my first taste of power. For three days I reveled in PMS status, then nearly had a disaster. Instead of being told to "police," the PMSs were told to give their charges close-order drill. My sole experience in drill was as a student marching in the St. Patrick's Day parade. But I was brash, had a loud voice, and somehow blundered through by following the lead of a legitimate PMS. This experience taught me the great importance of front and decisiveness in essentially bureaucratic societies, particularly those that feature uniforms. I avoided many onerous duties and actually advanced rapidly by being bold and authoritative..

I received my commission at Fort Benning, graduating Number Two in my class. Assigned to an infantry camp, out of sheer boredom I volunteered for Ranger training, which I received under Colonel Tiny Hewitt, a rather famous football player.

In May 1942 I was shipped to Europe. My active Army career began and ended with the 1st Infantry Division—terminated by a hand grenade that exploded a foot above and to the right of my face. This happened the morning of December 28, 1944, in the Battle of the Bulge. Twenty-seven pieces penetrated my carcass. Only one hit a very vulnerable spot, my left eye. The eye was removed in a field hospital in Liège, Belgium. I was declared a "high eye" priority, flown to Prestwick in Scotland, then to New York, where I arrived by New Year's Day, 1945. The miracle of flight immediately became apparent to me. I went on to El Paso, Texas, for plastic surgery. Though a remarkable job was done, the lids and tear ducts proved irreparable.

Fortunately, a short-lived law called Public Law 18 was still in force, and I was able to apply for retirement. By that spring, I was back in civilian life in great health and good spirits, considering myself lucky to have escaped the mess with one good eye. My status as a retired U.S. Army officer gave me two-thirds pay for life (tax free), plus all the other benefits available to officers retired after twenty years' service. I could even be buried with full military honors!

The deepest change in me, however, was psychological. Unable to see at all for two days, I resolved never to complain if I came out with one good eye. I did, and I haven't.

While on terminal leave, before seriously seeking a job, I entered Columbia University in the School of General Studies. At that point I was wearing an eye patch (I still do), had a new wardrobe, and was one of the first combat veterans in the school, and so my popularity was assured. Later, as success came my way, I became a favored alumnus. I was greatly honored while at Curtis to be invited to make a commencement address to the graduating class at the School of General Studies.

A comment that impressed me when I returned, and one that had much truth in it, was made by John Forshey, the sales manager of the Royal Typewriter Company, for whom I worked a short time. He expressed no sympathy for me. He said, "As long as they didn't interfere with your chin music, you'll be all right." That was accurate, for a great deal of what success I've had was the result of my innate Irish facility for conversation. I can recall many turning points in my career at which my sales ability gave me the edge.

I gained a reputation in New York for great wit when I said, in all innocence, "If I had to lose one of all the things of which I have two, I'm glad it was an eye."

Such was the background I brought to Harry Chamberlaine in our first meeting, set up by Glover Young. Chamberlaine hired me on the spot as a space salesman on *Good Housekeeping* at the lordly salary of $100 a week. *Ladies' Home Journal, Good Housekeeping*'s principal competitor, was then being edited by Bruce and Beatrice Gould, the acknowledged editorial leaders in the field. The *Journal* was published by Curtis, *Good Housekeeping* by Hearst.

I was an instant success as a *Good Housekeeping* space salesman because I arrived at just the time, 1945-1946, when the government was relaxing the stringent wartime restrictions on paper for advertising. Every call got an order. I learned how to enjoy my expense account, the "in" crowd, the clothes, and the association with a friendly organization that reflected the fine qualities of its leader. I still see Harry Chamberlaine often, and never fail to feel warmly grateful to him for taking a chance on a rather flamboyant, uninformed, inexperienced, one-eyed Irishman. His kindnesses did not end there. He helped me all along the way, sponsored me for the Apawamis Country Club to which I have belonged ever since, and remained my friend.

Before I became hopelessly spoiled by my initial success, I had the good fortune to be exposed to another extraordinary man, John Kingsley Herbert. Jack Herbert had been with *Good Housekeeping* before the war, and was made Eastern sales manager when he returned from the Marine Corps. He became my boss.

Jack, as the saying went, "could really make the spit fly"—he was an excellent vocal salesman. He helped me in many ways, but in one particular he did me a great service. He was the first to tell me that I was not nearly as good as I thought, and that most of my success was a break of timing. He also warned me to get the New Yorkese out of my accent, and the vernacular out of my oral presentation. In addition to what he did for me at *Good Housekeeping,* Jack was to be helpful to me later on.

Two other managers at *Good Housekeeping* and Hearst were to be significant in my development: Luke McCarthy, the marketing director of Hearst, and Ed Timmerman, known as Timmie, then the sales promotion head of *Good Housekeeping.* Luke McCarthy taught me how to drink martinis, along with imparting much knowledge about the then-new business science of marketing. Timmie opened up the vista of sales promotion to me while taking me on tours of New York night life, generally with one or more New York City detectives. Timmie was a police buff, never as happy as when he could enter a bar, sidle up to some customer, flash a bogus badge, and submit the victim to a frisk. He ceased this pastime when he found a victim who was armed. Luckily, the man was a small-time hoodlum, more frightened by the confrontation than Timmie.

Finally, at Hearst there was Dick Berlin, the president, a great salesman himself. He had come to the attention of Mr. Hearst through a fantastic sale of scores of color pages to a single advertiser—easily the biggest order Hearst had ever had up to that time. Tough, smart, and partial to salesmen, Dick heard about me from

Jack Herbert, asked to meet me, and thereafter took a strong interest in my progress. Although I left Hearst in 1949 because I felt that my progress was too slow, and Dick Berlin doesn't admire people who leave his company, we have remained warm friends over the years. He taught me one great lesson. He could concentrate more force against a single objective than any man I had met so far. He also had great patience, and intense loyalty to those who served him or Hearst well.

I went from Hearst to Ziff-Davis Publishing Company, mainly because I was offered a vice-presidency and management role. Even when I made this change, however, I, like everyone else at that time, was feeling the first fever from the bite of the television bug, and I resolved to get into television as soon as I could. I probably remembered my experience at Fort Dix, and wanted to step away from the mob of space salesmen.

Sam Davis was the business brain of the company. Bill Ziff undoubtedly was a prophet. He literally predicted the United States' problems with the Soviet Union over Berlin. He was also a brilliant advance thinker on air power. When the first atom bomb was dropped, he walked into the office of the science fiction department and said: "Gentlemen, science has finally caught up with your imagination."

At Ziff-Davis I got a taste of the fun and excitement of the "comeback" in business. My first assignment was *Modern Bride* magazine, a bad second in a two-book field. *The Bride's Magazine* was the miles-ahead leader. The losses on *Modern Bride* had reached the scale where a decision to liquidate was imminent. It took me less than nine months to turn the magazine around, get the advertising income to support new editorial investments, and gradually chip away at the leadership position of *Bride's Magazine.* We did pass it in advertising pages, although not in editorial excellence. The feat was achieved mainly with aggressive salesmanship and merchandising. I made one momentous sale to the Associated Merchandising Corporation, a central buying office for about thirty powerful department stores. A wonderful girl named Irene Bender of AMC helped me engineer this sale, which amounted to around twenty pages in a single issue of *Modern Bride.*

A neat little presentation trick was developed at this time; that is, I built such a strong merchandising support program for each ad that I was able to boast, "Even if we forgot to print your ad, you'd get results because of the promotion and merchandising!"

The management experience and the credit for the revitalization of *Modern Bride* were the beginning of the building of my reputation as a comeback artist. My chance to get into broadcasting came with the move of Jack Herbert, my former boss at *Good Housekeeping,* from Hearst to NBC. I went to him and literally begged for a job. He had none for me at the time and suggested that I get experience in motion pictures or some other field allied to broadcasting.

I took his advice and joined up with John Sutherland, who had a motion picture production company bearing his name. Sutherland produced excellent films, some for television. I learned the lingo, made numerous contacts as head of the East Coast Division, and kept nagging Herbert about a job at NBC until the break came.

It came in the form of another near-disaster, the "Today Show" on NBC-TV. This great concept of Pat Weaver's—he was then president of NBC—had fallen on evil days despite a beginning attended by unprecedented advance ballyhoo. The first few shows were dreadful—talent and guests completely overwhelmed by equipment and technique. The press, still jealous of television, rapped it savagely. Dave Garroway finally settled the show down, new producers were hired, and the show did improve. However, the initial momentum had been lost. The first brave advertisers retreated and, worst of all, the ratings had not improved. The earlier boast that "Today"would change the viewing and living habits of America was a source of great embarrassment to its author. Losing at the rate of $1.5 million a year, "Today" seemed fated for the graveyard.

Jack Herbert hired me as a sales specialist on "Today," with the thinly veiled admonition to make it pay or liquidate it. He hired me directly, without first getting the approval of George Frey, sales manager. Frey was furious and would not permit me in the Sales Department for several months. He also refused to put me on the regular Sales Department payroll. With the help of Dick Pinkham and Mort Werner, I found a tiny office in the RKO Building on Sixth Avenue, in the space used temporarily by the "Today Show" production unit.

Since I was not independently wealthy at twenty-six, I

needed money for living expenses. When I told Jack Herbert about the payroll problem, he had me put on the Talent payroll. I lined up every week with writers, producers, actors, and female performers, who handed in vouchers and got paid in cash. After five delirious months on the Talent payroll, I left for the regular payroll with great regret.

My exile at the RKO Building was no hardship—quite the reverse. While there, I met and developed enduring friendships with some delightful people. Gerald Green,who was to write some best sellers—*His Majesty O'Keefe, The Last Angry Man, The Lotus Eaters*—was a particular favorite. He was earthy, Jewish, natural, talented. He could panic me at any time with his one-man imitation of the Hearst newsreel, doing the voices and sound effects, plus an unbelievable range of facial expressions and gestures.

It was there I met my first secretary, Ethel B. Smoak. She has stayed with me through all my ups at NBC, Interpublic, and Curtis—and my downs.

There were serious moments during my NBC-TV tenure too—illness, death, mental breakdown, successful romances that led to marriage, failures that led to heartache, one to suicide. It was a microcosm of life in the world of creative people.

At what appeared to be the eleventh hour for the still experimental "Today Show," two developments reversed the trend and started it on its way to a decade and a half of success. One was my doing—I began using Dave Garroway in my sales presentations to advertising agencies. He was superb at telling them about "Today" with style and charm.

The other development was the result of a "way-out" idea of my two friends and colleagues in charge of programming, Dick Pinkham and Mort Werner. They discovered J. Fred Muggs, the charming chimpanzee. Muggs got the publicity and editorial promotion going again, the press responded, and almost immediately "Today" got a rating increase. My sales blitz with Dave Garroway also caught on. Within a year "Today" was virtually sold out, grossing $10 million annually; and Pinkham, Werner, and I were on our way up at NBC.

Pat Weaver was, by all measurements of which I am capable, a superior gentleman. He was strong enough always to be himself, and as himself he was most engaging. Tall, slim, urbane, witty, very good-looking in a highly individual way (ears like jug handles), Pat was the coolest man around even before the term was invented. A towering figure compared to his contemporaries, he exploded on the advertising world early as advertising director of the American Tobacco Company. He also built the Radio and Television Department of the Young & Rubicam advertising agency, one of the best agencies in the country.

Some of the knotheads who made fortunes out of broadcasting were light-years behind Pat Weaver in intellect, creative ability, leadership, and responsibility. Had Pat survived the corporate political contests at NBC, I believe all broadcasting would be vastly better now. Many aspects of United States society would also be better because broadcasting under Pat would have been much more responsible.

Pat was great for morale at NBC, particularly in any time of crisis, which was every other hour. One meeting in particular will never leave my memory. He held a weekly managers' meeting at which each department head would report, ask for decisions, gripe, whatever. On this particular morning, everything seemed to have gone wrong. We all sat around gloomily awaiting Pat. He arrived, greeted everyone breezily, and opened the meeting, giving the floor to the head of Sales, George Frey, who started the round robin, which was a litany of failure. Each manager reported more funereally than the last, until a pall hung heavily over the room. But Pat listened attentively, permitting each manager to finish. When they were through, he stood up and, covering the room with one all-embracing smile, said, "Gentlemen, it would appear that our problems are insoluble." Then he walked out of the boardroom!

Feeling as silly as we deserved to feel, we all went back to work and henceforth were more sanguine about our problems.

Pat attracted extraordinary people to his enterprises—bright, articulate, loyal, highly motivated. Typical in style, even abler than most, was Richard A. R. Pinkham.

He handled all his assignments with distinction. He was a Weaver man, however, and his days at NBC were numbered when Pat left.

Part of the tragedy of the early days of television was the injustice of the "revolving door" employment policies of the networks. If a man was on the wrong team, and his leader fell, he was washed out with the tide, either directly or indirectly. Dick Pinkham was not fired, but he was treated shabbily by others at NBC who happened to be in the ascendancy. He resigned and joined the Ted Bates advertising agency, becoming one of the agency men who, with Oliver Treyz, made a network out of ABC. Pinkham rose steadily to a top position at the Bates agency.

Mort Werner was a one-of-a-kind operator who got more individual things done a day than most people accomplish in a week. He had been brought to NBC by Weaver when Pat, to his credit, put his brother, Doodles Weaver, on NBC television. Doodles was a charming nonconformist.

When the "Doodles Weaver Show" was scheduled for NBC, Pat arranged for Mort Werner to come East from Los Angeles as producer. The show was a failure. Pat then reassigned Werner to the "Today Show," where he made huge contributions, not the least of which was to get the New York Police Department to permit "Today" to do extraordinary things. Huge animals were paraded before the studio windows; tons of snow were dumped on the street to provide a background for an air-conditioning commercial. Rugs and carpets were left out on the street in foul weather to prove they were colorfast; new models of automobiles were driven by during announcement time. Mort had his own wonderful way of getting these things done, some of which were highly original.

A nonconformist, Mort despised rote and routine. When Booz, Allen & Hamilton, a management consultant firm, was brought in to organize NBC as a business, they came to each of us for job descriptions. When they got to Mort, he was scornful. "Job description," he snarled. "How the hell can I give you a job description! The other day a goddamned dog we had on the show crapped in the middle of the studio during a commercial. The camera was due to cover the area within a half minute. The producer wouldn't clean it up, the stagehands all looked the other way. Who had to rush out and clean it up? I did. Do you want that in your goddamned job description?"

Mort was very good with talent and creative people generally—he was an excellent piano player himself and had once been a vocal coach. With the casting of the first "Tonight Show," Mort carved a niche for himself. In addition to Steve Allen, selected by Pat Weaver, the first show opened with Steve Lawrence, Andy Williams, and Eydie Gorme. Allen was already established but the other three, given their first TV exposure, all became stars in a relatively short time.

What beautiful days they were under the warm, tolerant, understanding leadership of Pat Weaver! He had no equal in conceptualization in broadcasting. Now, even a decade later, no one remotely like him has developed.

Dave Garroway was a dream to work with, although his schedule was brutally tough on him. J. Fred Muggs, aging and cantankerous, eventually became a hair shirt to Dave, even bit him one day. Broadcasting and communications, generally, owe Dave Garroway much. I was and still am deeply fond of him. He is now making a comeback, and all who know his abilities and personal qualities are in his rooting section.

There were at NBC, during my years there, numerous breakthroughs—"Peter Pan," "The Show of Shows," the teaming of Chet Huntley and David Brinkley (an idea of Davidson Taylor's). Taylor never got proper credit for that gamble, which started the breakup of the CBS News domination of network television.

We all worked like madmen, had no schedule of hours or working days. There were bone-wearying problems and mind-crushing pressures, but with Pat in command there was always the break that came from his humor. I dwell on him and the years at NBC because my exposure to Pat led to my developing a constructive attitude about business and realizing that grimness was not to be equated with efficiency. Even Mort Werner, with his passion for getting things done, could be warm and funny.

Mort went into a decline at NBC after Weaver left. He resigned to join Kaiser Industries, then went on to Young & Rubicam. Later, he returned to NBC in a key programming position, and now Mort is head of the Programming Department. We three advanced together in our separate ways—Pinkham in Programming, Werner in Program Operations, and I in Marketing. To a degree we were in competition, but we kept the competition honorable. As a result, we remain friends to this day.

I spent eight years at NBC, had seven jobs and seven raises. After reaching the top of the marketing force in television, I accepted the job as head of NBC Radio from Robert Sarnoff, son of General David Sarnoff, who was then president of NBC. We agreed that I would be returned to television after I had done my job in radio. As head of NBC Radio, I threw out the soap operas, live bands, and personality shows; I launched "NBC News-on-the-Hour," personally created "Emphasis," and revitalized "Monitor."

The good memories of my NBC radio days are rekindled many times a week because of the now permanently entrenched "NBC News-on-the-Hour," a breakthrough concept pioneered by NBC. It was a daring and dangerous idea, since it invaded, for the first time, the prized time of 7:00 and 8:00 A.M., theretofore the exclusive province of the local stations. We also had to dislodge the famous "Three-Star Extra" show of the Sun Oil Company, a fixture in the early evening all across the United States.

We needed an audio symbol for "NBC News-on-the-Hour." Many suggestions were made, all the way from the hypoed traditional sounds of a newsroom to ear-splitting electronic bleeps and fizzles. I discarded them for a variety of reasons. The final audio identification I invented myself. After hearing one of our editors talk about "The Heart of the News," I had the sound engineers get me a magnified heartbeat—kathump, kathump, kathump. Over this I asked them to superimpose a high-pitched electronic whine. The effect was magical—ear-catching, arresting, even a bit menacing. Robert Lewis Shayon, a perceptive and at times acid writer, later described it in an article in the *Saturday Review,* as a cross between *Rebecca of Sunnybrook Farm* and *The Hound of the Baskervilles.* Anyplace I go in the United States even now, fifteen years later, I am certain to hear the identification of "NBC News-on-the-Hour." I must admit to some ego gratification when I do.

Programming improvements were not enough, however, for network radio (in the words of Pat Weaver) had become "invisible wallpaper." We badly needed some attention-getting promotion. I spent a great deal of time mining for a single breakthrough idea. One came, finally, when I was doing some reading about ESP and psychic phenomena. Technically, it is called "closure" and "demand impulse." I coined the term "imagery transfer," and it clicked. NBC Radio sold television advertisers millions of dollars' worth of ten- and fifteen-second commercials that would cause a "transference of imagery" because of the subconscious drive for "closure." I took the most direct line for selling this concept, selecting some very good full-page, four-color advertisements from *Life,* where a page then sold for about $32,000. One, in particular, was a smash hit—an advertisement for the Cunard

White Star Line. Its beautiful photographs depicted the line aflutter with pennants, alive with gay, happy people in the midst of bon voyage parties. The ad headline said simply, "Getting there is half the fun—go Cunard!"

I got my best sound man to dig up evocative sound effects from dockside—river traffic, tugs' whistles, orchestra music, in the background hundreds of animated voices, and, just at the end, the foghorn, the purser's gong, and his voice saying, "All visitors ashore." One more big blast of the foghorn; then the most archly elegant British-accented voice said, "Getting there is half the fun—go Cunard!

Magically, the entire printed ad would be recovered from just this brief, rapid commercial. This, plus other samples, made selling NBC easy.

"Imagery transfer" survives. It is today the basis for the majority of radio commercials. I now boast about it—I am damned proud of it, as I am of the still potent "NBC News-on-the-Hour" and "Emphasis."

After I had moved into the radio job and turned it around, Bob Kintner, former president of ABC Television, was hired as color coordinator, a thin disguise for the coming czar of NBC. Within six months he was running the Programming Department, then the network. Tom McAvity, an outstanding programming executive, was bypassed—very unfairly, I thought—and Kintner became president. Kintner and I were incompatible.

I resigned soon after, and accepted an offer from Marion Harper to join Interpublic, Inc., a world network of communications companies. Harper had been after me for seven years with various offers. This time he let me construct my own job. He said good-naturedly at the time, "I gave Culligan four raises even before he came to work for me."

My three years at Interpublic were exciting. I remain convinced, after working closely with Marion Harper, that he has a kind of genius. I had thought that Interpublic would be a semi-permanent home for me, that I would stay there long enough to become independent, then move into some public service activity. Interpublic was the brainchild of Harper, a creation to serve the global needs of the supercorporations of the future.

In June of 1962 I was forty-two years of age, married, and had four children. In business I was respected, a key executive of

Interpublic, fond of and highly appreciative of my associates: Harper; Bob Healy, whom I nicknamed "Mr. Clear" because of his forthrightness and clarity of speech; Paul Foley, a delightful, irreverent Irishman who was marvelously creative. I had a huge salary for that time, a large stock position, and the prospect of world travel, which was a driving ambition. My RCA options were becoming extremely valuable, giving me the first "capital gains" formation of my business life.

Then came the offer from Curtis.

Why did I listen to it? I guess because I was not satisfied that I had tested myself enough. I had reached next to the top rung at NBC, as one of the five executive vice-presidents. Even if I had the ability for the presidency of NBC, it was foreclosed to me because there was another forty-two-year-old there named Robert Sarnoff, a more-than-worthy contestant for the presidency. I came into the advertising agency field near the top, but there again, the top position was not available. Marion Harper, only a few years older than I, filled that job better than I could have hoped to do for many years.

I had never been Number One—I wanted a try at it.

2

Considered quite a good public speaker, I received many invitations from schools and colleges. Emerson College in Boston, a special communications college, invited me to speak. In April 1962 I flew there to make an address.

In the line at the airline counter was Gardner (Mike) Cowles, founder of Cowles Communications. He was also the president and editor of *Look.* Cowles and I had known each other for about ten years. He buttonholed me and said he had meant to call me about something important having to do with Curtis. He had been asked to find out if I'd be interested in joining Curtis in a major executive capacity.

It came as no surprise to me that Mike Cowles of *Look* would be trying to help Curtis, whose *Saturday Evening Post* was a competitor. All the top people in publishing were constructive. They knew, as did all top agency people, that the failure of Curtis would hurt all magazines. I had to tread lightly with Cowles, for he was a close friend of Marion Harper, and his major effort, *Look,* was an Interpublic client. I said I'd let him know.

I admired Mike Cowles and knew some of his top aides quite well. Donald Perkins, his chief sales executive, had offered me several jobs at *Look.* They always seemed to come at the wrong time—I'd just received either a promotion or a raise where I was. Mike Cowles impressed me because he was waging a hard, successful battle against the giant *Life* and riding over the ailing *Saturday Evening Post* en route.

I told Marion Harper about the encounter as soon as possible, and got a surprising reaction from him—he asked if I'd be interested. I replied that I hadn't given such a change any serious thought because I had a contract with Interpublic and was quite happy with my activities. Harper said, "If you really want the job, I'll help you get it."

Harper's remark set me to thinking seriously about Curtis. But before I had time to get back to Mike Cowles, *The Gallagher Report,* a Madison Avenue newsletter owned and edited by Barney Gallagher, started plugging me for the job as president of Curtis.

Gallagher had most efficient and aggressive methods of extracting information about organizations that were having difficulties. Such companies fire people or have them quit, often in anger, frustration, or rage, and these displaced persons need reemployment. Gallagher would offer free help to them, either interviewing them himself or having Jack Mann, his unusual long-time assistant do so. It takes no imagination to guess the kind of response Gallagher would get when he said: "Well, to help you we have to know why you left [in this case] Curtis." What could the job applicant do—say it was his own fault, that he was stupid, disloyal, or dishonest? Naturally the answer was generally an outpouring of invective, insult, and criticism against Curtis, the person's superiors, and his associates.

Gallagher always had enough facts, or half-truths, to sound authoritative, and he assured himself of being right once in a while by predicting everything that could possibly happen. For example, on November 11, 1964, *The Gallagher Report* predicted:

CBS INC. TO MAKE HEADLINES SHORTLY. 1) President Frank Stanton expected to resign. CBS-TV president Jim Aubrey to take Stanton's job. V-p & assistant president Frank Shakespeare to replace Aubrey. 2) On the spot: v-p programs New York Mike Dann, v-p program development Hollywood Hunt Stromberg. 3) Merger with McGraw-Hill still under discussion. 4) CBS ownership of Yankees will doom baseball's favored anti-trust tax status. Senator Stuart Symington (D. Mo.) and Senator James Pearson (R. Kan.) plan Congressional investigation.

This prediction was 180 degrees wrong. Dr. Frank Stanton did not resign. James Aubrey did not take Stanton's job; in fact, James Aubrey left CBS within a few weeks of the "prediction."

Gallagher had a good source at Curtis, and there appears little doubt that he was useful to the corporate raiders gathering to move in on it. For example, this report appeared in March 1962:

March 19, 1962.

THE CURTIS CRISIS. Major changes in Curtis Publishing management and ownership expected shortly. Financier Peter G. Treves has been quietly buying Curtis stock for more than a year. Has acquired sizable holdings.

Not helpful to advertising sales or Curtis morale problems, this one also came in March 1962:

GRIM TALE. MacNeal has nothing but bad news for stock-holders. Operating losses were $11.2 million at close of third quarter. Editorial changes and promotion push for *Saturday Evening Post* fell flat. *SEP* begins twelfth year of steady de-cline with a year-to-date loss of 20.4% in advertising pages. (In same period, *Life* is down only 3.9%; *Look* up 5.7%.) First quarter figures show *Ladies' Home Journal* off 21.3%. Competing *McCall's* is down 15.6%. By stressing circulation quality over quantity *Good Housekeeping* is up 4.4%. In first three months *GH* carried 77 pages more advertising than *LHJ*, 21 pages more than *McCall's*. Final blow: resignation of *LHJ* editors, Bruce and Beatrice Gould.

The first mention of my name was made in May 1962. It read:

CURTIS SWEEPSTAKES. Doubleday out in front to get control of Curtis. Change in ownership calls for shift in top management. Possible candidates to replace president Bob MacNeal: Jerry Hardy of Time Inc., Joe Culligan of Inter-public.

The whole episode with Gallagher is tinged with the same kind of irony that has marked so much of my business experience. I hardly knew Gallagher. In fact, I generally avoided people like him—the snoopers and the peepers. I met him in the spring of 1962 at the request of Marion Harper, who didn't want to see him but was getting concerned about Gallagher's many criticisms. These had to do with overorganization, confusion, and so on at Inter-public. Marion felt that his refusal to meet Gallagher for luncheon was the reason for the digs, a kind of "Meet me soon or this will get a lot worse."

I did what Marion asked, met Gallagher for lunch several times, gave him some stuff for his report, and—sure enough— for a while he stopped picking on Harper.

Gallagher dressed foppishly, looked waxen, as though freshly embalmed. His favorite luncheon spot was the Canadian Club, and lunchtime was his favorite hunting hour. His power base was *The*

Gallagher Report. He also had an income base, his magazine-distributing companies. He has been able, somehow, to be retained and paid by some of the same companies about which he purported to report objectively.

A story Gallagher proudly tells about his success as a child member of a magazine subscription gang indicates his character. Some of the kids learned to walk like cripples, some to stammer or act dumb or deaf. Gallagher used falsehood and charm. His opening line to a new prospect, he told me, was "Do you know that fat lady down the street with the little white poodle dog? That's my mother." He would then go into his pitch for magazine subscriptions. Gallagher never forgot the lessons of his childhood.

Many inexperienced people support Gallagher by their subscriptions, considering him fearless because he attacks the top people in the advertising and media business. His *Report* is also read by out-of-town advertising and media people starving for information about the business in which they occupy a distant bleacher seat. Much of *The Gallagher Report's* income comes from the kind of subscriber who loves to see his superiors get their lumps from any source.

However, Gallagher *did* put my name forward as a prospect for the presidency of Curtis. Some Curtis directors were avid readers of the *Report* because, at that time, Gallagher was ripping the hide off the poor, defenseless president of Curtis, Bob MacNeal. My name got to Milton Gould, then a director of Curtis, and, instead of getting in touch with me directly, he asked Gallagher to arrange a date with me for him. I agreed to a meeting after I was assured that Gould could speak for the power at Curtis. Gallagher's dreary and to me unattractive office was the site of my first encounter with Milton Gould. It was a fascinating occasion.

Gould was then about fifty-six, five feet ten or so, chunky in build. He looked like what he was—a tough, smart, articulate lawyer from the streets of New York. He was colorful, grim, and compelling, and he used pretty strong language when it was useful. He knew an astonishing amount about the publishing and advertising businesses when we met. In just a few months as a new director, he had learned more than any other Curtis director had gathered in fifteen years.

Gould had gained his directorship by boldness and some guile. He had done legal work for Peter Treves, mentioned in *The Gallagher Report* as the broker who first scented trouble and opportunity at Curtis. When Treves and his group had assembled enough common stock to be impressive, he sent Gould to Curtis to demand seats on the Curtis board. MacNeal capitulated and so Gould became a director.

Gould was (and is) an exceptional man and an extremely good lawyer. He was also a good judge of people—at least of their motivations. Having apparently gathered a voluminous dossier on me and my successes, he sized me up in a hurry. I marveled at his ability to shift, halfway through a sentence, when I reacted nega-tively. He would go 180 degrees in the other direction. I told him about my contract with Interpublic, and admitted my severe reser-vations about *The Saturday Evening Post*, which, at the time, I did not think was salvageable—that was the consensus.

One experience at Interpublic had given me a negative feeling about Curtis. Marion Harper asked me to join a group of Inter-public executives to hear a presentation on Curtis from a team headed by Bob MacNeal.

In the Curtis group, introduced by MacNeal as vice-president, Editorial, was Clay Blair, Jr., who later played a major role in my career at Curtis. Blair was a Hollywood casting director's idea of a crusading editor in appearance and manner—hulking, rumpled-looking, with brows in a straight line across his eyes and the bridge of his nose. He gave the impression he was holding back tre-mendous energy, like a method actor, which—to a degree—he was.

In addition, MacNeal's entourage included Peter Schruth, the amiable ad manager of the *Post* at that time, and Ed Von Tress, the overall sales manager of Curtis. MacNeal looked unwell—his manner was distracted and he seemed almost anxious to get the meeting over with.

Blair was introduced also as the managing editor of the *Post*. He spoke quite convincingly about the magazine and its future, and made a reasonably good impression, but this was more than offset by the infectious hopelessness exuded by MacNeal. The *Post* presentation was designed to convince McCann-Erickson of the magazine's stability and promise, and of the performance of the great Curtis Publishing Company. It did the reverse. My colleagues and I left the meeting almost sighing "Requiescat in pace" over Curtis.

When I made it plain at my meeting with Gould that I was by no means sure Curtis could be saved, he turned my view around and used it on me: "Look, it is the very fact that will make it possible for me to sell you Curtis *at your terms.*" He practically assured me I could make at least a million dollars, even if Curtis failed.

He asked about my family, my finances, what I most wanted out of life, implanting in my mind the idea that this was a once-in-a-lifetime opportunity for me to write my own ticket because of the desperation of the Curtis board. He took me up to the Mount, "showed me the riches of the world," and I went for it hook, line, sinker, pole, and creel. Peter Treves, whom Gould represented, joined the meeting toward the end, saying almost nothing while he stood by a window listening and looking thoughtful.

They both all but said the job was mine if the Executive Committee could be sold. Then we parted. I tried to get back to work, but found it very difficult.

Now I was in an unusual role for me—that of the buyer; Milton Gould was the salesman. I did what all the buyers I knew did: launched a research program to put me in a better position to make a decision. I started this research immediately by asking Gould to tell me all he could about the Executive Committee— when and how it was formed, who was on it, what its authority and function were.

As he gave me the story, I began to see what an extraordinary quid pro quo artist and strategist I was dealing with. When Gould forced the board to fire MacNeal without having an immediate replacement in the wings, it became necessary to vest the power of the chief executive officer somewhere. Gould suggested the technique standard in industrial organizations, the formation of an executive committee of the board of directors. But he knew the Philadelphians were bruised and sulking because he had forced them to fire one of their own sons, and so to placate them, and also to put himself into the pivotal position, he refused to be a member of the committee and recommended only the old Philadelphia directors. However, he had himself named legal counsel to the committee. By this device, he became the true power at Curtis through May, June, and early July of 1962.

Gould admitted that there was also a side benefit: All the official members of the committee got for their service was a hundred-dollar fee per meeting; as legal counsel, he was in a position to charge his regular fee per hour.

Gould kept the Executive Committee in an uproar by reporting real or potential developments in New York. While I continued my research and evaluation of Curtis, he conditioned the Executive Committee on my behalf, warning them that I was just about the final hope and softening them up for my salary demands and fringe benefits. He actually assigned one of his associates to write my contract for me!

It was Gould who arranged my first meeting with the Curtis Executive Committee, an amazing quartet:

Albert Linton, chairman of the Provident Mutual Insurance Company.

Walter Franklin, former president of the Pennsylvania Railroad

Walter Fuller, former president of Curtis Publishing Company

Moreau D. Brown, head, Philadelphia office, of Brown Bros. Harriman & Co.

We met them at the stately offices of Brown Bros. Harriman in Philadelphia. This venerable private bank was managed by Moreau D. Brown, a descendant of the founder.

I was startled by the appearance of the group. Walter Franklin, who seemed ten feet tall, was about six feet eight—bald, bony, gangling, self-deprecatory. He wore a hat with a huge brim, which settled rather far down on his ears. Fond of describing himself as "an antique," he had a friendly manner and a twinkle in his direct, deep-set eyes. However, he knew nothing about advertising or publishing. He kept insisting that maybe the answer to the *Post* was to go back to a nickel cover price. Since he was rather hard of hearing, that may have been the reason my explanations why the *Post* could not go back to a nickel were unavailing.

Walter Fuller, though also bald and bony, was tiny by contrast. He had been president of Curtis during its prosperous days, and even though he was responsible for the sins of omission and commission that started Curtis on the road to ruin, he constantly deluged me with the financial figures from the years when he ran the company. Bob MacNeal was his protégé. Fuller had recommended him for the presidency when he himself retired. This had to be the worst decision of the post-World War II period. Well over eighty years old, Walter Fuller was very nervous and couldn't sit still. He would squirm and fidget and pick at his fingers, rub his hands, drum on tables, get up, walk around, look constantly about. He too was hard of hearing, and would drift off during meetings. He had the disconcerting habit of suddenly coming back to full awareness and making some comment related to a previous subject. The other directors would studiously overlook his remark. I suspect that Fuller used to tune out unwanted conversations by dialing down his hearing aid.

Albert Linton, chairman of the Executive Committee, was an outstanding executive in the insurance world. A Quaker, bird-watcher, skier, and amateur anthropologist, he was a splendid-looking man, lean and tanned, seventy-four years old when we met. He had a quick smile and friendly manner. Next to Bob MacNeal, however, Linton did more to harm Curtis than any other man alive, though his intentions were flawless. He truly believed he was the watchdog for the public stockholders. Albert Linton knew little about Curtis' publishing, advertising, circulation, or any other vital part of the business. In fifteen years as a director, he left no record of ever having asked MacNeal the right questions about essential matters. But he was the senior director in point of service; he was the strongest personality, and he was the closest to the Curtis family.

Moreau D. Brown was the best director and businessman of the group by far. Younger, with a very good financial background, he served on other boards and was not hidebound. Brown, nicknamed Doc, was also very tall—probably about six feet three. An enthusiastic yachtsman, he had the rangy, angular looks of a crewman, which, I believe, he had been. He also was baldish and bony, but very arresting-looking with deep-set humorous eyes. He wore metal-framed glasses that looked like a family heirloom. Brown was to become my favorite among the Philadelphians. He was a good director, an excellent chairman of the later-to-be-formed Finance Committee, as well as a complete gentleman with rock-ribbed integrity, a banker's conservatism, and a great sense of propriety. This last quality had prevented him from being an aggressive director before I joined Curtis. Doc Brown deferred to Albert Linton, who was from an older generation. This was a great pity, for Brown and Curtis Barkes, an "outside" director from Chicago, probably could have stemmed the tide of grief at Curtis, or at least rung the alarm a year earlier.

Our confrontation at Brown Bros. Harriman was hilarious. To Franklin, Fuller, and Linton, I must have seemed to be something from another planet. I was thirty years younger than Linton, thirty-five years younger than Fuller, and thirty-eight years younger than Franklin. After the introduction and an extremely effective presentation of my credentials for the job by Gould, we exchanged pleasantries, a few questions were asked, and then we lapsed into an uncomfortable silence.

Finally, Doc Brown asked some meaningful questions, one of which he later told me was pivotal. He knew that a major cause of the problem at Curtis was MacNeal's inability to delegate authority. He also knew that I was a specialist in marketing, with virtually no experience in papermaking, manufacturing, printing, high-level finance, and other pertinent fields. He asked how I expected to run a business as complicated as Curtis. I gave him a simple answer: "Delegation, the use of specialists, decentralization."

Linton, terrified that Curtis would collapse while he was in effect "running the show," was immediately willing to take Gould's recommendation. Franklin seemed agreeable to anything. Walter Fuller was doubtful, however, and refused to commit himself at that meeting, but he made a move that assured me the job. Despite his errors of omission as president of Curtis, Fuller did get around in business circles. He knew many advertising agency heads and top executives in consumer goods industries. Directly or through others, he approached a number of these executives with a list of people who were being considered for the presidency. The usual technique, described to me by Marvin Pierce, former publisher of *McCall's*, was to say something like, "Look down this list until you see the name of someone you think can save Curtis; stop there."

A sufficiently large number stopped at my name to satisfy Walter Fuller. A disquieting number commented, along the line, that it probably was too late to save the *Post* and Curtis, but if anyone *could* Culligan could.

After that first meeting with the Executive Committee, I went back to New York full of doubt about the future, not because of the known difficulties of Curtis, but because of my impression of Linton, Franklin, and Fuller. Gould had already greatly impressed me, and Doc Brown seemed to me a tower of strength. But I was concerned by the fear that Linton, Fuller, and Franklin, since they had been selected for the Executive Committee, might be the best of the Curtis board—a numbing prospect. If they were the best. . . . Then something happened that threw me into a tailspin.

Using a technique known as the "trial balloon," someone leaked my name to the press as the front-runner for the Curtis job. This had a bad effect on several Interpublic clients on whose problems I was working. A number of Marion Harper's detractors criticized him for not being able to hold people in his company. Now, without prior warning, I was suddenly all over the newspapers as practically in the presidency of Curtis, and Marion had not informed my clients of the possibility. Unwittingly, I had put him in a most awkward position. I told him I would tear up my contract, under the circumstances, so that he would not have to make explanations to bankers and clients. Almost immediately a coolness developed between me and some of the people who worked under my direction. There were about five days of backing and filling during which I did not have the Curtis job, and was rapidly losing control of my situation at Interpublic.

Gould, however, evaluated the press reaction to the trial balloon, considered it favorable, and pressured the Philadelphia directors to make a decision in my favor. They did, and authorized him, along with Albert Linton, to negotiate with me. I rushed to my friend and lawyer, William Coogan, of Sullivan, Donovan, Hanrahan, McGovern & Lane, and had him prepare me for the contract negotiations.

During the first week of July 1962, Gould, Linton, and I met for dinner at the Racquet Club in Philadelphia, and during the course of the meal arrived at an agreement giving me a salary of $120,000 a year, options on 50,000 shares of Curtis common stock, and designation as president and chief executive officer with practically unlimited powers. The deal was subject to the vote of the full board of directors.

From April through July of 1962, Milton Gould was in almost complete control of the Curtis situation, and he reveled in the role. He had his tents in three different camps, each with a different objective.

Since it will be impossible for readers to "tell the players without a scorecard," I must now introduce some people and organizations involved with Gould:

Loeb, Rhoades & Co., a leading investment banking house, which was also a brokerage house with multiple seats on the stock exchanges.

John Loeb, Sr., a personal friend of mine, the head of Loeb,

Rhoades, father of John, Jr., and two daughters. One daughter, Ann, was married to Edgar Bronfman, president of Seagram's. The Edgar Bronfmans were friends and neighbors of mine in Westchester. Edgar's father, Sam Bronfman, the distiller, was the builder of this great commercial empire.

Treves & Company, a small brokerage house, which was loosely affiliated with Loeb, Rhoades. It "cleared" many of its stock transactions through Loeb, Rhoades.

Peter Treves, head of Treves & Company, was a corporate entrepreneur with a group of associates who spent most of their time scenting stupidity, laziness, incompetence, or dishonesty in publicly held corporations.

Marvin Kantor, a partner of Treves at the time Treves detected the "odor of decay" at Curtis. Kantor left Treves and joined J. R. Williston & Company when his patron, Alpheus Beane, moved in and took over the reins. (The firm then became known as J. R. Williston & Beane.)

Robert MacLean Stewart, an oilman who had been a banker. He was close to Loeb, Rhoades. He was asked by Loeb, Rhoades to go on the Curtis board when Milton Gould made his moves.

The three camps in which Gould had pitched his tents were the Treves–Loeb, Rhoades group, which owned Curtis common stock and was ready to do whatever was necessary to protect its value; the Philadelphia directors, who were being advised by Gould, they being temporarily in a state of shock over a $19-million loss projected for 1962; and mine, the tiny third camp, the newcomers.

Gould manipulated me for a while, acting like the kindly old uncle, winning my confidence to a degree by telling me of certain events relating to Treves, Kantor, and others.

One item, particularly, Gould calculated would put him in a good light. As he described it, there was a strategy meeting of the Treves group during which he reported on his meetings with me and his progress with the Philadelphia directors. He told them about my record at NBC, the saving of the "Today Show," the launching of the "Tonight Show," my plan that revitalized NBC Radio and all network radio, my origination of "NBC News-on-the-Hour," "Emphasis," and so on. When he had finished, one of the group said, "Great. Culligan sounds like the perfect patsy. Let's get him to pump some life into Curtis; then we'll rape hell out of it." I felt a slight shiver. I couldn't get Gould to tell me who had made the remark.

Marvin Kantor was once described by *The New York Times* as a "mystery man of finance." I was astonished by this sophomoric label in the Financial Section of the *Times*—there really are no "mystery men of finance" in the United States. The rules of the game, both codified and unwritten, just don't permit it. One cannot be employed by a fine old brokerage firm like J. R. Williston & Beane and be a "mystery man." A man cannot be on the board of a public company and be a "mystery man." The reporter was just phrasemaking in writing his story as he did.

There was really nothing mysterious about Marvin Kantor. He was born, raised, and educated in New York. He worked in a series of sales and promotional-type jobs, veered toward finance and administration, and became good at both. For a time he was a partner of Peter Treves, a broker whose main claim to fame and protective coloration came from being loosely affiliated with Loeb, Rhoades, a truly fine investment banking house led by the elegant, urbane, brilliant John Loeb, Sr. With John Loeb in the top echelon, were such splendid investment bankers as Cliff Michel and Gene Woodfin. In the younger generation, maturing rapidly, was John Loeb, Jr. Treves maximized his tenuous connection with Loeb, Rhoades like an experienced name-dropper.

I heard about Kantor from Gould and Treves; then, by weird coincidence, from my father-in-law, Joseph A. Dernberger, who had been managing partner of J. R. Williston. He had announced his retirement after fifty-three years with the firm, and was "breaking in" Marvin Kantor as supervisor of the "back room"—in effect, the chief administrator of the firm. This was a very unlucky break for me. I had, over a score of years, come to respect, admire, and hold a deep affection for my father-in-law. He was the soul of integrity, a modest, conservative, effective manager who loved his firm in a manner alien to later generations. He liked Kantor, told me he was exceptionally bright, hard-nosed, and disciplined. He felt that the administrative function would be in excellent hands under him. My father-in-law thought we should meet; I thought so too.

My father-in-law asked me to join Kantor and him at lunch, and we met in a very good though modest restaurant in the financial district. My father-in-law disdained the "fancy clubs" that he considered outrageously expensive. I thought Kantor unusual-looking. He was small and olive-colored, with hooded black eyes, and he dressed both conservatively and well. Kantor was almost oddly calm, his eye-blink rate far less than average, which *can* mean inner tranquillity. That is what I judged it to be, at any rate.

Kantor was a good listener; also a good preparer. He spoke quite sincerely, it seemed to me, about *my* background, *my* record of comebacks, *my* great success at an early age. Coming at a time when I was periodically wondering about my sanity in taking the Curtis job, his words and almost reverential attitude were welcome and disarming. "Disarming" was the operative word for Marvin Kantor.

I checked his relationship with Gould. Kantor didn't seem overly impressed by him. I got the feeling that he thought of Gould as someone *he* employed.

Gould and I met twice and exchanged about half a dozen telephone calls while awaiting word from the Executive Committee. He talked effectively about "his fiduciary responsibility." His great objective in life, he told me privately, was to become a judge and his association with Curtis, particularly if the company was salvaged, could advance his cause.

I am the primary witness to testify that Milton Gould did contribute mightily to the saving of Curtis in the spring and summer of 1962. Without him, the Executive Committee would have vacillated about the selection of a president, and if Curtis had remained without a president for just one more month, I firmly believe it would have been in bankruptcy by the fall of 1962. Ten thousand jobs would have been lost and thousands of shareholders would have suffered irreparable loss.

All that remained at this point was for the Executive Committee to make the recommendation to the Curtis board naming me president. This move was put on the agenda for the July 9 meeting. I was asked to stand by in Philadelphia, but not in sight of the press or of Curtis employees. I was told to go to the Public Ledger Building across the street from Curtis, to the office of Walter Fuller (at that time he was running an employment agency for retired senior executives). I waited there for several anxious hours, not knowing there was a serious conflict on the board about my appointment, but concerned over the lengthening delay.

One of the directors, Richard C. Bond, president of Wana-maker's in Philadelphia, had been a schoolmate of Robert Kintner, president of NBC, the final reason for my resignation from NBC. Bond had called Kintner when he heard I was being considered for the Curtis presidency, and Kintner damned me with faint praise, cooling Bond's ardor completely—if he had any. But the resolution naming me president was finally offered. The acting board chairman, Albert Linton, asked all in favor to say "Aye." All but Bond said "Aye."* "Opposed," said Linton. None was opposed. The motion was carried. Linton requested the secretary of the board, Robert Gibbon, MacNeal's heir apparent, to "please ask Mr. Culligan to join us."

The telephone rar.g in Walter Fuller's office, his secretary picked up the receiver, then called me to the phone. The cool impersonal voice of Gibbon said, "Would you please come to the ninth floor? I will meet you there."

Suddenly enveloped in an Alice-in-Wonderland ambiance, I walked dazedly to the elevators of the Public Ledger Building, baroque and very old, through that marble lobby, across the street, up the sweeping stairs fronting the Curtis Building, between the towering columns, into the lobby of the Curtis Building. I scarcely noticed the lobby details as I got into the elevator and asked for the ninth floor. When I stepped off, the corporate secretary greeted me with "This way, please," and led me to the anteroom of the Curtis boardroom. Two magnificent, elaborately carved doors guarded the sanctum sanctorum. Gibbon opened them, stepped aside, and said, "Please go in, Mr. President."

I stepped into the cavernous, dimly lit, paneled boardroom. The twelve directors stood. Each extended his hand as I moved around the table. As I shook each hand, its owner said, "Welcome, Mr. President."

Albert Linton bade me sit at his right. I did. He continued as chairman of the meeting as I sat quietly at his side, studying the directors, most of whom I was seeing for the first time. Linton's long description of my background gave me time to settle down and look around. First I glanced at Bob MacNeal, who seemed to have shrunk since our previous meeting. He huddled in the massive boardroom chair, saying not a word and looking dreadfully ill. I

*Bond soon resigned as a director.

studied each director carefully and tried to imagine what lay behind his appearance.

Several times I asked myself, "What the hell are you doing here?" I knew I was in over my head running a company with the ninth biggest paper operation in the world, the biggest magazine distribution company in the world, loaded with the biggest headaches in the world, by consensus ninety days from oblivion. I recalled that John Burns, former head of RCA, who had also been senior partner of Booz, Allen & Hamilton and was one of the finest business intellects in the country, had turned down the job because he doubted that Curtis could be preserved as a major magazine publisher.

Some of my own friends had thought I was addled to take the job—one of them accused me of having a career "death wish." Even Marion Harper, who released me from my contract to accept the job, had said, "Win, lose, or draw, it will be the greatest experience of your life." Hardly a ringing endorsement of my decision! Such thoughts and opinions raced through my mind as the meeting wore on. Finally, Linton made a welcoming speech. I gave a brief acknowledgment, appearing, it was later reported, quite composed and confident.

So there I was on July 9, 1962, president and chief executive officer of Curtis. For better or worse, the Curtis empire, magazines, paper company, distributing company, 10,000 people, 30,000 stockholders, were in the hands of a relatively young marketing-communications specialist not qualified in all ways to run a sprawling, complicated, woefully mismanaged company that, though rich in tradition, was in desperate financial trouble.

There was no joy or elation at this point. What little pleasure there was dissolved when I sought out Bob MacNeal. I asked him into a private anteroom, shook his hand, and told him I had had nothing to do with his removal; that I considered the timing and method of his removal "unconscionable," and I wished him luck. MacNeal looked at me with great sadness and weariness, tears welling in his eyes. He said only, "Don't worry about me. Worry about my company." He shook my hand, then turned and walked dejectedly out of the room. I walked out in some dejection too. I was driven back to New York in a Carey limousine, alone, pensive.

The MacNeal episode weighed heavily on my spirit. He had been president for about fourteen years. No one questioned his loyalty, dedication, or administrative competence. Curtis had been profitable for most of his tenure, but the Curtis directors—friends, neighbors, members of the same church and social clubs—had fired him suddenly while he was traveling in Europe on Curtis business.

I asked myself, "What kind of people are these Philadelphia directors?" They did not even have a replacement standing by when they fired MacNeal. He could have been ordered back to Philadelphia and properly prepared for the numbing, debilitating shock of being kicked out of a company he had served for thirty years. But the Philadelphia directors capitulated. Apparently they feared most, in their world, public censure and loss of face. I now see, in sad retrospect, that something goes out of any man or group of men when he or they buckle. The Curtis directors "lost their nerve." Their later repetition of this pattern became inevitable.

3

The morning of July 10, 1962, I entered the Curtis Building at Sixth and Walnut streets to take over and run the quarter-of-a-billion-dollar company. I was somber, oppressed by the memory of the MacNeal meeting, full of doubts about where to start.

There were dozens of Curtis employees in the lobby, awaiting the new president. The lobby is spectacularly beautiful, with an enormous Maxfield Parrish mosaic mural covering a whole wall. I took in the scene quickly, noted in passing a marble bust of Benjamin Franklin. My gaze went by, then snapped back with what must have been an audible double take. Some beautiful nut—I never learned who—had put a black patch over the right eye of Ben Franklin. As I broke up completely and laughed aloud, I could feel the tension in the lobby dissolve. Everyone laughed. I raced into the knots of waiting people, introducing myself, pumping hands.

On the way to the elevator I passed a rack containing all the Curtis magazines—and realized with a mild shock that I had been so preoccupied with the *Post* I had almost forgotten Curtis also published the *Ladies' Home Journal, American Home, Jack and Jill,* and the highly prestigious *Holiday.*

The Ben Franklin bust in the lobby was no surprise. From childhood I had known that Franklin was intimately associated with *The Saturday Evening Post.* His picture was on the masthead, and was featured on the cover once a year, but the connection was much more than geographic or sentimental.

History does not indicate that Ben Franklin lost many battles in his earlier days. A story persists, however, that his first idea for a magazine of his own was "pirated" in what may have been one of the first examples of industrial espionage. His brainchild appeared, published by a competitor in 1728, under the title *The Universal Instructor in All Arts and Sciences.*

Franklin, aged twenty-three, gained possession of the publication and sometime later renamed it *The Pennsylvania Gazette.* This was the genesis of *The Saturday Evening Post.* It changed

45

format, ownership, and philosophy often, but like the four wheels on passenger vehicles, it survived because it was a basically superior idea. The permanent name, *The Saturday Evening Post*, was adopted in 1821.

Cyrus Curtis did not reach Philadelphia until 1876, and he did not acquire the *Post* until 1897, but on his way to Philadelphia and the *Post* acquisition, he had lived and accomplished quite a bit. Where did this amazing little man come from? What made him tick? I'll try to explain.

It may come as a surprise to most adults in business, publishing, and advertising that Cyrus Hermann Kotzchmar Curtis, the now bigger-than-life founder of the Curtis Publishing Company, was primarily a *salesman*. He acquired other attributes along the way from Portland, Maine, to Independence Square in Philadelphia, one of which probably stemmed from a creative nature. Curtis was born in 1850. His father and mother had a passion for music, and their modest frame house was a lively, noisy one. The priceless quality that supplemented the salesmanship of Cyrus Curtis was appreciation and understanding of the creative person and process.

He developed into a hard-nosed, pragmatic businessman, and a most demanding one, but he realized innately that the essence of mass communication was creative freedom. Editors blossomed under his leadership. The various "publics" to whom he appealed editorially responded to his editors. It was then that his superior selling ability paid its greatest dividends.

Cyrus Curtis was the first publisher in America to see the true relationship between advertising and editorial in public information media. He conceived the simple cycle, which, like trousers, proved not only permanent for men but increasingly popular with women, despite the difference in construction. What counted first and foremost was the editorial content of the publication. If that was good, the publication would be bought and read. If the publication was bought and read, it would be a good place for messages about products. If advertisers paid enough for their messages, there would be money left over after expenses to hire more and better editors, increase editorial services, show more pictures and color. Out of this instinctive belief in the duality of editorial and advertising came his conviction that advertising should be as honest as editorial material.

Curtis championed, alone at first, honest and fair dealing in advertising in the United States. He started this personal crusade in the 1890s, decades before it was accepted as a responsibility by the majority of businessmen. It took the Spanish-American War to bring to the United States the pure food and drug laws—but only after more Americans died of food poisoning than of enemy bullets. Additionally and independently, fair dealing in advertising was forced on the United States business community by this slight, bearded, intense little man whose equal has not been seen since. It was a towering achievement with the most profound effects.

Advertising, in most of the world, was largely unknown in the late nineteenth century. Where it existed, mostly in Europe and the British Isles, it was somewhat disreputable. In this country it carried much the same stigma as in England before Cyrus Curtis forced its improvement, gave it stature, even a kind of professionalism. National magazines in the United States burgeoned geometrically, rather than arithmetically, after Curtis set the pattern. He later put American advertising agencies on a sound economic basis by taking the lead in recognizing the bona fide advertising agency as the true representative of the client.

Curtis was not a simple man. How can anyone explain the seeming inconsistency in a man who was the product of a hard, canny, Puritan, conservative Yankee background, but who also had the nerve of a Mississippi riverboat gambler at times? He "tossed the dice" for hundreds of thousands of dollars when such sums were equivalent to millions in today's dollars. Some of his million-dollar investments were equivalent to ten million in current terms. His father, Cyrus Libby Curtis, had been only moderately successful in business—he worked for a retailer in Portland. Young Cyrus sold newspapers in his first commercial venture. He worked for the circulation department of the *Portland Press,* handling a newspaper delivery route. This chore took more than just ambition and industry. Only great stamina and iron discipline could have driven the pint-sized youngster out into the bone-chilling wind of those Maine winters in below-zero temperatures. He switched his alliance to the Portland *Argus* around the time of the assassination of Abraham Lincoln.

Walter Fuller, who remembered Cyrus Curtis well, believed that his first publishing venture was organized in 1865 while he was still in school. He issued his first newspaper, *The Young America,* on April 5 of that year. The format: book notices, fiction, and riddles. It sold for two cents per copy. The weekly printshop bill was around five dollars, so he couldn't make a profit because of costs. He supported the paper out of the earnings from his delivery route temporarily, determined to find a way out of the price bind caused by the printing bill.

The solution came with Cyrus' first capital investment—the sum of two dollars. For this amount he bought a handpress, liberated himself from the printshop cost, and converted *The Young America* into a profitable operation. Curtis never forgot this lesson. He followed the pattern of direct ownership to the ultimate. At his peak, he owned everything in the magazine field, from trees to distribution. It is clear that this indomitable man was to be overcome only by forces largely beyond his control.

Walter Fuller recounts a story about Curtis' first experiences with a delinquent advertiser. He was so enraged when Curtis demanded his money in person that he knocked him down a flight of stairs. Curtis went back; this time he did get paid, but the payment was followed by a second kick down the same stairs.

The great Portland fire of 1866 drove the Curtis family out of its home and young Curtis out of the publishing business for a time. He followed his father into retailing and became a salesman in a dry goods store, working at that dull, prosaic job until he was almost twenty. Then he left Portland for Boston with a better job offer in hand, and was on his own in 1869. Though he continued to sell dry goods, he started moonlighting as an advertising salesman. It was not publishing, but much more to his taste. His record as a part-time salesman was impressive enough to win him a full-time job with the *Traveller's Guide,* a newspaper. His days of selling ended when he and a partner launched their own magazine, which they called *The People's Ledger.* E. B. Thornton, his partner, promised to put up the money and supervise the editorial content. Curtis was to handle operations and sales.

The Boston of the 1890s was an ideal setting for Curtis. The community was literate, culturally inclined, and bustling economically. All sides of his personality were exercised and developed. Eventually he worked on all three Boston papers: *The Traveller's Guide, The Boston Times,* and the *Boston Independent.* It is difficult to know to what degree Curtis' rocklike integrity was innate as opposed to acquired. Advertising in those days was a chancy business. Perhaps he learned by example, both good and bad. In any case, he was decades ahead of his time in responsibility to the public.

I wondered, as I researched Cyrus Curtis, where his dramatic sense came from. The biggest single event in his life, up to that point, took place in 1872. It was the World Peace Jubilee. More musicians and artists assembled in Boston than had ever met in one place before, certainly in United States history, possibly in world history. Over 20,000 participants gathered in a series of extravaganzas that must have left Cyrus Curtis gasping and may have started his interest in the bigness and drama he favored in later years.

Thornton neither put up the promised $20,000 nor did he edit the magazine. Curtis found himself doing everything on a shoestring, and his habit of making a virtue of necessity surfaced again. He sold his printer on himself and his magazine. He built up a circulation of 30,000, paying the printer what he could, when he could.

Again fire destroyed everything. This time it was the terrible Boston fire of 1872. Curtis lost *everything*—records, possessions, manuscripts, artwork, all on one bitter Sunday. He found a new office on Monday and started producing the next issue of *The People's Ledger.*

If two major fires could not stop Curtis, and fierce economic problems failed to slow him down, one could assume that he feared nothing—not even marriage. He had no money, and a struggling new enterprise just barely surviving. Undaunted, he courted, won, and married Louisa Knapp, a lively, intelligent career girl—unusual for that day. They were married in the spring of 1875.

A bit over one year later, Curtis, then just twenty-five, took the most dramatic step of his life. The Curtis family numbered three by that time, a daughter having arrived—whom I was to meet almost eighty years later in Philadelphia—Mary Louise Curtis, who became Mrs. Edward Bok, then Mary Curtis Zimbalist. *The People's Ledger* had survived a move from Boston to New York, and now it had to survive a transplant to Philadelphia. It did survive, but not as a Curtis enterprise. Curtis has become such a legendary figure that later generations considered him almost omnipotent and invulnerable. He wasn't. He made mistakes, he occasionally dared too much, he moved around too much to suit the "play-it-safe, play-it-small" contemporaries who snickered at his failure. He could not make the magazine a success; costs outran income, even in reasonable Philadelphia.

Selden Brothers of Philadelphia acquired *The People's Ledger* from Curtis in 1878, and Curtis returned to selling. He landed a good-paying job selling space for *The Philadelphia Press*, and could support his wife and daughter and start dreaming again.

As my research continued, I was struck by some of the following coincidences with my own life. I certainly was not following exactly in his footsteps. We were from totally different backgrounds, though we both did come from modest circumstances and grow up in lively, noisy homes. We both started earning money very early in life. We both were sales oriented and both worked in retailing. And we both were advertising salesmen at around twenty-eight years of age. But his defeats came early in his business life. I had none until I was forty-eight years old. We both "moved around" to gain our objectives and were criticized for it.

Among other differences between us, Cyrus Curtis had a well-to-do brother-in-law who advanced him $2,000. With this sum, Curtis launched *The Tribune and Farmer.* He attracted Thomas Meehan, an outstanding agricultural editor, from *The Philadelphia Press.* This was the true beginning of the Curtis Publishing Company. *The Atlantic, Harper's Weekly,* and *The Century* dominated the magazine field when *The Tribune and Farmer* thrust itself into the fringe of the limelight.

With the exception of a few top-level magazines, the field was dreary at that time. There were no circulation or advertising standards. Failures were frequent, unpaid printing bills abounded. Printers ended up owning magazines in default. Magazine publishing at the turn of the century bore little relationship to the glamorous, prosperous, influential giant it has become.

Some gigantic enterprises of the twentieth century had modest beginnings in the nineteenth. For example, *The Ladies' Home Journal* began as a brief section of *The Tribune and Farmer.* Curtis named it "Women At Home." It was his own idea, and he wrote the first few columns himself. Nowhere could I find out why he did this—why he thought it necessary. He lost his job to his wife when she chided him about the misdirection of his efforts. He turned "Women At Home" over to Louisa Knapp Curtis.

"Women At Home" became a full page, then a unit distributed with *The Tribune and Farmer.* It was then that a name change took place. The inspiration for the name came from Curtis during a conversation with the composing room chief. Curtis suggested calling it what it was—*A Ladies' Journal.* The engraver added the word "Home."

The riverboat-gambler aspect of Cyrus Curtis emerged again in 1883 during a period of stress with his partner. *The Tribune and Farmer* was senior, safe, and profitable; *The Ladies' Home Journal* promising but speculative. In the breakup he chose the riskier path. Cyrus Curtis was predictable in one way—whenever he got into serious financial trouble he *sold* his way out of it. When big rewards were possible, he welcomed big risks.

His daughter, Mary Louise, seems to have exerted a certain influence on Curtis Publishing while still a youngster, since Mrs. Curtis felt it necessary to retire as editor of the *Journal* to raise her. Forced to find a new editor, Curtis located and hired Edward Bok.

Bok was a successful editor of *The Journal.* He had to be, for in 1889 and 1890 Curtis made two risky changes, which were opposed by almost all his associates. He raised the *Journal* subscription price dramatically, and when that did not ruin the *Journal,* he took another step that seemed suicidal—banning from the pages of the magazine all proprietary medicine advertising. It was a shocking decision, far ahead of its time in terms of business responsibility.

The ban on financial advertising followed. In both instances Curtis acted to protect the readers of his magazines against harmful or at least ineffective medicines and fly-by-night schemes that bilked the public shamelessly. His next dictum was different and quixotic. He banned cosmetic advertising because *he* did not approve of powder and rouge.

Incredibly for that time, the *Ladies' Home Journal* circulation hit over 500,000 copies monthly in 1900. Five years later, circulation zoomed to the magic million mark.

From 1905 through the end of the 1950s the *Ladies' Home Journal* was the Victoria of the women's magazine field. *Woman's*

Home Companion came, had a period of success, then collapsed and disappeared. *Good Housekeeping,* with a great inbuilt gimmick—the Good Housekeeping Guaranty Seal—plugged along, its major emphasis being on service, and became the most profitable for somewhat mechanical reasons. The *Ladies' Home Journal, Woman's Home Companion,* and *McCall's* all published 680-line-page magazines. The *Good Housekeeping* page was 429 lines in size. It used about 25 percent less paper and 25 percent less ink, and saved on postage (until the law changed).

In about 1880, basic changes in the United States spurred the conversion of local magazines to national forces. Transportation and marketing commenced their maturation as *national* forces rather than local and regional ones. Magazines *could* be sent across the United States, and advertisers *wanted* their messages to travel where the people were. It was a great marriage, transportation and marketing; and, to a degree, national magazines were its first fruits. The government, aware of the political possibilities, lowered postal rates and speeded the process.

The *Journal* succeeded in all respects, mainly financially, and by 1897 Curtis had the once-in-a-lifetime opportunity to expand at a reasonable cost. In that year, in what turned out to be a brilliant move, he bought *The Saturday Evening Post* for a thousand dollars—just one thousand dollars for what, in time, became the most influential single publication in the Western Hemisphere, perhaps in the world! Authors and illustrators were "made" by an appearance in the *Post.* The knowledge of new products and services swept the country within months, instead of the years it had taken for them to penetrate the awareness of consumers across the United States in earlier days.

Cyrus Curtis was president of Curtis Publishing Company from 1883 to 1922. He died, eleven years after retirement, at age eighty-three, on June 7, 1933.

Editor Edward Bok gave the *Ladies' Home Journal* maximum thrust by breaking old strictures surrounding the intimacies of life, courtship, mating, childbirth, and interpersonal relationships. He was daring in the extreme for his time.

George Horace Lorimer performed this function for the *Post.* Curtis hired him in 1898 though he had no previous experience with Lorimer and only very superficial knowledge of him. Still, after one meeting described as "a two-hour conference," he hired

Lorimer as editor pro tem while he himself went abroad to recruit Arthur Sherburne Hardy, then a United States diplomat, as editor of the *Post.* Hardy had established a fine reputation as editor of *Cosmopolitan* magazine. Curtis failed to get Hardy and stayed in Europe longer than expected. Lorimer officially became editor when he received a cable from Cyrus, still in Europe, ordering him: "Put your name on the masthead."

Curtis was now satisfied with the editor he had, but the editor was not satisfied with the magazine. Curtis gave Lorimer a completely free hand, and Lorimer used his authority with great skill, judgment, and taste. He was contemptuous of anything of questionable taste. He became committed to the proposition that the reader of the *Post* must get more of worthwhile written product than was available in any other place. Lorimer filled the *Post* with the works of Owen Wister, Frank Norris, Joel Chandler Harris, Alexander Woollcott, William Winter, Luther Burbank. He gave women their first mass market for literary output, employed the talents of Madame Schumann-Heink and Mesdames Jeritza, Calvé, and Nordica—towering figures in the music and operatic worlds. Other famous women whose writings Lorimer used were Mary Roberts Rinehart, Cora Harris, and Edith Wharton.

Walter Fuller, former president of Curtis, in a speech about the company, quoted Irvin S. Cobb, who commented on the success of the *Post*:

> The uncanny soundness of its literary judgment is demonstrated firstly by the fact that more people on this planet read the magazine and like it more than any other magazine; and, secondly, by the fact that it buys nearly everything I write.

Horace Lorimer used great fiction as his lever to success as an editor. He opened up a new area of opportunity by popularizing the competitive enterprise hero—the business leader. But it was great fiction by the world's greatest writers that became the hallmark of the *Post.* Fiction, articles, and of course artwork.

Lorimer seems to have made a major mistake, one of omission. Either he was disdainful of the pictorial approach espoused by *Life,* or he simply did not care to research the changing pattern of reading in the United States. He appears not to have anticipated the effect of television as well, as did all Curtis management. He certainly did not anticipate its effect on *reading*. *Life* apparently did, and produced a magazine that could be looked at quickly and pleasurably.

Life also pulled a razzle-dazzle trick that doomed the *Post* to erosion of its advertising support. The promoters of *Life,* its sales force, and the outstanding advertising agency, Young & Rubicam, developed and exploited "pass along" circulation, in contrast to primary circulation—that is, total audience rather than total circulation. They employed good researchers to find out how many people, on the average, handled or scanned each issue. Then they multiplied the circulation figure by the number of people who were exposed to each issue. That became the total audience of *Life.*

The *Post* was trapped in a unique struggle. As a text magazine, it was, of course, held longer by the purchaser, and therefore there was much less time to pass it along before the new issue came out a week later. *Life's* sale of this "pass along" idea must be acknowledged as an outstanding feat.

George Horace Lorimer resigned January 1, 1937, and turned the *Post* over to Wesley W. Stout. On March 16, 1942, Ben Hibbs was named editor. The *Post* lost its undisputed position as circulation leader in the field—*Life* became Number One, first in circulation, then inevitably in advertising.

Look, even when a poor product editorially, was wonderfully well promoted. Ultimately, its editorial quality caught up with its advance promotion, and today it is a first-class magazine that in some issues surpasses *Life.*

Robert Sherrod, journalist-author, who was editor of the *Post* when I arrived at Curtis in July 1962, knew Ben Hibbs better than anyone else at Curtis. I talked to Sherrod at length about his career at Curtis, his relationship with Hibbs and Hibbs's successor, Robert Fuoss.

Ben Hibbs had hired Bob Sherrod in early 1952 to cover the Far East. Sherrod lived in Japan until the fall of 1954. He performed very well and was rewarded by appointment as managing editor of the *Post,* reporting to Robert Fuoss, who moved up to a new post, executive editor. The pressure on editors, in a world getting more troubled and complicated, was steadily increasing. In a big editorial operation, an editor is a purchasing agent, logistics expert, first sergeant, administrator, marriage counselor, father image, arbitrator. He concerns himself also with art, copy, layout, scheduling, proofreading, libel, and manufacturing. A trio—Hibbs, Fuoss, and Sherrod—spread the load somewhat, but Sherrod made it plain to me that Hibbs saw and approved all important decisions.

Sherrod genuinely loved Ben Hibbs—his own words show it:

> Ben Hibbs was a great editor in the context of his earlier times. He is also warm, generous, and impeccably honest with every human being he deals with. The *Post* was a reflection of its editor, as every magazine must be if it achieves success.

By mid-1961, however, Hibbs was tired. He started advising Robert MacNeal and his close associates that he wanted to retire, setting the end of 1961 as the time for his amiable transition. That transition should have been uneventful, for Robert Fuoss was a seasoned veteran of nineteen years' experience, and behind him, showing huge potential, was Sherrod. Fuoss, Sherrod, and most of the *Post* editors were enraged by the grossly unfair press charges that Hibbs was fired.

Ben Hibbs made the *Post* more successful, more profitable, than when he took it over from Lorimer. He did it by producing a balanced magazine that contained, in a typical issue, eight articles, two serials, and four short stories. This "formula" was obviously right for the days before television, the automobile, longer vacations, paperbacks, and the specialty magazines made their inroads on the reading time of the typical *Post* reader.

The team of Fuoss and Sherrod took over around January 1, 1962. Here is Sherrod's personal appraisal of the *Post* from an editorial viewpoint:

> The quality of the paper, which our critics described in their milder moments, as "blotting paper." Whenever the subject was mentioned, the answer invariably came back, "too expensive to change." Meantime, *Life* and *Look* continually brightened their product.
>
> The shortage of top-notch personnel, which was directly related to the location of our editorial offices in Philadelphia. In Lorimer's day the *Post* could buy fiction from the world's greatest writers and publish it from Philadelphia with a staff of nine editors. Alas, by the 1950s competition was forcing

magazines increasingly into staff-written products. And it was impossible to lure the best magazine staffers to Philadelphia without making them managing editor and paying them high salaries.

It fell to Bob Sherrod to make what, for him, was a brutally tough decision. Though his personal courage was king-sized, he was a "softie" about other people, but he had to make the decision to move the *Post* editorial department from Philadelphia to New York. He has never gotten credit for this courageous change.

Five years earlier, Sherrod had had a fateful visit from a young editor who had worked for him at *Life*. It was Clay Blair, Jr., still young despite having been with *Life* for ten years. Blair asked Sherrod for a job on the *Post*. Sherrod later described this decision:

> Blair had been my assistant when he was about twenty-five years old, circa 1950. I knew him as energetic, enthusiastic, and resourceful—the very type I thought we needed on the *Post*. As I recall, my first wife introduced Clay Blair to the girl he was to marry. I classed him as my friend, despite the sixteen years age differential.
>
> The *Post* had no job open. But a couple of months later we had an unexpected opening in the number two slot in the Washington office, and I received Ben Hibbs's permission to hire Blair. He became one of the most prolific contributors to the *Post*, specializing in articles about the military, especially submarines, and in skin diving, which was his hobby.

Sherrod had, among an array of good qualities, modesty—perhaps too much modesty. I found he had a tendency to blame himself far too much for the failure of the *Post* to modernize its paper, format, art, and copy. I reminded him that he was third man in the editorial line; Hibbs and Fuoss were more responsible. But it is difficult now, looking at the record, to be very critical. Used as indexes of their abilities were circulation, cover price, and sales. However, profits were the responsibility of management, and management failed dismally, as witnessed by one fact. In 1956 advertising sales were $86.8 million, profits $13.5 million. In 1960 sales were up to $104 million, but profits were down to less than $2.4 million. Sales increased because *Post* circulation, the responsibility of the editors, increased. In 1956, the *Post* circulation was 4.9 million. In 1960 it had increased to 6.3 million. That is why Hibbs, Fuoss, and Sherrod need not indulge in much self-criticism. They really did their jobs quite well.

The policy of editorial freedom established by Cyrus Curtis had provided the atmosphere in which the *Post, Ladies' Home Journal,* and *Holiday* became great and successful magazines. Though Curtis was primarily a salesman and businessman rather than an editor, he saw early, earlier than anyone else, that the key to success in publishing was the quality and validity of what was between the covers of the magazines—i.e., editorial content. He apparently had the correct instinctive judgment about editors and content. He selected the right editors, and from that point on controlled them with the lightest rein.

Bob MacNeal, president of the Curtis Publishing Company from 1950 to July 1962, maintained the spirit of editorial freedom, but he lacked the knowledge, judgment, and instincts to supply any supervision. His most serious failure was permitting editors to stay on long after they had overmatured. Some old tired editors, old tired writers, lost touch with their audiences. A "generation gap" developed before the term was invented.

I also drilled into the statistical history of magazines—Curtis magazines, particularly. Assembled for me by the McCann-Erickson Media Department were these data:

The circulation of *The Saturday Evening Post* in 1935 was 2,808,000, with two-thirds of the circulation in single copy sales. By 1942 it had reached 3,327,000; but a marked change had occurred in the source of circulation. The total was almost evenly divided between single copy sales (newsstand) and subscribers. In 1952 the *Post* circulation reached 4,220,000, and now the balance had swung to subscriptions. More than a million more people subscribed to the *Post* than bought it on the newsstands.

In 1962, when I took over at Curtis, the circulation of *The Saturday Evening Post* was 6,652,000. In that year, however, newsstand sales had shrunk to less than 800,000. Circulation had become a commodity to be purchased, even if uneconomically. In 1950 the circulation box score in the general weekly field, in rounded, second-half averages, had showed the *Post* at 4 million, *Life* at 5.3 million, and *Look* at 3.15 million. Five years later the

Post had 4.7 million, *Life* 5.52 million, *Look* 4.1 million—nothing really dramatic as yet. However, by 1960, there was a marked change. The *Post* and *Life* were very close—*Post* 6.4 million, *Life* 6.7 million—but *Look* had climbed to the level of the *Post*. By 1962 the *Post* with 6.65 million was last; *Look* with 7.2 million was first, and *Life*—for the first time in its history—was second to *Look*.

The *Life* crowd refused to admit the competion with *Look*. They claimed *Look* was not in the same field, being a biweekly, and there was something to their argument. During this period *Look* had a great inbuilt advantage in its biweekly frequency. Its dramatic growth and its move ahead of the *Post* and *Life* in 1961 reflected both editorial improvement and its biweekly frequency.

It is important to note here the competitive situation in the women's field. The *Journal*, edited by the Goulds, dominated the field until the late fifties. The picture changed—or, I should say, was changed—by a slight, feisty, innovative editor named Herbert Mayes, editor of *McCall's*, by far the best women's magazine editor in modern times. His magazine, after trailing the *Journal* for decades, caught up with it in 1960, passed it in 1961, and moved dramatically ahead in 1962. By the second half of 1962 *McCall's* circulation reached 8.215 million. The *Journal* was a poor second with 6.865 million, and *Good Housekeeping*, Herb Mayes's former home, was at an all-time high of 5.25 million.

Holiday was unique, created at Curtis, skillfully and lovingly edited by Ted Patrick, the editor's editor. It grew soundly from a base of 425,000 in 1946 to a little under 1 million in 1962.

It is axiomatic that, in consumer media, advertising follows circulation. Only rarely has a new medium shattered the pattern. Television did this in a jolting manner. It got huge amounts of advertising *while* its circulation was building. Network television became a meaningful factor in advertising in 1949, only four years after the Federal Communications Commission "Television Station Freeze" was lifted.

At this time, magazines had reached the staggering total in advertising revenue of $440 million. TV had less than $12 million in network time revenue. Yet, by 1962, during the period in which magazine advertising revenue nearly doubled to $875 million, TV burgeoned to around $800 million. Even so, almost all through the fifties the Curtis momentum carried it forward. From 1943 through 1959 Curtis averaged between 17.7 and 18.8 percent of all the advertising revenue in all consumer magazines. The legacy left by Cyrus Curtis to the later generations of management was a bountiful one.

Horace Lorimer, Edward Bok, Ben Hibbs, the Goulds, Fuoss, Sherrod, and Ted Patrick were all excellent editors. The Curtis problem was not editorial—it was management. Management failed, and the old Curtis board also failed to function adequately as protectors of the stockholders. The old Curtis directors did not really know the publishing business or the editorial areas or advertising. Year after year, the board of directors saw the company first lose momentum, then become static, then start to slide, and then continue sliding to the edge of bankruptcy.

The Curtis-Bok family abdicated control but retained their board of directors posts for years, rarely attending meetings.

Even the banks were slow to see and act.

Milton Gould and Robert MacLean Stewart, acting for Loeb, Rhoades, Treves & Company, and Williston & Beane, invaded the closed circle of Curtis. Once they were on the board, it took only five board meetings for them to "smell the decay" emanating from the helplessness of MacNeal and his management. They brought MacNeal's management down—victory by ultimatum. I tried to build a new one. How, and how well, I will now attempt to describe.

4

My first week at Curtis was frantic. Just touring the facilities, meeting the 900 managers, and reading emergency correspondence absorbed most of my daylight hours. I raced between New York and Philadelphia, since editorial (except *Holiday*) and all sales and promotion were in New York. The corporate office, circulation, manufacturing, and the paper company were in Pennsylvania. Nothing constructive was done by *me* during the week, but a generous and quite typical act by Marion Harper enabled me to end the period on the "up" side.

With characteristic thoroughness and speed, Harper called together the best media brains in the agency and told them I had accepted the job as president of Curtis. He asked them to contribute their best cerebration and intuition to the problems of Curtis, and to develop a set of recommendations. Paul Foley, my favorite creative man in all advertising, was task force head.

When the report was finished, Harper invited me to his office and gave me the benefit of the accumulated experience and judgment of a dozen of his best people. The report was fascinating. In essence, it said that Curtis could not survive in the form in which I had inherited it—with the same magazines, same circulations, same frequencies—under the economic conditions then prevailing at Curtis. The task force recommended that the *Post* go biweekly; that *Holiday* be sold to generate working capital; that *American Home* be folded into the *Ladies' Home Journal*, saving millions in subscription costs. The final recommendation was to get Curtis out of the paper and manufacturing business. I accepted the Harper report with overflowing gratitude and rushed back to Curtis as though I'd found the Holy Grail. Calling in my inherited key men—Bob Gibbon, secretary of the Executive Board; Ford Robinson, head of Operations; Leon Marks, head of Manufacturing; G. B. McCombs, Number Two man in Circulation—I discussed the report with them. My soaring spirits plummeted as each of the Harper recommendations was shot down in flames, not because the ideas were faulty, but because of artificial, legal, or financial strictures that appeared to block every turn.

60

The *Post* could not go biweekly because of the contract the Curtis Publishing Company had with its own paper company, the New York and Pennsylvania Co. New York and Penn was owned by Curtis, but in a mortgage arrangement for earlier financing, Curtis Publishing had agreed to purchase enough paper from New York and Penn to keep the mills going full time, with a guaranteed 6 percent profit regardless of other considerations. In other words, New York and Penn had to make a profit, come hell or high water, depression or disaster, at Curtis Publishing.

Holiday could not be sold, the legal eagles warned, because of the "negative covenants" of the two issues of preferred stock outstanding. To get that needed financing, Curtis had committed itself not to pledge assets against loans. (It later turned out that their legal advice was amended. Curtis could not *pledge* any of its assets for borrowing purposes, but could sell any assets.)

American Home could not be folded into the *Journal* because of paper and printing schedules. My experts at Curtis, the old management team, advised me that we could not get peanuts for the New York and Pennsylvania paper company because it was falling apart with age and infirmity. The final charming news was that Curtis was nonunion, blessed to be so, and any cutbacks in personnel because of the folding of magazines or merging of magazines that resulted in decreased production would certainly bring in the big, bad unions.

I hid in the Warwick Hotel in Philadelphia for several hours after that meeting, fearful that my dismay would be infectious. For the next few days I ranged over Curtis, talking to each of the department heads, asking questions about rapid changes that could be made to break out of the pit into which Curtis had been permitted to fall. One startling fact became apparent: Bob MacNeal was probably the world's greatest accountant. He knew everything there was to know about the mechanical and administrative aspects of Curtis. He carried a little black book that was completely up-to-date, though most of the time he did not have to refer to it. He had a prodigious memory. He knew the drying time of every ink, the running time of every type of press, the number of meals served on the average Thursday in the company cafeterias, the length of the fibers of the fine black spruce trees Curtis grew in Canada, the temperature at which the wood chips were "cooked" to make pulp, and even the number of miles the ancient battery-driven Curtis trucks could travel in heavy traffic without recharging. A question to MacNeal elicited a torrent of statistics and explanations. I began to understand the dilemma of the directors. Every manager of Curtis followed his example. Each had his own "little black book" with all the facts about his own division. I did not meet a single department head who had been appointed by MacNeal and trained by him who believed there was anything wrong with the way he ran his operation. The automatic response to a question was the reaching for the "little black book" and a flood of data. If the answers were questioned, the manager would pull into a shell and sulk.

The only exception was Clay Blair. He dogged my footsteps, even met me on a Sunday at church to have an emergency meeting. He *knew* an astonishing amount about Curtis, but at that stage he did not *understand* most of what he knew. He fired suggestions at me about who should be fired or promoted, what facilities should be sold, closed down, "burned down," or "blown up." (Blair was given to violent verbal imagery.) In the Curtis world of tired, dispirited, resigned, even hopeless people, Blair stood out like a beacon. He wanted to do *something*—anything—to change Curtis. Apparently he was one of those rare people willing to "go through the wall" to get to an objective. The trouble was that he did not always know *which* wall to attack. I felt that if he could be harnessed in some way, he could be like Mort Werner of NBC—the great doer. And, God knows, I needed a doer more than anything else during my first six months. If Blair could get the facts to go with his drive, I was prepared to keep him my Number Two man in Editorial and Operations. However, since at that time I could not be sure of Blair's competence and objectivity, I decided I needed outside help.

I turned to Fenton B. Turck, of F. B. Turck & Company, whom I had known for quite a few years. I was sure Turck, an industrial engineer who had done a score or more consultant jobs for Time Inc., could be trusted to probe for me with maximum tactfulness, to keep old Curtis employees from having nervous breakdowns.

Immediately there was resistance from the MacNeal holdovers in management, and I decided they would have to go. They went, as quickly as I could decently remove them. Turck and his associates were employed. This was my best, very early decision.

During these first days, the press reports on my appointment as Curtis president were excellent from July 9 through July 19. There generally is a honeymoon period with the press when such changes are made, but mine was one of the shortest honeymoons on record. *Time*, on July 20, just eleven days after my appointment, ran a full-page story with a picture of me in the press section. It was hostile and clever. I could see immediately that I had become the victim of "the *Time* system"—a technique that made for some very good writing, but not always such good reporting.

Here's how it worked in my case: A lovely, ingenuous girl researcher called for a date at my office. Her opening comment disarmed me. She batted her deep blue eyes at me and said, "How did anyone as young as you get so far, so fast?"

We talked, and she asked some innocent-sounding questions, one of which was: "Why do you keep leaving safe, secure positions for such terribly difficult jobs like this?"

I jokingly replied: "Well, some of my friends say I have a career death wish—they say I'm psychotic." I went on to explain that I was something of a loner, liked the freedom one is given in potentially disastrous situations. The interview ended on a friendly note.

Then a *Time* photographer called and asked about pictures, suggesting that they be taken at my home. I agreed. The photographer came out to Rye, New York, and started taking routine pictures. He noticed that I had a battery of three telephones clustered in one corner, one flat on a small table, two others hanging together on the wall, and he expressed considerable interest. I explained that the telephone arrangement was a holdover from the days at NBC. We all had several telephones at home because of the demands of the news operations and the impatience of General Sarnoff, or his aides, who monitored the NBC television and radio networks. It was unsatisfactory to get a call and have to say "I'll call you back" when something went wrong. So we all developed the habit of saying "Hold on a moment," grabbing the other phone and getting the facts, and then relaying them to the inquirer on the first phone.

The *Time* photographer asked me to hold a phone against each ear for a picture. I agreed, and he took the picture. This photograph reached the desk of the editor in the press section at about the same time the raw data from the girl researcher arrived.

With fiendish skill, the editor paired the picture and the quote—
"They say I'm psychotic." The article itself was destructive and
harmful, but the worst part was the picture showing me with a
telephone in each hand, a frantic stare in my one eye, and the
caption—"They say I'm psychotic"—as a direct quote from me.

Clay Blair, who at this point called me "Dad," was sympathetic about the *Time* story. He used some colorful expletives to
describe his former associates at Time Inc. He despised *Time*.

My attitude toward Blair *after* I became president was one of
wary hopefulness, as I have already implied. He actually had come
off quite well in the meeting at Interpublic, described earlier. The
second time I had met him was in late June, 1962, just days before
I was offered the presidency. This meeting was the oddest I had in
almost twenty years in business. It was conceived by Milton Gould
without any advance warning to me. The setting was Brown Bros.
Harriman, before the final meeting with the Executive Committee
at which they made a verbal commitment to me, subject only to
board approval. Gould knew that Blair wanted to be president. In
fact, Blair had given Gould a memo naming himself as president.
Gould didn't want to tell Blair about me, so he decided just to
throw us together and see "who'd come out on top."

Blair walked into the conference room, saw me, said, "I'm
Clay Blair—aren't you Joe Culligan?" I pleaded guilty. He started
talking, letting me know that Milton Gould had asked him to
come to the office in which I was waiting. Assuming Gould had
told Blair about me and my approaching appointment to the presidency, I started asking him some questions about Curtis, which he
at first answered. As the probing got deeper, he suddenly fixed me
with a suspicious stare and demanded: "What is your interest in
Curtis?"

I said, "I may join Curtis."

"In what capacity?"

"As president," I answered.

Blair's reaction was violent. He gasped and went ashen, star-
ing at me with an expression I could not quite read. Had Gould
warned me of Blair's ambition to be president, I would have been
prepared.

Believing that Blair was in a mild state of shock, I took the
offensive immediately. He was quite easy to handle, and within
about a quarter of an hour he had sworn fealty to me. Later, I

confronted Gould. He laughed the matter off with the comment that he knew I'd come out on top. I then pressed him for full information about Blair. The tale he told was a disquieting one in some ways.

When Blair had been moved to Philadelphia from Washington, he had got the bug about taking over Curtis several months before MacNeal was fired. He knew Admiral Lewis E. Strauss, former head of the Atomic Energy Commission and a most important citizen. (Blair had written about Strauss favorably when covering the Washington beat.) He secretly went to Strauss, told him of MacNeal's loss of control and the impending power struggle that was shaping up. Strauss talked about the situation to Douglas Black, president of Doubleday, a leading book publisher that would have been a logical organization to take over Curtis. Profitable and stable, with a huge printing volume, Doubleday would have given Curtis the new profile it needed, and enabled the company to solve some of its paper and printing problems. The four banks to which Curtis owed $22 million would have welcomed Doubleday with open arms. Most of the Curtis Philadelphia directors, tired, frightened, would have welcomed Douglas Black in order to get out from under the fast-approaching potential failure. Black actually agreed to study the Curtis situation. Blair took this information to Gould and became a galloping white knight for a short while. Gould proposed that the Curtis board of directors elect Blair vice-president, Editorial, which they did at the same meeting at which MacNeal was fired. Blair read this appointment as the green light to the presidency of Curtis.

He went so far as to lay out a complete plan for the reorganization of the Curtis management, filling the key spots with editors he had hired and recommending himself as president. At Gould's insistence, the Executive Committee met with Blair and discussed several critical matters with him. They quickly wrote him off as a candidate for the presidency.

After I became president of Curtis, Blair was (as I have said) underfoot wherever I turned. At this period he looked awful most of the time. He ballooned in weight, seemed distracted sometimes, drank coffee and smoked incessantly. He attacked almost all the Curtis executives in discussions with me—but seemed to know more about Curtis than any other person there.

Blair had been exposed to some great and effective men as a

Washington reporter. He was particularly impressed by Admiral Hyman A. Rickover, and often decried the "terrible treatment Rickover was given by the Navy 'brass hats'." He undoubtedly developed an implacable hatred for the "Establishment" during his days as a Pentagon correspondent and, particularly, while he was researching and writing the book on the Polaris submarine. Blair frequently expressed to me his disdain for the Curtis board; he despised bankers and public relations people also. Though he rebelled against authority, discipline, success in others, he sought it for himself. Believing that "knowledge is power," he obviously was determined to become the most knowledgeable man at Curtis. His position as vice-president, Editorial, gave him a hunting license there, and he used it effectively, going into the various departments, asking questions, gathering facts and fancies, and developing a considerable, though superficial, knowledge of Curtis.

During my first two weeks at Curtis, Blair acted like a raging lion. He rushed into my office, practically screaming about real and fancied errors being made. I feared for his welfare, and looked for some therapeutic method of settling him down, getting him out of my hair, and possibly using his ability as a reporter to gather additional facts about Curtis. Hoping that, working inside with other Curtis people, he would develop information that could be confirmed or denied by my consultants, Fenton B. Turck & Company, Inc., I assigned him to set up what we called a Study Group, which consisted of four members of the editorial staff. I gave the group broad powers to call for records, reports, engineering data, sales figures, financial figures, production data—in fact, anything needed to review Curtis operations. Most important, I gave the group the authority to call individual witnesses into the project headquarters for interrogation.

Blair set the group up like a congressional investigating committee. The large room I assigned him became known as "the tank." It was not air-conditioned, and the Study Group did much of its work in August. The furniture was arranged as in a courtroom, even with a "witness" chair. A tape recorder was in constant use. Blair and his team sat on one side of the table and grilled the "witnesses" to the point of exhaustion.

The spookiest aspect of the Study Group was the attendance of MacNeal at the interrogations. At the direct request of Albert Linton, I had agreed to let MacNeal stay around Curtis for several weeks. (This was a mistake that I corrected.) MacNeal sat there, day after day, watching and listening, as Blair and his team bored in on each manager, always implying incompetence and past mistakes, and often directly challenging witnesses on the accuracy of the information given. It must have been a horrible experience for MacNeal. The Study Group adjourned the end of August, and Blair moved rapidly to get himself into a position to dominate Curtis editorial and move into the editorship of the *Post*.

As the reports from the Study Group came to me, often with harrowing recommendations, I rushed them to Fenton B. Turck for analysis. His responsibility was to tell me if Curtis could do what the group recommended and not lose its capacity to print and distribute magazines without ruinous increased cost. The plan worked admirably, and within a month two avenues of great cost reduction appeared possible. I needed them desperately, for after two weeks in the job I was warned that the creditor banks were in a state of shock and anguish over the financial figures coming from Curtis and the press reports coming from *The Gallagher Report* and the advertising trade press.

Director-banker Moreau D. Brown received "friendly tips" from the four banks to which Curtis owed $22 million that they were exceedingly concerned about their loans. This was not the kind of news I needed at this time, but it could not be ignored. Brown suggested that I call on the banks and try to give them a feeling that *I* knew what I was doing, and some assurance that they would not be in the embarrassing position of financing Curtis losses with loans.

I called on all four banks with a carefully designed presentation, which accomplished its objective, a one-year renewal of the $22 million Curtis indebtedness. Here, again, my talent for vocal presentation was pivotal. I judged that the worst possible thing I could do was face these hard-nosed bankers, after such a brief time in the job, with a full program for Curtis. Their logical suspicion that I was just a salesman would be confirmed by such lack of judgment. So I made a straightforward vocal presentation of my background as a kind of "doctor" for sick media properties, and put heavy accent as well on my plan to spend the first six months in a sales blitz to save our present advertisers and gain new ones. I parroted some of the excellent business logic of John Burns, dealing with delegation, decentralization, and use of consultants in highly technical areas. Most significantly, I made the flat-footed promise that there would be immediate massive cost reduction programs to reduce losses until the advertising revenues could be increased. The four banks bought my plan, gave Curtis a twelve-month extension of the loan, and, miraculously, a commitment on an additional $4 million. This was my first major contribution to Curtis. The First National City Bank of New York let me know that time was running out, however, and that they were not entirely convinced Curtis could be saved. Their negative attitude surprised me at first, but I learned a bit later what caused it.

Despite the relatively poor standing of the New York and Penn paper company, it did have great lumber holdings in Canada, some modern equipment, and what was considered to be one of the best group of papermakers in the industry. It also owned thousands of acres of hardwood forests in Pennsylvania. The technology of papermaking was advancing at a rapid rate, and it was thought that hardwoods would become usable for magazine stock within several years, a development that would make the Curtis timber in Pennsylvania valuable indeed. Contiguity of timber with mill facilities is a key to low-cost paper production, and competitors had paper mills in Pennsylvania and neighboring states. Some of them looked covetously at New York and Penn, but were unwilling to pay what Curtis would have needed to sell the mills.

One company in particular, run by a ruthless president, thought it saw a way to pick up the New York and Penn paper company, on the auction block. This man was quite close to a top official of First National City Bank, and he kept up a barrage of negative dope to his friend about Curtis, stressing the hopelessness of the situation, and bringing home the nagging worry that Curtis would go bankrupt and leave the great First National City Bank with egg all over its face. The bank's credit officer responsible for Curtis, Ted Gardner, was not a particularly affirmative type. He apparently did not like the Kennedy family, and when the *Post* ran an article by Eunice Schriver about mentally defective children, Gardner called me and complained that Curtis was giving the Kennedy family too much exposure. I suspected he had not read the article and did not even know for sure what it was about. A chill swept over me at the prospect of having my fate and that of Curtis even partly in the hands of this man.

Even more damaging to Curtis was the action of a financial officer of Time Inc. He was interested in less competition for *Life*, as well as the chance to pick up the *Post* subscription lists for *Life* on the auction block. This man, too, reported negative data and rumor to a top executive of First National City Bank. Together, these two anti-Curtis forces more than offset the trickle of good news starting to emerge from Curtis. The despair about Curtis filtered down from the top to the middle management of the bank, and Gardner and his immediate boss started to put the pressure on me for repayment of the $7 million Curtis owed them. When I said we could not pay it, they first suggested—then demanded—that Curtis sell one or more of its assets to get the money. They warned me in writing that they would not renew the note at the end of the grace year.

The other banks became somewhat infected by the First National City Bank attitude, though they had a different kind of involvement with Curtis. All three were Philadelphia banks, with strong economic and emotional ties with Curtis. Ten thousand jobs were at stake in a city in which the economy had crumbled, and so civic pride was an effective deterrent to their following the lead of First National City.

I was now on the hook with the bankers, having promised immediate massive cost reduction. They had taken copious notes about that part of my presentation. It was certain that my creditability would be permanently impaired if I did not deliver on so definite a promise.

The Study Group reported there were two activities at Curtis that were costing the company nearly a million dollars a year and contributing nothing essential to its operation. I asked Fenton B. Turck to confirm this. He did—almost by return mail. The two departments were Job Press, an in-house specialty printing company, and the Industrial Engineering Department, a particular favorite of MacNeal's.

The charter of Job Press was to produce for Curtis all the special material it needed for sales, sales promotion, merchandising, internal and external communication, etc., and also to get and fulfill outside contracts for printing. The theory was that there would be enough profit from contract printing to support the activity and give Curtis low- or no-cost service. Instead, Job Press costs were out of line with its competition; it got no outside business. Its people, in order to perpetuate themselves in their jobs, appealed to Curtis departments for more and more work. When I arrived, there were over seventy-five different letterheads being used throughout the company, and hundreds of special memo pads, forms, and the like that were of no practical use.

The Industrial Engineering Department was composed of forty graduate industrial engineers who were supposed to keep Curtis modern and profitable through constant evaluation of its operations and of the advancing technology in publishing. This had to be the saddest joke in American industry in the fateful year of 1962. Curtis was to lose $19 million in that year, and had been spending hundreds of thousands of dollars a year on an Industrial Engineering Department whose charter was to keep the company modern and profitable.

The astonishing ineptitude of the old Philadelphia Curtis board of directors started dawning on me with that realization. Job Press and Industrial Engineering were costing Curtis a million a year, contributing little, and the board did not know enough about the business to ask why.

As soon as Fenton B. Turck told me that Job Press and Industrial Engineering could be eliminated with no loss of service to advertisers, readers, or distribution customers, I made the decision to eliminate them completely rather than reduce them gradually. The shock power of such a bold move would, I knew, be of maximum use with the banks. But when I told the Executive Committee members about it, they refused to believe such a drastic move was possible, and resisted it.

Linton, particularly, realized the significance of the development. Obviously, if I could in two months eliminate two entire departments and other operations, at a saving of a million dollars, the board should have done something about it years ago. He suggested a face-saving device, a "gradual reduction with a check after the first step to see if there was any damage to Curtis." I flatly refused to consider any alternative, and started working on individual board members, using Fenton B. Turck as my support. He was great in this role, and he gradually convinced the new directors that I was right. He also warned them of the possible effect of a refusal to accept my recommendation. When I made the formal recommendation to the board for the complete elimination of the two departments, the motion was carried unanimously.

These initial moves did more than save a million dollars on an annual basis. They demonstrated that Curtis was loaded with excess personnel and that massive cost reduction was indeed possible. They also alerted me to the inadequacy of most of the old Curtis Board of Directors, before Curtis Barkes, Milton Gould, and Robert MacLean Stewart joined the board. Linton's performance gave clear evidence that he was especially concerned with his own personal reputation and might be a problem in any cost-reduction program. In addition, the moves convinced me that I needed a newcomer to replace Brandon Barringer, MacNeal's treasurer—someone who was tough as nails and particularly experienced in cost reduction and control programs. I advised the board of my need, and employed Booz, Allen & Hamilton, the management consultant firm, to search for a top financial officer for Curtis.

It took only two board meetings and some quick research to learn that Brandon Barringer was hopelessly out of his range in the Curtis situation, though he had undoubtedly been an able man at one time. His own ill health and that of his wife, and the worsening situation at Curtis, sapped whatever strength he had. He and Albert Linton snapped at each other in board meetings like a pair of grouchy old maids. There was much for the directors to become irritated about, however, and Linton's criticism was justified. Barringer would deliver a financial report to the board giving the current results and the anticipated results for the coming quarter. At the very next board meeting, he would admit that he had been off as much as a half-million in his estimate, but always on the down side. That is, his errors were never in the company's favor. Between meetings, I tried to find how he could be so wrong over the short term. His answer was flabbergasting. Under MacNeal he had worked in a very specific manner: MacNeal would advise him of the financial results he intended to represent to the board, and Barringer would bend his figures to suit the MacNeal figures.

Then fate again took a hand. At home one evening, after I had been at Curtis about six weeks, the telephone rang and the long-distance operator said that J. M. Clifford was calling from Santa Barbara, California. I knew that he was living there, having been "put out to pasture" by RCA, where the finish of his career was not pleasant. Clifford was at odds with Robert Kintner—a relatively easy state to achieve—and got into an opposite position to him at NBC during the period when Bob Sarnoff was enthusiastic about Kintner and all was going well. Clifford was moved upstairs to RCA, from which he had originally been sent as a mentor to Bob Sarnoff when the time arrived for Bob to move up into the top position. I was sure that one of Clifford's missions had been to undermine Pat Weaver at NBC. He succeeded. Pat lost out there, and for a brief time Clifford was quite powerful at NBC. But he was not powerful enough to buck Bob Kintner, and so was thrust out of NBC and assigned to the West Coast office. His salary was drastically reduced, and he was given an assignment having to do with a contract for the United States Department of Defense "Distant Early Warning System."

Clifford was about as subtle as a punch in the mouth, and his opening line—"I just called to congratulate you on your new job"—did not fool me at all. I was immediately sure that he was looking for a job with me. When I brought the conversation around to that, I got a quick affirmative reaction.

I was elated because Clifford was the perfect man for the cost reduction and control job to be done. He was a known quantity, efficient in cost reduction and control, and available immediately. His liabilities were equally well known to me from personal observation at NBC. He was blunt, doctrinaire, not very sensitive. His principal fault was complete lack of comprehension of creative people.

I fed his name into the Booz, Allen & Hamilton search. They confirmed that he would be excellent for the job, admitting that their search had not surfaced anyone of comparable experience. So I told the Executive Committee about him, and advised them that Barringer had to go—and quickly—and that Clifford should be hired as executive vice-president for Finance and Administration.

I asked Clifford to come East for meetings with me and the Executive Committee. These meetings were held; the committee was impressed with his background, appearance, and apparent toughness. He pulled a neat trick, I learned much later, when it came to his compensation. Even though his salary was then about $30,000 a year at RCA, he did have a large amount of accumulated compensation from previous years, which was paid out in installments. His W-2 income tax form for the year 1961 showed very close to $100,000, and he used that as his salary base. I wanted to pay Clifford well because he would deserve all I could do for him if he carried off what I had in mind. I had little trouble getting him a base salary of $100,000 a year, and I also got him 20,000 shares of Curtis common stock on option.

John MacLain Clifford—short, chunky, crew-cut, white-haired, steely-eyed, and tight-lipped—wore dark horn-rimmed glasses that did nothing to soften his look of machine-made efficiency. Educated as a lawyer, he had veered into labor negotiations, then finance and operations. RCA had trained him well. Clifford was married to a lovely woman, and had one daughter. He had few friends, and fewer hobbies. The most important one was flying his own plane, and that he seemed to enjoy more than any other activity.

Over the years, Clifford had become hardened and cynical, and was actually the near-perfect instrument to top corporate management. He would take and follow orders to the letter and could fire hundreds, even thousands, of people with no outward show of emotion. After he had been with Curtis for six months, he showed me a small, cheap trophy one day. It had come through the mail, he said, obviously from someone at Curtis. On its base was inscribed—"J. M. Clifford #1 Bastard." He thought that was very funny.

Clifford moved into Curtis in October 1962, with full authority as executive vice-president, Finance and Operations. He spent about a week looking around before he reported to me that we were in much worse shape than he, the board, and I had thought. He had made the shattering discovery that Barringer was keeping a different set of figures from those kept by the very able comptroller, Cal Nichols. Unfortunately, only Barringer's figures were getting to the board, and Barringer was consistently overrating the Curtis liquidity by some $4 million. This may be hard to understand, but after all Curtis was a complex operation with $40 million in transit at any given time from advertisers, subscribers, and distribution customers.

Clifford told me we had to move immediately on the cost reduction program, and recommended a "no exception 20 percent cut across the board." It was tough medicine, but there was no alternative. Without it, Curtis would be out of money by the end of the year, unable to meet payrolls and with no chance that the banks would reopen its credit.

At this point, we had a great stroke of luck: Almost every

major accounting firm called me about getting the Curtis account. They correctly assumed that I would change accountants, though Curtis had used Brown and Company for decades. Knowing that Clifford was en route, I told them nothing would be done until my new financial officer arrived. One of the callers was John O'Hara, manager of the Philadelphia office of Price Waterhouse. He took me at my word, but did not sleep on it. He made a detailed examination of Curtis financial statements and found that Curtis was not handling "deferred subscription income" in the same accounting method as *Time, McCall's*, and other publishing companies used. "Deferred subscription income" is that from subscribers on time-payment plans. Accountants and the Internal Revenue Service permit some latitude in how this income is handled. The more alert publishers had modernized their methods. Curtis had not. After O'Hara discovered this Curtis omission and prepared himself well, he made a presentation at our request. Superior both in person and presentation, he got the assignment and performed magnificently for Curtis. O'Hara engineered a multimillion-dollar tax refund, changed our methods and procedures, and was able to report several months later that Curtis financial controls were equivalent to those of the top third of Price Waterhouse's clients.

With the appointment of Price Waterhouse as public accountants for Curtis Publishing, an immediate side benefit accrued. They had for years been public accountants for the New York and Pennsylvania paper company owned by Curtis, but so compartmented was Curtis that Price Waterhouse was permitted no information about the parent company. Now, with both in Price Waterhouse, their problems could be equated with the overall corporate problem.

Almost without exception, critics of Curtis cited the paper in its magazines as a major flaw. I knew nothing about papermaking, but the editors' and advertisers' problems were immediately plain to me. Editorial freedom was limited because of a requirement to use a certain amount of poor-quality paper that would not take color and was slightly off-white. Nobody liked it—editors, advertisers, papermakers themselves, or printers—but Curtis was locked to it because of the integration and the failure to modernize.

I knew there would be a barrage of questions for me as I started performing my outside duties, primarily leading the marketing operations, so I decided to take a cram course in paper-making. I also told Clay Blair to put paper and the paper company high on the priority list for the Study Group. He obliged, and I had the Study Group's report on paper by the end of August 1962. An excellent piece of work, it is summarized here.

Paper is to magazines what earth is to farming, what film is to photography. Paper is the basic ingredient on which a magazine is created, the vehicle on which printed words and pictures ride.

It is also the most expensive single cost in the making of a publication. Even in the ad-lean year of 1961, Curtis Publishing spent $43 million for the paper that went into *Post, Journal, American Home, Holiday,* and *Jack and Jill.* In 1962, despite a continued thinness of books, Curtis will consume almost *190,000 tons* of magazine paper. Each copy of *The Saturday Evening Post* costs 17 cents to make and deliver. Out of every 17 cents the cost for paper alone is 9 cents, more than one-half the total. In the decade between 1950 and 1960 costs of magazine paper rose about 25 percent.

The reverse was true just after World War II. Boom was the byword in magazines, as in everything else. Publishers had been stockpiling ideas and ad revenues for expansion. But there was a shortage of the basic ingredient—paper. Many an ad never got printed only because the publisher did not have the material to put it on; the paper industry could not meet demand, and because paper, machinery, and capacity, like presses, have to be planned for years in advance, there was no immediate remedy for the ad-rich, paper-poor publishing business. This time of shortage, in part, explains the overcapacity of today. In 1950 Curtis, the integrated giant, became even bigger with the full acquisition of its own paper company.

The biggest reason for calling Curtis "captive" is that we have to buy the magazine paper New York and Penn would make, and what New York and Penn can make is: (1) more paper than we can consume and (2) a quality of paper inferior to the product of other manufacturers.

Curtis has been unable, therefore, to take advantage of the buyer's market in paper. Even though we are one of the biggest paper users in the United States, we cannot lean on the lever of competitive bidding in order to get the best price for the paper we need. Our mill continues to churn out its rolls and we continue to run with them.

More important to the magazines, the paper we do buy

is not the paper we would buy if outside sources were available to us. Since 1950, and the acquisition of New York and Penn, there has been a pronounced change in magazine papers from uncoated "free sheet" papers to coated "ground wood" stock.

Curtis cannot order ground wood because New York and Penn could not make it. The president of New York and Penn admits that cost of power, mill location, and impracticality of conversion makes ground wood manufacture impossible for his company. So New York and Penn continues to turn out free sheets.

There is one more area in which our subsidiary limps along with subpar quality. A valid and industry-wide measure of paper performance is the "web break" percentage. A web break is the tearing of a roll of paper as it passes through the printing press. Such breaks, of course, produce costly "down time" on the presses, increase paper consumption and delay in printing of the magazine. As a result, manufacturing costs rise.

In 1945, still hungry, Curtis bought into New York and Penn. A new machine was built at Lock Haven to make magazine papers for Curtis, and three other Lock Haven paper machines were "dressed," reengineered so that the rolls produced would best fit the Curtis presses.

It appeared logical that complete control would give us full access to the output of the mills (we then thought we could use as much paper as could be produced). The other owners, because of a market business that was diminishing in ratio to the increase of Curtis' magazine appetite, were happy enough to give us full ownership.

From a capital outlay standpoint, Curtis worked a fine deal. New York and Penn increased its bank loan from 6.3 million to 20 million, and, with a small amount of additional capital, bought up all the New York and Penn stock not then held by Curtis. Without acquiring any more shares than the number we held as 48½ percent owners, Curtis became the sole shareholder and, hence, full owner of New York and Penn.

Further, the acquisition fit Curtis tradition perfectly. It seemed only right and proper for the world's largest integrated publishing company to own its own paper mill, particularly since owning the mill also meant owning some timberlands from which the paper would eventually be made. And the mills were a ready repository for our paper waste—they could churn it back to pulp. From stump to bindery, a Curtis magazine is made of Curtis materials—only the ink on the pages is purchased from an outside source, and that omission, admits past management is one that had often been considered for correction.

Curtis failed to see the coming need for all-coated stock in the early 1950s; had the parent been more foresighted in time of prosperity, then all of New York and Penn's 680-line magazine papers could be coated today.

A simple shutdown would appear to solve any overcapacity problems. One way to shut down would be to reduce the operation from a seven-day cycle to a five-day cycle, have four weeks of holiday shutdown during the year. Indeed, if all the mills closed two days each week, the magazine papers produced would drop about 30 percent to 130,000 tons per year. But such a shutdown would raise the price of paper that *was* produced; New York and Penn, in fact, estimates that such a curtailment would raise the price by some $23 per ton, making its product exorbitant when compared in price to outside papers. It is not economical or practical to shut off paper machines two days a week— maintenance costs soar, production speeds drop, quality suffers.

As an alternative, we considered leaving one or two mills on a seven-day operation, closing the remaining mill (or mills) altogether.

The mills are unionized. Under the present distressed circumstances in the communities of Lock Haven and Johnsonburg, it is a sure bet that the shutdown of one mill, or a drastic reduction in head count because of a shortened work week, would lead us into new labor troubles.

The discarding of theoretical solutions brought the Study Group to the most final possibility—divestiture of the mills.

So although New York and Penn may approach $100 million in replacement value, $60-odd million according to survey, there is no hope of getting such money. In meeting with New York and Penn we arrived at a rough, round figure of $30 million as a price that might be acceptable to Curtis, that might be attractive to an outside buyer.

The biggest bonus of such a sale would be the freedom from free sheets; once more, the company could buy its most basic ingredient in the competitive open market. Most important, it would free Curtis to make decisions about its magazines based on the magazines themselves, not on the interrelated, integrated problems of a wholly owned paper mill. It is imperative to realize that, under the present captive conditions, Curtis can make no magazine decision on pure editorial or publishing grounds. It is no exaggeration to say that Curtis, as it has been constituted, might keep an inferior product on the newsstands merely to better absorb its inexorable ration of inferior paper.

Management has to have the freedom of making publishing decisions based on the publishing business and not the paper business. It is unfortunate that New York and Penn has been so intimately connected with Curtis prosperity, or lack of prosperity. When the magazine business was booming, the paper business boomed too. When the magazine business turned bearish, suddenly there was a glut of paper on the market. But this unhappy truth about the dependency of the magazine paper business does not mean that Curtis must be inextricably wrapped up in those paper problems. Curtis has to be free to succeed or fail on the strength of our products, not on the inherent and historical weaknesses of the basic industry from which these products are made. Curtis' future lies in communications—but communications *on* paper, not production *of* paper. An old bargain has become a very bum deal; now, when Curtis can still get out—and take some money with us, we must.

I studied the group report alone, and then with Fenton B. Turck, to learn what was fact and what was fancy. The overall report was surprisingly accurate. What Clay Blair did not know was that Curtis was hog-tied to New York and Penn by a mortgage agreement with the New York Trust Company, which blocked Curtis from any move to extricate itself from the deadly embrace of the paper company. Only in a recapitalization of Curtis, with the replacement of the mortgage, could Curtis move forward.

I learned two lessons early in life: First, the man who controls the money controls the situation; and second, you can't build a big future with timid partners. No one at or around Curtis really controlled the money. The Curtis-Bok family should have—it owned enough stock. The First National City Bank in New York could have, as the so-called lead bank for the $22 million credit. But this bank was disenchanted with top management at Curtis and just wanted out—after it got its loan repaid. So there was an obvious power vacuum. My instincts told me to try to fill it before someone else did.

However, that question about Curtis, all questions about Curtis, would be academic if I did not do immediately what I was best qualified to do—sell advertising. Curtis was bleeding to death.

Too much unnecessary expense and not enough advertising income would bury Curtis by January 1963, unless . . .

I was the "unless"; no one else was in a position to deliver. This statement is not intended to be boastful—the burden was actually on my shoulders. No amount of promotion, advertising, or sales calls by others would suffice. So I followed my instinct and decided on an unprecedented personal sales effort. I determined to do what no other executive in United States business had ever done—call personally on the heads of America's two hundred leading corporations within six months.

5

July and most of August seemed to evaporate. I worked twelve to fourteen hours a day, seven days a week, during that period. It was primarily a time for putting things in place. I had brought in Fenton B. Turck & Company, Inc.; the Blair Study Group was starting to complete its investigation and delivering its reports and recommendations. Price Waterhouse had been appointed, and most important, J. M. Clifford, who was to earn his nickname "Mac-the-Knife," was installed as head of Finance and Operations.

My next move was planning my sales blitz at all major advertisers in the United States. If our condition had not been so desperate that desperate measures were called for, I could have gone to the advertising agencies in the traditional fashion and tried to convince them to recommend Curtis magazines to their clients. But I could not truthfully tell the agencies our magazines were the best or even second best in their fields. So I decided to bypass agencies and go directly to the clients, admit that Curtis magazines needed improvement, and appeal for business *because we needed it*. I depended on the innate sympathy of most businessmen, their love for the *Post*, which many of them had sold as youngsters, and some spellbinding personal salesmanship.

However, I knew I needed an important weapon for my sales kit—some "gimmick" to justify calling together large groups of clients and agency people, and also to serve as a kind of "warm-up" to dispel the chill around most big business meetings. No point in thinking small: I selected as my gimmick the most exciting man of my generation—John Fitzgerald Kennedy, President of the United States. Unashamedly, I called in Bob Sherrod, then editor of the *Post*, and confiding my need of a talking point for the coming sales blitz, I asked him how I could get to see the President.

Sherrod said simply, "I'll ask him." He explained that President Kennedy, who revered courage above all else, had read and been greatly moved by his book *Tarawa*. Sherrod had an open line to President Kennedy. Within seventy-two hours, through Bob

Sherrod, I had an invitation to the White House from the President. I had not, up to this time, met him personally, and wanted to very much for all the usual reasons in addition to the very practical one of needing something unusual to talk about before selling Curtis magazines. There was not time for me to visit Russia, write a major magazine article on some important subject, or get an award, but I felt sure that a visit to the President might yield a few amusing anecdotes. I got much more than I bargained for.

Arriving at the White House twenty minutes early, I waited about five minutes in the round press room before Pierre Salinger, the President's press secretary, came in and greeted me. Salinger took me to his office for a brief, friendly chat. He is an engaging man, and I appreciated the "warm-up" from him. After another five minutes, he took me into the office of Mrs. Lincoln, President Kennedy's personal secretary. A small, dark, and concerned-looking woman, she moved around the office as if on wheels, assuring me often: "The President will be with you in just a few minutes." I was gearing myself for the meeting, expecting to be ushered into the famous oval room, but that was not the way it happened. Without warning, the door to his office opened and out the President strode, incredibly good-looking, with an athletic lope, a warm smile, and outstretched hand.

"Mr. Culligan," he said, "glad to see you. Wait in there for me, will you? I'll be back in a moment," and he sped by me, across and out of Mrs. Lincoln's office.

A bit dazed, I went into his office. Immediately I noticed his famous rocking chair, positioned near the end of the semicircular sofa. I dutifully sat down near the rocking chair and looked around, marveling at the simplicity of the room and the directness of the man who occupied it. It seemed hard to believe that this youthful, handsome charmer, only six years older than I, could possibly be *the man*.

I assumed that the President had gone to Salinger's office to be briefed on me. He was gone less than five minutes before he returned and strode vigorously across the room. We shook hands again, then he sat in the rocking chair, I on the sofa. He said, with a sly smile, "I'm glad to meet the president of the Curtis Publishing Company. I always have been interested in the long Republican tradition of your predecessors. It didn't seem to do them much good. . . .What are your plans?"

I mumbled something about my feeling of responsibility to inform and stimulate the public. But I was much more interested in hearing Mr. Kennedy talk, which he did—easily and gracefully. He asked what I could do about the Curtis losses. When I told him of the plan to reduce the work staff from 10,000 to less than 8,000 he looked startled, then thoughtful.

"Well," he said, "that is one advantage of being in the business world. You *can* reduce the payroll. That is not so easily done in government."

Then he asked about my earlier days and my war experiences; he knew how I had lost my eye. I told him of several humorous experiences I'd had as a result of my eye patch. He laughed appreciatively when I told him of the kid who yelled on first sight of me, "Mommy, look at the pirate."

We talked about twenty minutes; then the door opened, and Ollie Atkins, the *Post* photographer in Washington, entered. Reacting to my look of surprise, the President said, "I thought we might have Ollie earn his pay today."

Ollie took a number of pictures, one of which the President signed for me. It now has a permanent place on my study wall. When the picture-taking was over, I concluded the interview was over as well, and started to offer my sincere thanks to the President for the visit.

He stood up and put his hand on my shoulder. "You know, Joe, it's great to see an Irishman getting ahead in the business world."

It was exactly the kind of thing I would have expected from an old Irish uncle. "It's true, you know," he went on. "The Irish in America have done very well in politics and in the church, but it's only recently that they are getting to the top of the business world. My father was one of the first to make it in a big way."

Instead of leaving me at the door of his office as I expected, the President walked me through Mrs. Lincoln's office and into the office of Pierre Salinger, who stood up and grinned as we entered. The President, with a straight face, said, "Pierre, before Mr. Culligan leaves, would you tell him of your experiences with *Collier's?*"

The degree of the President's knowledge, recall, and humor were all summed up for me in this parting quip. Pierre Salinger had been with the ill-fated *Collier's* when it was finally interred. This marvelously subtle dig by the President at both Salinger and me was typical of his sly, mocking, ironic wit. Parenthetically, he asked me back a second time. I was immensely flattered having heard after my first visit: "The President was quite impressed by you." This second invitation seemed to prove it, particularly since this time it was for lunch in the family apartment on the third floor of the White House.

The lunch, less than two months before his assassination, was a delightful experience. The President took me on a tour of the floor. As we walked through the Lincoln Room, he explained that he used that room because of the regular telephone invasions in the dead of night. We had a brief chuckle when I noticed a copy of *Goldfinger,* the James Bond thriller, on his bedside table, and he agreed with me on the humor of the name of one of the female characters.

There was one regrettable incident during this otherwise charming meeting. Halfway through lunch, the President asked if there was anything upcoming on Washington in the *Post.* I told him there was an article by a military expert on MacNamara and the Pentagon. The atmosphere changed instantly. The President's face became stern, his eyes steely. He almost snapped, "Well, it won't be faaair" in his extraordinary Boston accent. He explained that the *Post* had done a serious disservice to the country with its story of the dropping of the Sky Bolt program. I had no way of knowing, of course, that the canceling of the U.S.-supported "Sky Bolt" program for Great Britain had caused a major problem with the British Government. The *Post* had scooped the press with the story that the Department of Defense had canceled the program, before the British Government had time to prepare the British people for the abrupt change in the plan to give Britain "deliverable nuclear weapons."

As quickly as the President's anger had come, it disappeared, as though he realized that the story had not been my fault, and that I was his guest. We talked about what he might do after leaving the White House, discussing the possibility of his getting into the communications business. I suggested that he buy control of Curtis Publishing, or move in on some major communications company. He did not dismiss the idea. Then we talked a bit about politics. I mentioned that I considered it part of my obligation to the two-party system to try to help force the rebuilding of the

Republican party. He did not say much in reply at the time, but two weeks later sent me a note. It was on White House stationery, and was addressed to "Dear Mr. Culligan." He had drawn a line through that and written in his own hand "Dear Joe." It said:

Dear Joe:

Thank you for your letter.

I know that within our separate areas of responsibility we share a common desire to advance the interests of our country.

As for "forcing the rebuilding of the Republican party" I wish you only limited success.

With best wishes.

Sincerely,
(*Signed*) John F. Kennedy

Here again, the dry, delicious humor came bubbling through.

My hunch that a visit to the President would be a great talking point for the upcoming presentations around the country was right. My description of my visit and the President's remarks, particularly about "Irishmen getting ahead in the business world," was a smash hit. The audiences warmed up quickly and were quite responsive when I started selling Curtis and its magazines.

After my first White House visit, I stayed in Washington two extra days, partly to rest and build up strength for the sales blitz, which would dominate my life for the better part of nine months. The second reason for remaining was the pressing need to analyze the final report of the Study Group I had set up under Clay Blair. I had insisted on having a preliminary draft to take to Washington with me, and I locked myself in a pleasant suite at the Mayflower to do little else but read, review, cerebrate, and sleep.

My instincts told me that it was dangerous to leave Curtis, with all its problems, on even so important a mission as sales. I hoped that, after reading the Study Group report, I would be able to identify the primary problems before I left, and issue instructions to various groups for attacking these so that everybody would be kept so busy they would stop whining and griping and politicking.

This remarkable document—the result of the decision on my part to set up the Study Group—is highlighted here.

The Study Group convened, at the request of Curtis president, Matthew J. Culligan, on Monday, July 16, 1962. It began without preconceptions, merely with a determination to explore any and all ways that might turn the Curtis Publishing Company into a profitable venture.

The procedure of the group was simple: It first surveyed in depth the operations of the entire company. The survey was conducted in three steps: (1) a study of existing documents and reports to help refresh individual knowledge of each department or division, (2) on-the-scene inspections accompanied by division heads, and (3) an exhaustive investigation of operations and costs, by interviewing the cognizant department or division heads who were usually accompanied by their chief subordinates. In all, the Study Group interviewed more than seventy-five people.

The Study Group labored under some handicaps. The first was a shortage of time in which to probe the immense complexities of the giant Curtis Company. Another was inexperience: no member of the Study Group had ever participated in a survey of this kind before; time was lost in developing a method, in learning to separate wheat from chaff. We lacked background in engineering and cost accounting. None of us had explored in depth before either a paper company or a printing plant; yet these two elements of Curtis loomed enormously in the forefront of every decision. Another complicating factor was the participation of Robert E. MacNeal, former president, in the Study Group. The background the ex-president contributed was invaluable. Yet he inhibited witnesses who appeared before the group; and, with his passion for detail, constantly submerged the group in minutia—details concerning "the diameter of Y Y press cylinders," "the head box of a paper machine," "the fibers in paper," "impingement burners on press dryers," "spare parts of electric trunks," "capabilities of obsolete presses."

The Study Group was dissolved on September 14, after nine weeks of operations. About half of those weeks were spent in researching the company; the other half in preparing reports.

The Study Group was dismayed by the method of ad revenue forecasting, a crucial function, since almost everything from financial statements to our 1963 order for paper hinges on the accuracy of these reports.

The general financial situation dictated to a large extent

every recommendation of the Study Group. Our last "fix" on this situation developed these general points: (a) that by the end of August, our old line of short-term bank credit of $22 million had been exhausted, (b) that Culligan had been able to negotiate a new line of short-term bank credit to the extent of $4 million by pledging certain accounts receivable and some intangibles of the Circulation Company; we in effect extended our line to $26 million.

In almost every report the Study Group has complained about the lack of exact money information; this uncertainty extends even to cash forecasting. Treasurer Brandon Barringer does a multimonth forecast once each month. Comptroller Cal Nichols has a seven-month forecast prepared each month. The two forecasts do not agree; sometimes they are nowhere near agreement. For instance: as recently as August, Barringer and Nichols were more than $1 million apart on the cash balance estimate for 30 September; for November of this year, the two forecasts are $2.2 million apart; for December, the difference is more than $3 million. Incredible? We think so. The assumptions in each forecast are different. Each man claims to be "accurate." The final outcome usually falls somewhere in between the two.

But what is important is that both forecasts have Curtis in grave money straits before 1963 is half over. Nichols' group forecasts that we will have exhausted our $26 million line of credit in January, 1963. Barringer forecasts that we will possibly have to use up our $26 million in March. [These estimates were all incorrect. New sales and cost reductions reversed the trend.] These forecasts, we assume, do not take into account the almost daily reductions in costs which have been in progress since July.

In regard to our money position, however, the Study Group saw no reason for despair or panic. The Curtis giant is rich in assets, some of which we need, some of which we do not need in order to engage in our primary mission of publishing.

The value of an asset is, fundamentally, that which a buyer is willing to pay at a given time—not necessarily that which *we* might think he would pay or should pay. Thus, for the purposes of its exercises, the Study Group assigned rock-bottom-type figures to Curtis assets.

Manufacturing facilities were valued at $45 million; New York and Penn company at $30 million; Curtis Circulation Company (including Keystone Readers Service, Moore-Catrell; School Plan; Telephone Solicitation) at $30 million; Electronic Data Processing (personnel; lists; equipment) at $10 million; *Holiday* magazine at $10 million; *Jack and Jill* at

$5 million; Securities at $5 million; Real Estate (6th Street) at $5 million. Total of $140 million.

It is apparent, that while the financial situation at Curtis may be serious, there are many courses open to us. We explored the idea of selling off the printing plant, the paper company, or selling both as a package.

A Crowell-Collier type operation on Curtis might work as follows. First, *Saturday Evening Post, Ladies' Home Journal,* and *American Home* would be folded. The very large fulfillment obligation for those magazines could be disposed of, we believe, by giving away the subscription lists, or, with luck, selling them. Following this, the paper company could be sold, generating enough net profit to curtail the existing short-term bank notes against the parent firm. Curtis could then be reorganized into four divisions: (1) Manufacturing; (2) Circulation; (3) Special Projects (Direct Mail, etc.); and (4) Magazine Division (*Holiday, Jack and Jill*).

Yet the Study Group does not now recommend this course for Curtis.

Although our magazines have sustained huge losses in 1962, we believe there is a continuing market for these products, and a profitable one at that—in spite of the historic decline in mass magazines. Only two years ago—1960—the *Saturday Evening Post* generated $106 million in advertising revenue. It can do it again, we believe.

The important fact to consider is that while our ad revenue picture is less than enchanting, the *decline* of the money flow which reached a nadir in 1962, has stopped. This *decline* stopped in the period July-September, when the Study Group was in session, and it is attributable, we believe, to the new company (Culligan) management.

This stop in the *decline* profoundly influenced the Study Group.

RECOMMENDATIONS:

I. *Paper Company*

Without reservation, the Study Group urges disposal of the paper company, and a new source for Curtis magazine paper.

The Study Group estimated a sales price for New York and Penn at about $30 million. The sale of the paper company would, in one stroke, dramatically modify the overall financial position of the Curtis Publishing Company. Thus, we would be in a position to refinance the company, if this was desirable.

II. *Manufacturing*

As with the paper company, the Study Group spent a

great deal of its time exploring the manufacturing operations of the Curtis Publishing Company.

In sum we recommend:

(1) That Manufacturing be set up as wholly owned but separate subsidiary, similar to the manufacturing element of Meredith Publishing Company.

(2) That Manufacturing be consolidated.

(3) That we explore immediately the possibility of printing a portion of the Curtis magazines in the Midwest, preferably Chicago or vicinity. We did not feel that it was practical at this time for Curtis to build its own plant in the Midwest.

(4) That we abolish Job Press. Although it was not able to arrive at exact figures, the Study Group believes that the above recommendations might bring Curtis a savings in the area of $2 or $3 million a year in manufacturing costs. The Study Group hopes that Fenton B. Turck could assess these recommendations from an engineering standpoint.

III. *Circulation*

The Study Group spent a major portion of its time exploring the Curtis Circulation Company and its subsidiaries, and the fulfillment organization at Curtis-Electronic Data Processing.

We believe it is overstaffed, "fat," and that the inept management up to now has cost us unnecessary millions. We urge that the sprawling, confused operations of Circulation be consolidated into a trim, efficient company, bossed by a single man. G. B. McCombs (Number Two man in Circulation) has begun his own Study Group, and already he has found methods of saving money—perhaps as much as $700,000 a year. We believe G. B., an exceptionally able man, needs help. We therefore recommend that some outside consulting firm—J. K. Lasser or equivalent—be brought in to make a study of Circulation Company similar to the Turck studies in the manufacturing area.

The Study Group would not be surprised to learn that savings of upwards of $2 or $3 million a year could be made in the Circulation Company—with no loss in cash flow.

IV. *Consolidation*

We exhaustively explored the inefficient geographical sprawl of the multifarious parts of the Curtis Publishing Company.

We urge that, as rapidly as possible, all New York elements be consolidated, either in our own Curtis Building (hopefully), or at 666 Fifth Avenue, whichever seemed most practical. We also urge a temporary consolidation of all Philadelphia nonmanufacturing elements in the Curtis Building on Sixth Street and a consolidation of manufacturing at Sharon Hill, as touched on earlier in this report.

V. *Marketing*
The Study Group has submitted a separate report on the Curtis advertising sales structure and personnel. We felt the president was best qualified to deal with this problem—as he has been doing almost daily—so we confined our report to notes of caution about a few potential trouble areas.

VI. *Special Projects*
The Study Group was frankly astonished at the lack of professionalism in this area. The Study Group has, among other things, urged:

(1) That we begin publishing hardback trade books (not paperbacks).

(2) That any books growing out of Curtis material return earnings to Curtis, not to individual editors.

(3) That we actively solicit joint ventures for direct mail merchandising.

(4) That we revise Curtis literary contracts so that we buy all rights to material, including foreign and television rights.

(5) That a *Holiday* travel club be established with Fugazy, if we see sufficient profit potential in the venture.

(6) That Curtis try to buy VHF television stations.

(7) That Curtis investigate the potential of UHF television, and if it seems profitable, buy in.

(8) That Curtis seek out—through Special Projects—profitable specialty magazines, which can be absorbed into the Curtis Publishing Company, to be operated by the editorial director.

(9) That we try to develop a staple item such as an encyclopedia (too expensive), or Bible, or dictionary.

(10) That we explore the possibility of publishing other children's magazines—especially a "news" weekly.

(11) That we explore the possibility of acquiring a textbook publishing company—if any are available.

VII. *"Overhead"*
The Study Group spent a portion of its time wrestling with the great problem of "general company overhead." This item (the cost of running the company) has risen from about $7 million to $12 or $13 million, a considerable increase.

SUMMARY:
The Study Group recommends that:

(1) An editorial director be appointed.

(2) Editorial staffs be consolidated at 666 Fifth Avenue; or failing that, that *Ladies' Home Journal* and *American Home* staffs be merged at 300 Park, and *Holiday* transferred to 666 Fifth.

(3) The *Post* maintain status quo: 45 frequency 6.5 million circulation.

(4) The *Journal* maintain status quo: 10 frequency 6.5 million circulation.

(5) *American Home* maintain status quo: 10 frequency 3.25 million circulation.

(6) *Holiday* remain at 12 frequency; be reduced in circulation from 900,000 to 800,000.

(7) *Jack and Jill* be increased in circulation to 1 million, and that advertising be accepted.

I considered the Study Group report a very good piece of work. At this point in time, I knew more about Curtis than any man alive because, in addition to the Study Group reports, I alone had the Fenton B. Turck & Company, Inc., reports, the historical records of Curtis, and the files of the former president, plus my own knowledge and experience accumulated through the years at Hearst, Ziff-Davis, NBC, and Interpublic. Thus, it was relatively easy for me to factor Curtis' problems, set an order of priority, establish new and improved reporting lines, and issue directives and time schedules. I set up a dynamic communications pattern with key department heads.

From late fall of 1962 through the spring of 1963, I ran Curtis almost entirely by telephone, memo, and crash personal meetings at airports, in cars roaring along turnpikes, in the Curtis plane (a sturdy old twin Beech), and even a helicopter, which I leased, to cut down the time wasted getting from New York to

Philadelphia. My luck almost ran out twice in the helicopter trips between New York and my home in Rye. Over New Jersey a blinding rainstorm, with high winds, caught us not far from Newark. We were flung around like a ping-pong ball. When the rain stopped and visibility returned, the pilot and I were horrified to see a jet airliner en route to Newark Airport blasting by us less than fifty feet away.

The second time, just above the George Washington Bridge, we were caught in a downdraft. At any other place it would have been no problem. But here we plunged down, apparently straight at the bridge tower on the New York side. The pilot swung the helicopter parallel to the ground and we sideslipped out of danger. I congratulated myself on forcing Curtis to give me a $500,000 life insurance policy as a fringe benefit.

Before leaving on my trip, I decided to bring in some surefire business-getters who could deliver while I rebuilt the sales force. I set up a corporate marketing department. John Miles was secured from Time Inc., Jack Leonard from McCann-Erickson, Jim White from *This Week*, Jim Fuchs from NBC, and Philip Ewald from *The New Yorker*. I also hired Bill Buckley, an experienced book publishing executive, in the hope that we could generate some income from diversification. These men reported directly to me and were assigned key sales targets.

Clifford and I became "Mr. Inside" and "Mr. Outside"—he seldom out of the Philadelphia office, I rarely in it. I was bringing in the money; Clifford was making sure that some of it stayed at Curtis.

The year 1963 was a great one, undoubtedly the most productive of my business life. I reorganized the company, with the help of Fenton B. Turck & Company, Inc., and of the lessons I had learned from John Burns while I worked for him at NBC. When I came to Curtis it had thirty-one divisions, sixteen of which reported to Bob MacNeal, the remainder to Ford Robinson, vice-president for Operations. No manager can properly administer more than a half-dozen divisions, I had been taught, so I set Curtis up in six divisions—the Magazine Division (Editorial, Advertising, and Promotion), Production (all manufacturing), Circulation (under G. B. McCombs), Finance and Operations (under Clifford), and Paper and Special Projects. The chief operating officer of each one reported to me. I reserved Bank Relations for myself, initially. Later I put this division under Clifford—a decision that turned out badly, as described later.

I set great hopes on the Circulation Company, after making G. B. McCombs its president. Jim Fuchs was moved into direct control of the Curtis School Plan, which was under serious threat from *Reader's Digest*. McCombs and Fuchs performed magnificently, and earned the perpetual gratitude of Curtis.

Jim White, to whom I assigned the southern part of the United States, did a heroic job, and I rewarded him with the job of publisher of *Holiday*. Leon Marks, head of Production, responded to new leadership and kept the presses going despite deep cuts in expense and personnel. I will never know how he did it without bringing the unions into Curtis.

Clifford relentlessly pursued the personnel reduction plan, and when it was completed we had removed from the Curtis payroll 2,000 people, as well as reduced and simplified operations and eliminated departments with an annual financial saving of $13 million a year. The reduction was, by my orders, humanely carried out, with retirement, advance retirement, and special relocation programs. Had we achieved these results and brought on a reduction of the number of magazines produced or a loss of customers, it would still have been a virtuoso performance. But we actually produced more and better magazines, sold more advertising, sold more magazines, and vastly improved the Curtis profile through some expert public relations work.

We supplied the public, trade, and industry press with progress reports, cost reduction reports, advertising sales bulletins. Gallagher and *Time* ceased, for a time, their funereal bulletins. Also, I was getting some advance credit for the upcoming sales caravan.

The sales blitz followed a carefully designed plan. I learned quickly and at first hand about the sales management and force I had inherited in a way that could not have been duplicated in less than a year. The salesmen were assigned specific duties in the program, preparing briefing reports for me, which they had to deliver immediately before each sales call, usually in a car taking me from meeting to meeting. Not only did I get to know the strong ones immediately, but I was able to evaluate the majority of the staff. It became painfully apparent that the Curtis sales force was as dreary as most of the rest of Curtis.

My sales blitz was great for the morale of Curtis. One episode in Toledo, Ohio, was particularly touching. I had planned to make my main calls in Cleveland, but the salesman covering Toledo begged me to come there and call on his accounts. Suddenly I realized that my appearance had become a status symbol for the salesmen. *Time* and other publications had made so much of my unprecedented trip and client coverage that each salesman now had to deliver me to *his* territory or lose face with his prospects. Despite the burden and my temporary exhaustion, I agreed to go to Toledo, though the only way I could get there was by a helicopter. We hired a small one and telephoned the salesman to get permission for us to land in the park in the middle of town. He did so, and we took off. The salesman met us and whisked me off to his three clients. After I made my presentations, he returned me to the park, where I boarded the helicopter for the return to Cleveland. As it took off, I turned to wave at the salesman below. Standing at attention, he threw me a snappy military salute.

Results from the sales blitz came in rapidly, and the spirits of the Curtis staff rose in geometrical proportions. The board also reacted to the stream of good news. As the increased volume was felt in financial statements to the banks, the mood of the three Philadelphia banks changed for the better, but nothing seemed to reverse the increasing chill from the First National City Bank. Warning signs were appearing in several places that the bad trend might be irreversible.

The sales blitz was also splendid for *my* morale. I visited about sixty-five cities in thirty states, to have personal meetings with 200 potential advertisers. Only a rampant national politician can appreciate the variety and depth of the experiences encountered in that kind of trip. There were excitement, drama, sadness, inspiration, and humor in abundance. I spent a large part of six months in airports, motel lobbies, scheduled flights, charter flights, the Curtis plane and helicopter, in cars and reception rooms and business offices. An occurrence in New Orleans gave me many a tantalizing memory. I was making a speech to a mixed group of leading citizens in which I commented on some of the less attractive aspects of contemporary life. My final sentence, delivered with appropriate drama, was a quotation from a preacher who said in a Sunday sermon, "Millions yearn for immortality, but don't know what to do with themselves on a rainy Sunday afternoon." I sat down to a good round of applause. As the luncheon moved toward conclusion, a waiter handed me a note. Written in a beautiful feminine handwriting, it read, "Mr. Culligan—I can tell you what we could do on a rainy Sunday afternoon!"

I looked carefully around the room. Sure enough, a quarter of the way across I spotted a beautiful brunette looking at me with the wickedest, most delectable smile imaginable. Unfortunately I had to run for a plane, so I never did learn what she had in mind.

I suppose the greatest compliment I got for my sales blitz came from Mike Cowles, head of Cowles Communications, principal architect of the success of *Look*. He told me he had cut short his Florida vacation because his publisher ran up a distress signal over the loss of about a hundred pages of advertising to the *Post*.

Contracts for a firm total of $78 million were the fruit of my tree-shaking in six months. Behind this total are some obscure facts. Not only the acquisition of new business for the *Post* was involved. Scores of old and loyal *Post* advertisers were starting to defect because of the shocking blunder made by the creators of the so-called New *Post*, which was variously described as "the work of a group of drunken art directors" and "the result of turning the *Post* over to the finger painters." The constant trumpeting by *Time* and *The Gallagher Report* of every bit of trouble at Curtis had also gradually undermined confidence in the company. Even the great professionals of Detroit were showing signs of wavering.

I am proud of my Curtis sales blitz. Nothing like it had been done by one man before, and nothing like it has been done since. However, I was to pay a high price for the sales blitz because, during my absences, a most lamentable schism developed between Curtis and the First National City Bank. It was caused by Clifford, and it could have been an acorn in importance. He made it an oak by one typical bit of abruptness.

While I was away, Clifford hired a man named Carl Meister for a marketing job in the New York and Pennsylvania Co. Meister had been employed by an appliance company in Philadelphia, but a "family" dispute broke out and the employees chose sides. Meister picked the wrong side, found himself unemployed, and disliked by the victors. Unfortunately, one of the Curtis banks was on the *winning* side. When the credit officer of the bank heard that Clifford had hired Meister, he called and criticized him for the action. One of the least tactful men in the Western Hemisphere, Clifford answered, "Just because we owe you money, don't try to tell me how to run my business." Hardly the right thing to say to a nervous banker.

Clifford's comment spread among the banks instantly, and the honeymoon with them was over. I do not doubt that Curtis would have been thrown into bankruptcy if all its lending banks had been in New York—they would have moved as a unit. But three of them were in Philadelphia. Two of these, each holding $7 million notes, were managed by delightful, constructive men—Bill Kelly of the First Pennsylvania for Banking and Trust and Fred Potts of the Philadelphia National. The extraordinary Bill Bodine of the Philadelphia National was also a stalwart. I judged that my only hope was to try to wedge the New York bank away from the Philadelphia banks, using loyalty to old Curtis as the lever. It worked; the Philadelphia banks did not jump all over me as the New York bank did.

Then a strange development indicated to *me* that the end was in sight for Curtis and First National City Bank. Ted Gardner started demanding that Curtis sell some major asset to get the money to pay off the $22 million debt, $7.5 million of which was its share. By odd coincidence, *Reader's Digest* appeared with an offer to buy the very valuable, very profitable Curtis School Plan.

I was struck by the irony of the situation in the spring of 1963. Curtis was vastly improved in some aspects, improving in others; but First National City Bank was not impressed, not interested in anything but the repayment of its $7 million loan. The credit officer was stone-cold to me. I started having daytime nightmares of a collapse of Curtis. My instincts told me Curtis and I needed new allies, and I started that spring to find them. I found one in Pat Clifford, then vice-president of the Franklin National Bank. At the conclusion of our very first lunch, he put out his hand and said, "Joe, you can count on me for $5 million when you need me." I was to need him less than a year later, and he was *better* than his word—he came in for $5.5 million.

However, though Pat Clifford was the best banker I had met up to that time, his bank, the Franklin National, did not have a commanding enough position in United States banking to carry the load completely. I searched for the one banker who could inspire others. In an unusual, unorthodox way, I found him in the spring of 1963. This discovery led to my single most important contribution to Curtis.

6

By the spring of 1963 I had been president of Curtis for less than nine months. Amazingly enough, most of the experiments I had tried panned out well.

The Study Group had done its work and produced reports on all phases of Curtis. Fenton B. Turck & Co., had reviewed these and confirmed which recommendations were sound. The Turck organization also rang the warning bell on recommendations that, though sound on the surface, would be ruinous if carried out. For example, the Study Group had recommended the dismantling, moving, and reassembling of some gigantic old presses from the Curtis building to the Curtis printing plant in Sharon Hill, some twenty miles away. The consolidation made sense, the presses could be moved. But Turck informed me that those presses had been rebuilt, propped up, experimented with, improvised, and—in his words—"were running from memory." "Joe," he said, "I will stake my career on it—you dismantle those presses, move them twenty feet, not twenty miles, and they'll never print anything again."

Clifford had succeeded up to the fullest expectation in cost reduction. About 2,000 people had been removed from the payroll. Payroll and other costs were down at the annual rate of $13 million, and the program was only 75 percent completed.

Clay Blair was whipping the Curtis editors into unprecedented action, and a new vitality was apparent in the *Post.* Circulation was up too, and I dared to think about, and soon put through an increase in the cover price.

Time had nothing to slam Curtis about and was very quiet.

The Gallagher Report, starting in the fall of 1962, had been complimentary. For example:

HOLD YOUR FIRE. Madison Avenue wiseacres too ready to criticize, Culligan is getting results according to schedule.(1) He's been all over the country convincing advertisers that Curtis magazines have a future. Already has close to $41 million worth of ads on the books. (2) Renewed the confidence of banks to the tune of $22 million. (3) Appointed new top executives in management, advertising, selling by promotion from inside Curtis. Now going outside. Has just hired Bill Buckley from book department of McCall's to head Curtis' new Special Projects Department. Has a new top financial officer in the person of J. M. Clifford, formerly of RCA and NBC. (4) Hired Fenton B. Turck & Company, Inc., industrial engineering experts, to go over Curtis' production and eliminate outdated systems and excessive personnel. (5) Made Clay Blair (protégé of Admiral Strauss) Vice-President and Director of editorial requirements to upgrade editorial on all magazines. [Point No. 5 was incorrect—Blair got the job *before* I joined Curtis.]

In January 1963, a signal honor:

ADVERTISING, MARKETING, MEDIA MEN OF THE YEAR. Selected by readers of *The Gallagher Report.* Matthew "Joe" Culligan, new President of Curtis Publishing, voted "The Man Who Did Most For The Advertising Industry During 1962."

And on July 9:

HIGH HOPES. Curtis now has promising future. Stock at present price (between 7 and 8) a good buy. Should double in next eighteen months.

Gallagher told me he bought Curtis stock before making the prediction. He later boasted that he sold the same stock at a much higher price.

All these good signs, however, did not impress the First National City Bank, and I felt the end of the relationship was coming. Fate again took a hand—its unlikely instrument the marvelous, inimitable Matty Fox. Matty, among the world's greatest promoters and salesmen, had been instrumental in the beginnings of pay TV. He had an explosively inventive mind, and he could sell almost anything to somebody.

Matty called me about "a sensational, multimillion-dollar deal," and I broke a date to see him, so fond of him was I. He rolled into my office, short, round, and bald with a black fringe of hair, and bouncing with energy. He described a heroic barter plan, which included thousands of tons of aluminum. I never questioned Matty during one of his presentations, partly because he was spellbinding and partly because he had a low boiling point about criticism.

When Matty was all finished, I said, "Matty, it's great, but I can't do it now. Let's give it a go after July first."

He accepted that, and then we visited as mutually concerned friends. I told him about my bank problems, and he was unequivocal in his advice. He said that a bank relationship was like marriage—once gone "sour," it was irretrievable. Continuing the analogy, he said, "Get a divorce."

Matty spoke of his devotion to the famous Serge Semenenko, then vice-chairman of the First National Bank of Boston. Even at that early date I knew a bit about Semenenko. He preferred anonymity, but some of his spectacular banking successes were well known. Most significant was the lucky fact that he and I had mutual friends whom he held in high regard.

I jumped at Matty Fox's idea and asked him to arrange an introduction to Semenenko for me. Through Matty I was invited to visit the banker at his sumptuous office in the Hotel Pierre. I don't know what I expected Semenenko to be like, but I was not surprised to find him warm, friendly, and generous. Within minutes I knew that he *had* to be my banker. He was fearless and used to fast-paced, highly competitive businesses. He knew publishing, paper, motion pictures, and television through working with Hearst, International Paper Company, and Warner Brothers, Seven Arts. He was reported to love challenges. I surely presented one. One other quality encouraged me. He was people-oriented. Fox had told me, "If Serge likes you, trusts you, you're in."

Serge Semenenko opened our meeting by expressing great affection for Matty Fox. I knew that he would have seen me as a courtesy to Fox, no matter how uninterested he might be in my problem. But a subtle change came over our meeting when I mentioned my relationship with Dick Berlin. Later I learned that Berlin, for whom I had worked at Hearst, was a close friend some twenty years before *I* met Serge, who had entered the picture at Hearst when Berlin was desperate for help. In that instance also, one of the banks had turned completely sour and was demanding payment of its loan. Semenenko came to the rescue, and advanced the necessary funds, enabling Berlin to save the Hearst Corporation. Semenenko gained Berlin's perpetual gratitude in addition to a balance at his bank, which at times reached $50 million.

Serge Semenenko's New York base at the Pierre was artfully designed for his comfort and business efficiency. He had a two-room office, with reception room, plus a lovely apartment beautifully furnished in an Old World manner, with Russian religious overtones.

Semenenko greeted me warmly. I noted his slight accent, and took in quickly also his medium size, trim build, excellently cut suit, alert eyes, and encouraging smile. He had an unusually interesting, high-domed face.

The first meeting was not very long and was mainly social. I told him about my troubles with the First National City Bank. He nodded but said nothing critical of the bank. I had been warned not to push hard in the early stages with Semenenko, who equated haste with panic. But I deliberately told him exactly how serious the problem at Curtis was and how difficult the solution would be. I described the situation I had found when I arrived there, as well as my initial moves and my hiring of Clifford, and gave him a timetable for the accomplishment of some of the initial goals. Naturally, I accented my program of direct contact with all the leading advertisers. He obviously enjoyed the report, and applauded my actions and the way I had gone about them.

When it became apparent that Semenenko did not intend to close the door on me, I decided to grab my minor victory and run. I asked if I could keep in touch with him and report on progress, and hope that some day in the future I might interest him in entering the Curtis picture. He agreed with some warmth, saying something that was characteristic of him throughout our entire relationship: "Serge Semenenko is always interested in a constructive banking challenge." The word "constructive" was one of his favorites and I never, in personal experience or in fact or rumor, heard of any variation in his entire career. I became his fan early, and my admiration grew throughout our relationship.

I put Semenenko on my "tickler file" and either called him or visited him at least monthly through late spring, summer, and early fall of 1963. I would not attempt to accomplish too much in each meeting, but I was able each time to show him the progress being made in advertising income, savings, and loss reduction.

This last point was especially dramatic. By stopping the loss of advertising revenue, even increasing it slightly, while saving what finally amounted to $13 million in 1963, we reduced the loss from $18.9 million, the 1962 figure I had inherited from MacNeal, to $3.4 million in 1963. Semenenko thought this was a fabulous achievement, particularly the cost reduction. In early summer he made a definite step in my direction by introducing me to two of his brightest assistants, Peter Reed and Bill Thompson. Not long after I met these two men, I realized why Serge had been able to make decisions involving scores of millions and never have a loan go bad, which was his record in over thirty years of banking for the most difficult industries, such as motion pictures and paper, in some of the most desperate circumstances. His staff work was superb. He asked if Thompson and Reed would be given freedom of movement at Curtis to conduct a study of all its operations, explaining that he could not possibly be interested in Curtis or any other company without a complete investigation. I was elated, for I felt that Curtis by this time was a vastly improved company compared to what I had inherited.

Reed and Thompson went to work within Curtis with incredible speed and thoroughness. Within three months they and Semenenko knew more about Curtis in most respects than the entire board combined, and certainly several times more than I knew, since a good part of my time was being spent in editorial and marketing matters. By September, they had completed their studies and compiled a voluminous document, which covered every aspect of Curtis' operations, including their evaluation of me and of my staff. The gist of it was that I knew exactly what I was doing in the areas in which I had experience and background, and had brought in good specialists in areas in which I did not have personal knowledge or experience. They made advertiser and advertising agency calls to determine the new profile of Curtis. Their conclusion—in fact, their recommendation—was that Curtis was well on its way to being revitalized; that profitability was indeed possible; and that there were enough assets around to protect the bank even if Curtis failed. The report to Semenenko came not a moment too soon. It stated:

> The writers feel that a credit of $40 million can be safely made to the Curtis Publishing Company. The job of reconstruction of an all but defunct company is well along and is in the hands of an extremely capable management. While this management has admittedly lacked finesse and

expertise in its financial relations, this was not nearly as critical a failure as a lack of top advertising ability or cost control would have been. The basic reasons for our conclusion can be summarized as follows:

1. Curtis has asset values far in excess of book values. We estimate a total value of between $80MM–$100MM, which in relation to our proposed loan of $40MM gives us reasonable coverage.

2. Any loan to a company of this nature must be based on confidence in the capabilities of management. The important problem areas have been attacked with vigor, and we believe management is equal to the tasks facing it in the future.

3. The financial crisis in which Curtis finds itself is a relatively recent one. The company has proved over a number of decades that it can earn satisfactory profits, and since the potential has not been lost, we believe that a proper and efficient utilization of its assets can once again produce a reasonable return.

4. The recent reports we have seen on advertising revenues indicate that the downtrend may have leveled off and we feel that the 1963-1964 ad budgets appear reasonable.

5. Once the company gets itself back on firm financial ground, there are a number of opportunities for profitable ventures through merger or acquisition. Our whole plan is based on the concept that Curtis is much more valuable as a corporate publishing system than cut up into its various corporate segments in order to provide a better credit picture.

6. Finally, the Curtis situation offers any bank the opportunity of performing a very constructive banking job and participating in the rehabilitation of a large nationally known corporation that for many years has been a common household word.

William Thompson
Peter Reed

At this point, communications with First National City Bank broke down altogether. Gardner was remote, and his immediate superior, Newton Cutler, the regional manager of the bank, was called into the picture, apparently with the instructions from upstairs to get the bank out of the Curtis situation with all possible haste. I was immediately sorry that I had not met Cutler earlier and under different circumstances. He was of much finer clay than Gardner. I felt that we could have had an excellent relationship if we had come to know each other before the activities of the paper company executive and the highly placed financial officer of Time Inc., cited earlier. By the time Cutler became involved, he had his instructions and could do little other than take orders.

The stern conversation with the First National City Bank took on substance in writing, and in an exchange of letters, Curtis was virtually told that its note would not be renewed, and the bank demanded to know what plans we had for paying the $7 million we owed. Once I was certain the trend was irreversible, I went to Semenenko for what certainly was the most fateful meeting for Curtis up to that time, taking Cutler's letter with me. Its harsh message was:

> This will confirm our telephone conversation on Friday, August 16, which was occasioned by the maturities on that date of notes of Curtis Publishing Company and Curtis Circulation Company. In accordance with our prior understanding, you have now received demand notes in amounts of $5,760,000 and $1,240,000 respectively. I telephoned you on Friday in order to be absolutely certain that the significance of these demand notes was clear to you and to your associates in the financial management of Curtis.
>
> We realize that you are faced with the immediate problem of determining what method of payment of both of these obligations you would elect in the event demand were made upon you. We request that you advise us as soon as possible what your plans for repayment would be if your banks forced you to take this action.
>
> In the meanwhile, and in order to bring this matter to an ultimate point of resolution, we request that you furnish us within the next thirty (30) days, or before September 16, with a plan satisfactory to us for the payment of both of the above-mentioned notes before the end of this calendar year.
>
> To avoid any possible misunderstanding, I should emphasize that in asking for such a plan before September 16, we are not indicating or even implying that we will not be forced to demand payment at any time. Clearly, we must reserve this right in the event that a reconsideration of our position or any adverse change in your own condition makes it necessary for us to demand immediate payment.
>
> *(Signed)* Newton Cutler
> V. P.
> First National City Bank

With a mien that was as serious as I could muster, I entered Serge's office at the Pierre. Quietly and soberly I told him of the position taken by Cutler, showed him the letter of ultimatum, and said, "Serge, it's now or never." I really felt as though my heart had stopped beating—I know I stopped breathing while waiting for his answer.

"Joe, my dear," he said, smiling, "you can tell our friends at the City Bank that Serge Semenenko has entered the Curtis picture." At that moment, the words did not seem as powerful as they were quickly proved to be.

I asked him if that meant his bank would "take out" First National City Bank, which would have been the usual practice. That was not at all what Semenenko had in mind. He did not just want a *part* of the Curtis loan; he wanted the role of "managing the entire credit in a massive capital reorganization of Curtis."

I asked him how we could proceed. He instructed me first to advise First National City Bank of his entry into the situation, adding that he would quickly get in touch with the three Philadelphia banks and attempt to hold them in line. Then, during the winter of 1963, he would work with Curtis in a brand-new credit, which would clean up some of the mess that had accumulated over the years. I said, "How do we pay off First National City, as they're now demanding?" He answered matter-of-factly, "Oh, they won't be in any hurry now that we have entered the picture." I found it hard to believe, but he was right!

I must admit that I derived a great deal of pleasure from my meeting with Ted Gardner of First National City. He condescended to have lunch with me on my invitation, no doubt assuming I was coming on bended knee to beg a reprieve. I waited until we had finished lunch—and until he said "Well, what about it?" (the "it" being his $7 million).

Then I let him have it right between the eyes, using the exact words Semenenko had authorized: "Would you please advise your associates that Serge Semenenko and the First National Bank of Boston are entering the Curtis picture?"

The magic words had a devastating effect on Gardner. Paled and speechless, he stared incredulously at me. Then he mumbled something and made a hasty, unraveled exit to get the message back to Newton Cutler and the brass at First National City Bank.

Serge Semenenko moved with great speed once he had made

the commitment to me. He spoke long-distance to Bill Kelly of First Pennsylvania Bank and Fred Potts of Philadelphia National Bank. They agreed to stay calm and meet him in Philadelphia to hear his plan for the refinancing of Curtis. I told Serge about the generous offer of Pat Clifford of the Franklin for $5 million. Semenenko seemed somewhat surprised by this, and so I insisted on confirming it. Clifford repeated to Semenenko his commitment, and a new respect for me developed.

Simultaneously, I told the Executive Committee and the Finance Committee of Curtis. There was first disbelief, then chagrin, that I had not informed them of my campaign to enlist Semenenko. Only Clifford had known of it, and he was involved because Semenenko wanted to size him up before making the final commitment. I had kept the Semenenko refinancing plan to myself because the Curtis board leaked like a sieve, though there were a few directors I was sure I could trust—among them Moreau Brown, Curtis Barkes, and Robert MacLean Stewart.

Through early November, the highest priority was the completion of the refinancing plan, a massive $38 million project. Semenenko got approval of the First National Bank of Boston for $10 million, and he and I persuaded the two Philadelphia banks to increase their participation to $7.5 million each. That made $25 million. Pat Clifford brought the Franklin in for $5.5 million, swelling the total to $30.5 million. The rest came from the Union of Los Angeles and the Houston Association of the Southwest, both called on by me personally—for a grand total of $38 million.

From the moment I told Ted Gardner about Serge Semenenko's coming into the Curtis picture, I never had a cross word from him or the bank.

It was now late November 1963, and all indexes at Curtis were up: Advertising increases were being achieved, the $38 million bank loan was virtually assured, circulation of Curtis magazines had been increased. Morale was generally excellent, and I, for the first time since July 1962, felt certain that the company was saved.

November and December of 1963 were the two happiest months of my business career. I had known the job as president of Curtis was too big for me when I took it, but I gambled on being able to grow into it. In November and December I thought I had.

The praise, prestige, the millions of dollars ahead, were exhilarating. Still, every so often I'd regard myself with some disbelief and ask, as I had on the day I first sat in the Curtis boardroom as president, "What in hell are you doing here?"

Some clouds were gathering, however, and not all of them inside the company. A group of preferred shareholders, who considered themselves the true owners of Curtis, organized a "vigilante committee" to protect their interests. They were quite secure, they thought, because Curtis could not borrow money by pledging assets. As long as the assets were uncommitted, the preferred shareholders would come first (after salaries and bank debt) in case of bankruptcy. The Semenenko-managed credit was conditional on pledging of Curtis assets. Somehow Curtis had to gain the support of the vigilante committee.

It was Marvin Kantor, then a Curtis director, who volunteered to "pull the teeth" of this committee of the preferred shareholders. He was very good at that sort of thing and had the proper instincts for the task. He knew the mentality of vigilante-committee types and also of the "strike lawyers" who often fatten their wallets with nuisance suits against public companies. Kantor did indeed achieve the promised results, aided by the fortunate fact that this particular committee was constructively inclined. Gould also helped, as did a task force of Curtis executives to whom I assigned the names of large preferred holdings for a telephone canvass and selling job.

I felt myself in Kantor's debt as a result of this episode. I repaid this debt later, to my great sorrow.

Then I lost a potential ally. Carl M. Loeb, Rhoades & Co., the huge investment banking house, had been interested in Curtis. Its head, John Loeb, Sr., had a particular interest. His daughter, Ann, was married to Edgar Bronfman, president of Seagram's, and Bronfman owned over 170,000 shares of Curtis. This stock was worth about $900,000 when I took over Curtis; within eighteen months it was worth almost $2 million because of general improvements. Loeb, Rhoades sold the Curtis stock, and when the Bronfman stock was sold and Loeb, Rhoades no longer had any stake in Curtis, I lost a valuable potential ally and an outstanding director, Robert MacLean Stewart. Kantor moved closer to me after Loeb, Rhoades left the scene. I found myself depending on him, as a director, for advice on financial affairs. In fact, Moreau Brown had run a check on him at my request. The Brown report bore no negatives.

When the "salad oil scandal" broke in the summer and fall of 1963, I felt genuine concern for Marvin Kantor. His firm, Williston & Beane, was involved in a minor way with Tony DeAngelis, the central figure in this astonishing mess. Kantor was not personally involved in the situation even within his own firm, but he was vulnerable, as were all executives, if the firm were swamped, and it was. Small oceans of salad oil had disappeared, and many sophisticated organizations—American Express, Ira Haupt & Co. (a brokerage firm), and half a dozen banks—were holding "paper" that was worthless without full tanks of salad oil.

Williston & Beane was relatively small and not overly financed. It could not survive the suspension forced by the New York Stock Exchange, or the loss of customer confidence, which sent hundreds of its clients scurrying off to other brokers. The only solution was to find refuge in a larger firm. It did—Williston & Beane was "absorbed" by Walston & Co., a large, strongly financed brokerage and investment banking firm. Kantor was thus out of work. He had a family to support and obviously lacked reserves, and he appealed to me for a job.

I checked the Executive Committee first. There was no objection, so I hired him as chairman of the Magazine Division. Only Milton Gould expressed any reservations about hiring Kantor. He later threw it up to me in an "I told you so" comment.

Here, again, fate took a hand. The bank loan was in preparation at this time, *but not signed.* If it had been signed and in effect, I could not have hired Kantor without specific approval from Semenenko. Semenenko, I am sure, would have talked me out of hiring Kantor. When I told him, after the fact, he looked at me with great sadness and disappointment and said, "I'm afraid you will regret this move, Joe." It was too late then; Kantor was an employee and had a contract. I was to regret this decision more than any I made in over fifteen years in business. I paid dearly for it.

While I was making that mistake, Clifford was continuing to make his mistake with the editors, through his staff. There was no one major affront to the editors, but a continuing stream of petty irritations. Credit cards were canceled without notice, expense accounts were questioned, salary increases were delayed for weeks, even months. Rules and regulations about working hours and vacations, sound enough in normal business operations, were attempted in editorial areas in which they had no validity or use.

Readers familiar with magazine publishing know that there is always a conflict between the editorial and business sides of the enterprise. The editors insist on complete freedom, sometimes even license. The business office is responsible for profits, and tries to influence the course of the magazine to whatever degree possible, to make it acceptable to advertisers. The editors also want to close the magazine as *late* as possible in order to accommodate late-breaking stories; the business office wants to close as *early* as possible to avoid overtime.

The two sides are naturally antagonistic. Effective top management generally keeps the operations on an even keel, but almost always by being partial to the editors. That was my policy at Curtis. Clifford, for all his time and experience in business, had a blind spot that had become apparent at NBC. He acted as though creative people were no different from other types in business and treated everyone about the same, which was mainly with rudeness. Almost always when the top man is rude, his subordinates seem to feel they must outdo him in his specialty. As a consequence, some of Clifford's subordinates were grim, blunt, abrasive, insensitive "machines" who followed orders to the very letter.

I had deliberately directed Clifford's cost reduction program to the other departments of Curtis first, leaving Editorial to the last. He had moved into the other areas like an avenging angel. First he dictated, with my approval, an across-the-board 20 percent cut in personnel. If any department head could prove that a 20 percent cut in personnel was absolutely out of the question (and this was damned difficult), Clifford would accept an equivalent cut in the department budget in dollars.

The agonized howls of old-line Curtis managers reached every corner of Philadelphia. Appeals were made to the Curtis-Bok family. The Philadelphia banks received pleas to "stop the madmen (Culligan and Clifford) who were ruining Curtis." I had to hold off the directors, who were constantly questioning the reductions. They could not believe Curtis could function under such cuts. It was only after months, during which we produced more and better magazines and the losses started to show steep reductions, that the awful truth finally dawned on some of the old Curtis directors. They had been sitting on the Curtis board, theoretically protecting the interests of the public stockholders, while MacNeal and his staff spent millions of dollars a year over a ten-year period.

Small wonder they were terrified—and grateful, at least for a while. Their gratitude was evident in many ways, the most pleasing of which was a bonus of $30,000 to me for the year 1963, and a salary increase of the same amount for the remainder of my three-and-a-half-year contract. In net dollars, that gesture, an official act of the Curtis board at the December 1963 meeting, was worth $135,000 in *new* income to me. *Time* never reported this sign of Curtis' gratitude, though it was well known.

Clifford did a monumental job in cost reduction and control through most of 1963. In the spring he had started installing his cost reduction and control procedures in the Editorial Department. I thought—and hoped—that he had learned something about handling creative people after his experiences at NBC. At least, he seemed to be listening to and agreeing with me when I described the problems of cost reduction in an Editorial Department. But he and his people blundered into Editorial. Within a few months the editors were in a rage.

Most of these editors had had reservations about Clay Blair when he assumed the role as vice-president, Editorial—that is, those who were not in the close coterie of friends Blair had personally hired. Ted Patrick, the late, great editor of *Holiday,* was disdainful of Blair, saw right through him. In former days, when he had his full vigor, Patrick would have "brushed Blair off" in any controversy. By this time, however, Patrick was old, ill, and rapidly losing interest. Now Clifford made Blair the hero of the editors. It was Blair to whom they would go with their complaints about the rudeness of some of Clifford's people and their lack of understanding of the problems of editing magazines. Blair acted on this development as a gift of the gods. Editors who did not particularly trust or respect him trusted and respected Clifford even less, and Blair used this situation to cement his position as the editors' spokesman. He was their white knight, defending them against Clifford and his staff.

Blair would come to me with complaints, some of which

were picayune and silly, but there were always several bona fide items that I could see were alienating the editors. I would call Clifford on these, and he would generally agree with me that they were unnecessary harassments and promise to talk with his people about them. All would be peaceful for a time. Then another batch of complaints would accumulate, Blair would come to me, there would be another meeting with Clifford—the whole routine repeated.

In October, after an unusually rugged period for the editors, they rose in rebellion with Blair as their chieftain. While I was traveling on advertising business, the editors met and drafted what they called an "Editorial Manifesto," which they bade Blair bring to me. In what became a comedy of errors, Blair gave the Manifesto to Philip Ewald, public relations chief. Ewald called Marvin Kantor and told him about it. Kantor grabbed the document and held it for my return, in the meantime telling Clifford about it. Kantor was not then an employee of Curtis, but he and Clifford were fairly close. Kantor called me long-distance, tracked me to an airport, and in a state of alarm and excitement said, "Joe, you have a palace revolution against Clifford on your hands." Then he read the Editorial Manifesto to me:

October 9, 1963

The editors of *The Saturday Evening Post, Ladies' Home Journal, Holiday, American Home,* and *Jack and Jill* are finding it increasingly difficult to function effectively because of the steady encroachment into editorial operations of the Curtis business department, the comptroller's [Maurice Poppei's] office, and the office of the executive vice-president [J. M. Clifford]. In order to concentrate our thought and energy on producing a good editorial product, we must have the undisputed right to control editorial personnel, make prompt and necessary staff replacements, negotiate editorial contracts, and control all editorial budgets within limits previously determined. Business office delays, interference, and harassment are undermining the Curtis editorial operation, lessening its ability to compete with other publications, occupying too much of the time of the editors, and lowering the quality of our magazines. The Curtis Editorial Board asks for immediate and permanent relief from this interference, and a return to the editorial freedom granted by Cyrus H. K.

Curtis to George Horace Lorimer and Edward W. Bok, which has been a traditional policy in this company until the past six months.

THE CURTIS EDITORIAL BOARD

s/Clay Blair, Jr., Vice-President, Editorial
  Charles D. Thomas, Editor, *Ladies' Home Journal*
  Caskie Stinnett
  Asger Jerrill, Art Director
  Ted Patrick, Editor, *Holiday*
  Norman Ritter, Assistant to Clay Blair
  William A. Emerson, Jr., Managing Editor, *Saturday Evening Post*
  Frederick Moffitt, Editor, *Jack and Jill*
  Don A. Schanche, Assistant Editor, *Saturday Evening Post*
  H. G. Walker, Editorial Assistant to Clay Blair

After I got the editors calmed down, I had one final heart-to-heart talk with Clifford. Instead of showing concern and contriteness, he was abrasive and vituperative. He described the editors as "a bunch of goddamned lunatics." He refused to back up an inch. I had to conclude that there would be no change in his approach and treatment of editors. So, as an expedient, I moved him one step away from Editorial by interposing Bill Buckley, whom I had brought over from the McCall Corporation to head up the Curtis Book Division, between Clifford and the editors. Buckley was acceptable to them and seemed to get along well with Clifford, and the plan worked well through the early part of 1964. The steady improvement of Curtis did much to relieve the pressure caused by Clifford's intransigence.

Here again, my gratitude and sentiment misled me with Clifford. I knew what a superb job he had done for Curtis from November 1962 through 1963. Alone, I could not have done the things that had to be done during that period, and I was deeply grateful to him, and sympathetic also, since his health was a matter of concern. He had had some kind of internal growth years before and the problem flared up again. It seemed to me not at all unlikely that the long hours and worry connected with his job contributed to his poor health. I should have retired him with full honors and rewards—but I didn't. Clifford resented my decision to back the editors and never forgave me for it.

In spite of everything, the month of December 1963 was delightful. All the hard work of eighteen months paid off in huge dividends. A special meeting of the Curtis shareholders was called during that month to present the Semenenko finance plan, which was voted on in a most exciting meeting. There was vocal opposition from individual shareholders, but no organized opposition thanks to the great work of Kantor with the preferred shareholders' vigilante committee. I received a standing ovation from the stockholders. Personally, I considered the Semenenko bank loan and the establishment of $38 million credit as my greatest single sale, accomplished alone. The effect on the trade and industry press was electrifying. Advertising increased, and a profit was achieved in the fourth quarter. This was followed by a modest profit in the first quarter of 1964. *Curtis had six consecutive months of profit,* a near-miracle considering the 1962 loss of almost $19 million. *The New York Times* selected me as "one of the men who left a strong imprint on U.S. business in 1963."

Had Curtis built on this foundation, there is no doubt in my mind that the company would have been returned to good financial health by the close of 1964. That was not to be.

7

Aphorisms can be useful. In a very funny book titled *What It Means to Be a Politician,* by an erstwhile West Coast politician named Stimson Bullitt, there is an amusingly touching description of a political defeat: "The moment of truth for a man comes when he learns whether he's the bull or the bullfighter." I was both at Curtis.

At first I was the bullfighter, in full control, with a choice of time, companions, and weapons with which to meet the bulls. I had the power of promotions and raises. I could hire and fire executives, close down whole divisions, employ consultants, change accountants, influence purchasing, change suppliers for everything from ink to insurance. For almost two years I was the bullfighter. I had the power. I ran Curtis.

Then Curtis started to run me. I became the bull. Exactly when and precisely how the change occurred, I do not know. What I do know is that it happened between March and May of 1964.

I reached my peak at Curtis in December 1963, but I lacked the experience and wisdom to capitalize on it. At that point in time, with the backing of Serge Semenenko, I was in virtual control of Curtis. I should have forced the Curtis-Bok family to sell its stock to a syndicate organized by me, or to give me voting control of that stock, but I didn't.

I should have asked Linton, Franklin, and Fuller to resign from the Curtis Board to open opportunities for me to attract younger, trusted, talented new directors, like Harry C. Mills, whom I brought in as a director, but I didn't. I should have retired Clifford because of his troublemaking with the editors and his intransigence, but I didn't. I should have dissolved the position of editor-in-chief of all Curtis magazines and restricted Blair to editing the *Post,* but I didn't. I should have realized that to Cary Bok and the Philadelphia directors I was an outsider, but I didn't.

No bullfighter can make that many mistakes and remain a bullfighter, or a live ex-bullfighter. No chief executive officer can make that many mistakes either, and survive.

I did not make all or any of these pivotal moves that might

have saved me for a variety of reasons. Like others of my particular type, I am usually at my best when conditions are at their worst. Everything looked so positive in January and February of 1964 that I felt it was time to let Curtis run like a well-organized business, which by this time it was.

The Curtis organization chart looked like a Booz, Allen & Hamilton model. Curtis was decentralized in four profit centers. First was the Magazine Division under Marvin Kantor, its primary functions being Editorial and Marketing. Kantor, the chairman, was actually the administrative officer, a post for which he was qualified. Clay Blair was editor-in-chief, as well as editor, of the *Post.* Each magazine had its own publisher and sales staff. The publishers were Jesse Ballew, the *Post;* John Collins, *American Home;* J. Michael Hadley, the *Journal;* Jim White, *Holiday;* and Bob Young, *Jack and Jill.*

The second profit center was the Curtis Circulation Company, ably led by G. B. McCombs. New York & Penn, the paper company, also operated as a profit center, as did the much smaller Special Projects Division, under Bill Buckley.

The fifth division—Finance and Operations—was a service center, which served the profit centers and was supported by them via contributions according to services rendered, size, and past history. J. M. Clifford headed up that division through January 1964, when I had to remove him.

There were two powerful committees: one was the Curtis Executive Committee—Linton, Brown, Fuller, Franklin, and me, with H. C. Mills as a nonvoting added member. This committee was authorized to "act for the full board between meetings." Its decisions, however, had to be ratified by the board at the regular monthly board meetings. The second committee, the most useful and effective one, was the one I recommended and with which I worked in complete harmony. This was the Curtis Finance Committee—chairman, Moreau D. Brown.

With the signing of the bank loan agreement in December, Serge Semenenko, as representative of the "lead bank" (the most money and the organizer), had "approval of management" rights; the Curtis management needed advance approval for any major changes after January 1, 1964. As agent bank, the First National Bank of Boston would receive one-eighth of one percent of the total $38 million loan for its services. Semenenko also had me insured for $5 million, with the banks as beneficiaries.

The Curtis cash position was good, better than at any time since 1959. The fourth quarter of 1963 had been profitable—a fourth-quarter profit had been forecast and was, in fact, delivered. The gloom and doom sayers had been routed, and the survival of Curtis was no longer in doubt. The subterranean forces, however, some of which I underestimated, were regrouping.

The Philadelphia directors, holdovers from the dismal past, were inseparable—Linton, Brown, Fuller, Franklin, and Cary Bok moved as a cohesive unit. There were three neutral directors, fine men all, who were not always completely informed since they attended only the monthly board meetings. They were Harry C. Mills, the retired head of Merchandising of the J. C. Penney Company; Curtis Barkes, chief financial officer of United Air Lines; and Ellsworth Bunker, a United States diplomat of ambassadorial rank. As this book is being written, Bunker is the United States Ambassador to South Vietnam.

Blair and Kantor were close, and trying to move even closer, to the office and power of the presidency. Gould was playing a lone hand.

Clifford, "his man" Maurice Poppei, and the corporate secretary, Gloria Swett, were a close-knit trio. Clifford had appealed to me shortly after I hired him to approve his hiring of Poppei and Swett from RCA. I agreed—another of my early errors. Maurice Poppei I had met briefly at NBC. He came down from RCA in a cost reduction and control program as a "budget director." He was a strange, sullen, morose type. Great industrial corporations need people like Poppei, and somehow always seem able to find them. He took his lead and inspiration from Clifford.

Bill Emerson drove Poppei to distraction. Poppei would enter Emerson's office already mad, since Emerson never made a date with him *before* 4:45 P.M. Emerson knew Poppei was a nine-to-five type, and would make the meeting as brief as possible. But when Poppei would walk in, Emerson would rush up and give him a welcoming slam on the back, which would propel Poppei forward, and invariably drive his eyeglasses down his nose. When he recovered, Emerson would walk him with a one-arm embrace, and say loudly, "Well, Maurice, are you getting much these days?"—

with a wide leer. Poppei, the squarest of men, would be flustered and embarrassed, anxious to flee as soon as possible.

Gloria Swett, Clifford's secretary at NBC, was a compatible personality.

The corporate counsel, Pepper, Hamilton and Scheetz, representing both Curtis and the Curtis-Bok family, was protecting its prerogative against Milton Gould. Gould had been slowly building a record against that law firm—for what reason, I could only surmise. He had collected little ammunition up to November 1963. Then the Wally Butts case was tried in Atlanta, and Curtis was found guilty of libeling Butts. The jury socked Curtis with a $3.06 million judgment—Gould had his wedge.

The debilitating Wally Butts–Bear Bryant libel case started, routinely enough, January 12, 1963, with an article about unnecessary roughness in college football. It was a good article by Furman Bisher, and a necessary one. College football coaches, totally preoccupied with winning football games, had perfected the offensive art to a high degree of mayhem. Paul "Bear" Bryant, coach of Alabama, mentioned in the article, sued the *Post* for $500,000. There was no undue concern at Curtis over this suit, nor at Pepper, Hamilton and Scheetz. Because the suit was filed in Alabama the corporate counsel, in the person of Philip Strubing, employed a local attorney in Birmingham to act for Curtis. This lawyer, T. Erik Embry, commenced his pretrial search for support of the statements in the *Post.* It was during the course of this search that Embry first heard about a telephone call allegedly overheard by an insurance agent in Atlanta.

According to the insurance agent's testimony, he became part of the electronic freak known to laymen as "crossed wires." He claimed to have become accidentally hooked into a conversation between Wallace (Wally) Butts, athletic director of the University of Georgia, and coach Paul "Bear" Bryant of the University of Alabama. In this conversation, he testified, he overheard Wally Butts giving vital information about his team to Bryant on the eve of their annual game. This testimony was reported to Clay Blair and Bill Emerson, managing editor. (Later, the United States Supreme Court held that incomplete investigation led Blair and Emerson to grievous error.)

Clamping a lid of tight security around the project, Blair ordered a "cover" story of the same length inserted into the make-up of the issue in which he planned to put the Butts-Bryant story, so that even his own editorial staff would not know about the story until it was in print. He even ordered a secret foundry set up so that only a handful of trusted aides would know of its production.

I was unaware of the story until the first proofs arrived from the secret foundry. Blair seemed comical to me in his approach with the proofs. He entered my office, closed and locked the door, said, "Hold on to your hat," and laid the proofs in front of me in his finest dramatic manner. Though Blair seemed almost ridiculous, what I read was not. I am sure I gasped when I read the headline—"The Story of a College Football Fix." I may have trembled with excitement when I looked at the art work and read the captions. When I dove into the story itself, I was startled, angered, and sickened by its content. I looked at Blair when I finished and asked: "My God, can we print this?"

"You're damned right we can," Blair assured me.

"Has it been checked by libel counsel?"

He said it had, and I made him explain that, which he did. I specifically pressed him for the assurance that libel counsel had read this particular version and approved it, the headlines, and the captions under the pictures.

I also made other direct and indirect inquiries about the libelous nature and actionability of the story, first calling libel counsel personally in Philadelphia. They confirmed what Blair had said about the origin of the story and the clearance from them as chief libel counsel for Curtis.

I did not kill the story mainly because it came from our own law firm, and because of their opinion that the *Post* was safe in printing it. This was a unique situation. Up to then, I had never known a story to emanate from a publication's own libel counsel. That fact, more than any other, led me to accept the recommendation of Blair and Emerson that we run the story in the *Post*. It appeared in the March 23, 1963, issue, boldly announced on the cover.

If we had taken more time, called in other counsel, done more research, either the story might not have run at all, or sufficient changes might have been made to make it nonlibelous and unactionable. One libel expert later told me that if the title had been "The Story of a Strange Telephone Call" or something like that, and if about a dozen or so sentences had been altered, the story would not have left the *Post* so horribly exposed.

Even after Butts and Bryant had filed suit against Curtis for $10 million each, there was no panic at the *Post* or at Curtis or at the Curtis board level. Some shock, yes, at the size of the amounts being asked. Milton Gould, however, was not at all sure about it. Almost immediately after the story appeared, he registered with me his concern over the way it was written from a technical libel viewpoint.

Immediately after Butts and Bryant had filed suit, a lot of other investigations started, including one by Georgia's Attorney General. What appeared to be supporting evidence started flowing in. Many leads reached Curtis, some anonymously. As Strubing, chief libel counsel, recounted these supposed supplements to the vital evidence, a sense of euphoria developed. Blair and Emerson delighted in the press coverage of the *Post* story—they were, indeed, the hottest young editors in the United States. At what a price we were to learn much later! Blair had by this time adopted the "sophisticated muckraker" label, and he posed as the young, fearless, crusading editor. He made one incredible blunder, which might have been the single most damaging bit of physical evidence that found its way into the hands of Wally Butts's lawyer, William H. Schroder of Troutman, Sams, Schroder & Lockerman.

For several months after the national press coverage of the Butts-Bryant story, Curtis was hit with million-plus libel suits after the publication of virtually every issue. Almost every public figure who was the subject of a *Post* article rushed to the courts and the press with libel suits. A total of $18 million in suits, in addition to the $20 million of Butts-Bryant, was filed against Curtis. Blair, who once stated that he feared nothing in the world, proved it by writing a memo to his *Post* editorial staff in which he boasted about the number and size of these suits, closing with the immortal statement, "We know we are hitting them where it hurts." This statement, as well as the whole tone of the memo, had malice written all over it. During the actual trial, Bill Schroder, who had superb courtroom technique, introduced Blair's memo to prove malice, a necessary requirement in libel action when punitive damages are involved. He also grabbed Blair's own phrase, "sophisticated muckraking," but made it sound like "mudslinging." I did not attend the trial but had three different observers reporting to me on it.

The Curtis defense was a comedy of errors. In the pretrial work, Curtis failed to get the earlier witnesses to restate what they had allegedly said; a principal defense witness was not stalwart either. Schroder introduced some evidence that tended to undermine the *Post*'s star witness. Courtroom eyewitnesses say that Schroder's summation was most telling and effective. He followed it with a description of the final scene of the eventual funeral of Wally Butts. Schroder had Butts laid out in his coffin, surrounded by the colors of the University of Georgia, with a banner across his chest reading "Georgia forever." There was hardly a dry eye in the courtroom.

The *Post* seemed to be on trial rather than the Butts-Bryant story in that courtroom in Georgia. A member of the jury later described the scene in the jury room after the judge had sent the jury out to decide on the verdict. One of the panel, we were told, sat down, snapped his galluses, and said, "I'm going to teach those nigger-loving sons-of-bitches what I think of their magazine." He and the other jurors "showed" us by voting for a $3 million judgment for punitive damages and $60,000 for compensatory damages.

When the verdict was announced in the courtroom, Strubing said, "Oh, my God"; Blair said, "Did he say three million?" The judge himself was so startled by the verdict that, on his own responsibility, he reduced the punitive damages to $400,000, letting the $60,000 compensatory damages stand. This was no victory for Curtis in November 1963; but the reduction of the judgment created the illusion of an impending one in the Appellate Division appeal. If not there, we were sure that victory would come in the Supreme Court. We adopted the self-comforting notion that the Atlanta jury had been biased and that the Appellate Division of the Supreme Court would undoubtedly reverse the decision.

The Butts decision started a chain reaction at Curtis, among the board, among the law firms serving Curtis. In retrospect, I believe it was the pivotal element in the reversal of the favorable trend of Curtis during my stewardship. The Atlanta decision that the *Post* was guilty did things to people inside and outside Curtis that hurt both the magazine and Curtis deeply. For the first time in the history of the *Post* since the days of Benjamin Franklin, the honesty and integrity of the magazine were exposed to serious question. The full import was somewhat delayed because everyone thought the *Post* would be vindicated in appeals. Still, the lash had been laid on the backs of the magazine's editors, and it stung.

The public and trade press turned savagely on Blair and the *Post,* as though thoroughly ashamed of them for the damage done to the entire press of the country. Many advertising agencies lost faith in the *Post* as an advertising medium because of the "guilty" verdict. Bill Bernbach of Doyle Dane Bernbach, Inc., was particularly critical of the *Post*. David Ogilvy, of Ogilvy, Benson and Mather, never a fan, was also very critical. The Curtis board of directors was staggered.

Gould's performance in this instance was excellent. In addition to telling me at the very outset that the story was not properly protected from libel, he said the same to other board members long before the verdict in Atlanta. He was in a perfect "I told you so" position. He used this issue as the wedge to interject his law firm into the Butts-Bryant case "for the good of the corporation."

I had little choice at the time, since Strubing's position and that of his firm seemed indefensible. I thought of getting rid of Pepper, Hamilton and Scheetz outright, but abandoned the idea after consultation with the Executive Committee, on the grounds that the Bryant part of the case was still to be heard, and the firing of counsel would be extremely damaging to our cause in that trial in Birmingham, Alabama. However, we had to do something to placate Gould, who had scared the wits out of the directors by making guarded references to an unknown party in New York who was threatening to use the Curtis directors for failing to fire Pepper, Hamilton and Scheetz for its role in the case, and for the recovery of monies spent in the action.

Gould insisted on inserting his firm (Gallop, Climenko and Gould) in the Butts-Bryant situation. A totally unnatural alliance was formed at his insistence that put overall strategy for the rest of the Butts-Bryant matter in Gould's hands, with Strubing in charge of tactics. Strubing was to have the "assistance" of Jesse Climenko, one of Gould's partners. In all fairness, I must say that

Climenko was very constructive, honorable, and—I am sure—effective under the awful circumstances involved. The man most adversely affected was Phil Strubing.

Strubing was an honorable man too, and a leading figure in his community. The Butts decision must have been his bitterest career experience. I was the one who had to tell him of the decision of the Executive Committee to move Gould and his firm into the picture. He must have felt that most of the thrust for this move came from me, since Gould had been so instrumental in my being hired. In any case, Strubing moved close to Blair and Kantor, and performed several services for them in April and May that hurt me badly. (They will be described shortly.)

The only important figure involved in the Curtis situation who was not panicked or upset by the Butts-Bryant case was Serge Semenenko. His performance throughout this period won him my permanent respect and affection. As luck would have it, he was in the process of assembling the $28 million from the other banks, which, with the $10 million from his own, would make up the total credit. On the very day the Butts decision came from Atlanta, Serge was in Philadelphia calling on the First Pennsylvania Banking and Trust and the Philadelphia National, to get them to enter the new credit for $7 million each. During the precise hour in which Blair called me from the courthouse with the shocking news, Semenenko was in the boardroom of the Philadelphia National with the bank's top management, discussing the credit. I could not let him be surprised by the news or grabbed by the press before I had told him of the developments, so I called the bank and asked the secretary to take him a note requesting him to come to the telephone. That quarter-hour between hearing the scalding news from Blair and getting Semenenko's reaction was the worst in my business career up to that time. Some later blows at Curtis put it in perspective.

I told Semenenko of the decision, of the fact that the press was in full cry after him and me, and that the fate of Curtis hung in the balance. If he failed to get the other banks, Curtis was doomed to bankruptcy.

Serge asked me for a few moments of reflection, then came back on the line and gave me instructions to call his Boston office and have his secretary issue a statement to the press that the decision in Atlanta really had nothing to do with the financing, and that he would continue to head the group for the new credit. He went back into his meeting, calmly told the bankers about the decision, and proceeded to get their commitment. Surely the phrasemakers must have had someone like Serge Semenenko in mind when they coined the term "a cool man." He maintained his calm, constructive attitude then, and later, when the very serious problems erupted in April and May, 1964.

The irreparable break in communication between Clifford and Blair came in late January, 1964. Blair refused to permit any of Clifford's staff on the editorial floors of the Curtis Building in New York. Clifford retaliated by refusing any cooperation of the corporate finance or operations areas he supervised in Philadelphia. This absurd situation had to be changed. Blair and the editors were "at the barricades," and I had to make a choice. It was a fateful one. There were (and still are) many imponderables in the magazine business, but one fact is incontrovertible—for a brief time a company can put out good consumer magazines without timberlands, paper mills, printing plants, distribution companies, corporate executive vice-presidents, budget directors, publishers, and accountants. But it cannot put out readable, acceptable magazines without editors. All the Curtis editors were in a smoking rage about Clifford and Poppei. Blair lashed them into further frenzy at every opportunity. At this time Clay Blair himself was not the issue. It was all the editors—Ted Patrick and his group on *Holiday* included. The rupture was complete. I tried once more to get Clifford to understand what had been done to Curtis, to me, to himself. The effort was futile. So I removed Clifford from his post as executive vice-president, Finance and Operations, and gave his financial duties to Maurice Poppei, then treasurer. The duties of Operations, mainly manufacturing, I temporarily took over myself.

Clifford took the change badly and sulked for a time; then he appeared ready to perform his new duties, which were by no means inconsequential. I assigned him all acquisition and merger activities, and he was chairman of the board of the New York & Penn paper company.

I should have gotten Clifford out of Curtis entirely instead of demoting him. He brooded, and waited. Soon he started moving closer to Albert Linton. They had in common their dislike of Clay Blair, and gradually they became close. Clifford found an ally in Allison Page, the young partner of Pepper, Hamilton and Scheetz, who became Curtis' corporate counsel. Page was willing, I believe, because of the anti-Culligan feeling at the law firm resulting from the Butts-Bryant affair. Clifford waited until the propitious moment. It was to come in October of 1964.

I was diverted about that time by a splendid merger possibility. It took little acumen and experience to see that the one, simplest, quickest solution to virtually all Curtis problems was a merger with a well-financed, glamorous company.

Of all the possibilities, I was most attracted to the Columbia Broadcasting System. Its management was superior. William Paley, Frank Stanton, and Jim Aubrey gave CBS unparalleled management strength.

I devised an original plan as the catalyst for a merger of CBS and Curtis.

CBS would add great strength, financially, and be aided in exchange by Curtis magazines.

The *Post* was in a declining field, the general weekly field. On the other hand, the news weekly field was burgeoning rapidly. There was room for a *Saturday Evening Post* converted to a news weekly. In my plans I invented a new magazine, *Time*-size, and called it the *CBS News-Post*. It would be created by the combined staffs of CBS News and *The Saturday Evening Post*. There would no longer be the huge losses caused by the expense of maintaining subscriptions in a declining reader-interest field. The *CBS News-Post* would concentrate on newsstands and be distributed by Curtis Circulation Company. Its circulation would be reduced to 3 million with all its subscriptions in hand from the old 6 million *Post* subscribers.

I had a good relationship with Frank Stanton, president of CBS. We shared an interest in architecture, and he was then working on the upcoming CBS building. I told him of my hope for a CBS acquisition of Curtis, and explained that I'd accept any reasonable role, or no role at all, if CBS didn't want me. This was not altruism. If CBS did acquire Curtis, my 70,000 shares of Curtis option stock would have been worth several million dollars.

Stanton bade me proceed and develop the plan, promising to discuss it with Bill Paley, board chairman of CBS. I made up a complete dummy of the projected *CBS News-Post*, even using the CBS eye in the logo, and wrote scores of pages on operations, including marketing and financial information, to support the logic of the deal.

Stanton appeared quite impressed by my presentation, and as promised, set up a date with Paley. I knew damn well I never would have got to Paley unless his screening force, including Stanton, was bullish about the idea. The power base of CBS was brilliantly illuminated in this meeting. Paley listened carefully, even intently, when the *CBS News-Post* was shown. I thought he was hooked. Not so. When I concluded my presentation, he took some time to talk quietly with Stanton; then he announced that he was not in favor of the idea because—and these are his exact words—*"The magazine business is too hard."* He went on to say that the same time and money invested in broadcasting, Broadway shows (CBS was preening in the glitter of their astonishing success as backer of *My Fair Lady)*, or "even sports" would return far greater dividends. It became clear several months later that Paley had then, through Mike (Killer) Burke, been negotiating to buy the Yankee baseball team, an acquisition that has not, up to this time, proved to be one of his better moves. However, his decision to put Mike Burke in charge probably ensued the eventual success of the Yankees. Burke is a helluva man.

For one wild month, an attempt was made to interest the Ford Motor Company in acquiring Curtis. The entrepreneur in this case was Frank Ryan, whose father was one of the first worldwide-venture-capital Irish-Americans to make the grade. An OSS man during World War II, Frank spent some time in Spain, fell in love with the people and the country, and set up operations there, in Madrid. A handsome man with easy grace and exquisite manners, Frank is one of the most impressive and charming people I met in the postwar years.

I tried to revive the Doubleday Company merger proposal, another ideal match for Curtis, when Douglas Black retired and installed John Sargent as president. Sargent did not respond.

There were others—Warner Brothers, Seven Arts; Gulf & Western, and so on—but Curtis looked so incredibly messy from the outside that all efforts—mine; those of Serge Semenenko; Loeb, Rhoades; the directors; various brokers—were futile. In desperation, I even had involved conversations with the head of Dominion Tar and Chemical of Canada and with the huge Italian publishing complex, Mondadori. Finally, I shelved this activity for a year, having learned the essential lesson: Nobody wanted to "buy" the headaches so painfully apparent at Curtis. We'd have to go it alone.

At about this time, the penalty for my diversion from supervision of Sales became apparent. The *Post*, particularly, started to "cool off" as an advertising vehicle. The question of why does a magazine get "hot" and then "cool off" has bedeviled magazine experts for decades. The space-buying apparatus for magazines is dispersed geographically, the volume spread being about as follows: New York, 65 percent; Chicago, 15 percent; Detroit, 7.5 percent; West Coast, 2.5 percent; all the rest of the United States, about 10 percent. There can be argument about these estimates because, for example, Coca-Cola is in Atlanta, Georgia. However, the buying of space is done by its agency in New York. In addition to the geographic dispersion of the buying apparatus, there is also a dispersion among hundreds of buying groups. An agency like J. Walter Thompson has dozens of buying groups for its individual accounts.

At the time I took over Curtis, in July 1962, the *Post* was almost "stone-cold dead in the market," as the calypso song had it. My sales blitz of late 1962 and early 1963 heated it up. Then I put Bud MacNelly in as publisher, and he kept the temperature up for a while. After the Butts disaster hit in the late fall of 1963, the *Post* did not show the effect immediately because most advertising schedules were "locked in" through the first quarter of 1964. But in April and May the chill started. When I demanded explanations, I got some studied evasion. One seemingly bona fide excuse was the continuing confusion over the frequency of the *Post*.

Gallagher, who for years had been shrieking for a biweekly *Post*, seemed to take it as a personal insult that I had delayed the move. The *Post* sales department, not the sturdiest in history, was dispirited because of the uncertainty about the frequency of the *Post*. They complained that the first half of every sales call had to be spent dodging questions on that subject.

On April Fools' Day I made the decision to keep the *Post* at forty-five issues through 1964. I wrote the board of directors, with appropriate copies for others:

April 1, 1964

TO THE BOARD OF DIRECTORS

Speculation continues around the advertising business about the frequency of the *Post*. Our agent bank has also expressed an interest in the matter.

Gallagher has taken a public position for a biweekly *Post*.

I initially favored a biweekly *Post*, considering the *Post* as an island, without relationship to the rest of Curtis. Marion Harper of McCann-Erickson recommended it to me. George Gribbon of Young & Rubicam has expressed the view that the *Post* should be biweekly.

I engaged our management in a massive study of the problem. We examined the *Post* first as an individual magazine, then as part of the Curtis family. The conclusion was inescapable—the *Post* should stay at forty-five issues through 1964. Here are the reasons:

(1) 1964 is a Presidential election year and it would be impossible to keep on top of developments as a biweekly. For this and other reasons the Editorial Department was opposed to any reduction in frequency.

(2) The New York & Penn would be forced into a different and less favorable economic base with sharply reduced production. Its value to a potential buyer would be proportionately reduced.

(3) Sharon Hill would similarly be forced into a less favorable economic base with the loss of a large part of its production. Its value in sale or sale and lease back would be reduced proportionately.

(4) Keystone Readers Service, one of our most promising businesses, must have a weekly *Post* in its inventory in order to maintain its stability and growth.

(5) The Curtis School Plan also needs a weekly *Post* in its inventory in order to prosper.

(6) The decision to go biweekly would have been irrevocable and considered the last stand of the *Post* (and Curtis). If it were not an immediate success the "undertakers" would have once again tried to bury us.

We still have that option ahead of us if conditions change, and they could change. For example, if we sold New York & Penn, one barrier would be removed. A sale and lease back of Sharon Hill to another printer who could phase production with other magazines could remove another. We could use *Life* in our Keystone and School Plan Package and eliminate that negative, though giving a great plus to a competitor.

In conclusion, I would say that a biweekly *Post* is not an impossibility down the road, but at least through 1964, the forty-five-issue frequency is justified on sound business logic as well as instinctive, emotional "feel."

The announcement that the *Post* would stay at forty-five issues a year did not serve to halt the increasing "cooling off" of the *Post*. Advertising schedules were reduced, some canceled; other expected schedules did not materialize. No buyer or group of buyers said, "The *Post* lost its integrity and authority in Atlanta to Wally Butts"; but, in retrospect, I felt certain that affair was an underlying cause of the ill-timed decline of *Post* advertising.

Unfortunately, at the same time, the *Ladies' Home Journal* started having newsstand sales problems. This was as much attributable to the superiority of Herb Mayes, editor of *McCall's*, as it was to the performance of the editor of the *Journal*, Blair appointee Davis Thomas. The two developments—*Post* sales decline, *Journal* newsstand sales decline—turned the second- and third-quarter figures around, and gave Clifford some arrows to shoot at my distant, unprotected back, even though his close friend and protégé, Maurice Poppei, was by this time chief financial officer. Clifford started telling Linton that the disappointing financial picture was the result of his removal. This was utter nonsense, but Albert Linton was easy prey for such hunting because he still, in mid-1964, knew almost nothing about publishing and Curtis.

With the first signs of some bad news, the John Veronis-Clay

Blair feud erupted. Veronis, the hard-driving, effective president of the Curtis Magazine Division, started pushing for *Ladies' Home Journal* editorial improvement to offset the newsstand problem. He also bewailed the loss of *Post* integrity and authority because of the (there it was again) Wally Butts defeat. Blair reacted by screaming to Kantor, his immediate superior, and to me, Kantor's superior: "Veronis is trying to destroy me." Blair and Veronis both reported to Kantor. Now *he* had a choice to make, like the one I had had between Clifford and the editors. He chose Blair, and recommended that Veronis' contract be settled liberally. This was during a period in which Kantor was performing well and before there was any sign that he and Blair were becoming partners with me as the target. I accepted his recommendation; I should not have.

By March 1964 I felt like Horatio, but not at one bridge. There were several bridges to be defended *at both ends*. And more unpleasant shocks were on the way.

The legal team became feverish again as the "Bear" Bryant libel action in Birmingham, Alabama, approached. We all were very much depressed because of one inescapable conclusion—if Butts had received an initial jury verdict of $3.06 million in Atlanta, then Paul (Bear) Bryant would, we felt, get a huge jury judgment in Birmingham. Strangely enough, though there was great sympathy for Butts in Atlanta, he was not particularly popular with many Atlantans. Bear Bryant, on the other hand, was nearing beatification in Alabama. No new evidence was discovered, most leads having evaporated. Milton Gould started talking settlement quite early. His partner, Jess Climenko, echoed the theme. Philip Strubing, with his own and his firm's reputation at stake, wanted to win in Birmingham. Obviously, if Bryant lost in his part of the suit, the Butts loss would be minimized. Blair, of course, was opposed to settlement, saying, "A settlement would destroy me."

Two days before the start of the trial, Bryant's lawyer contacted the *Post* legal team and indicated Bryant would consider a settlement. This information was rushed to me. I advised Jess Climenko to find out what Bryant wanted. We were pleasantly surprised at the news that he would settle for $300,000. The settlement was made, and the *Post* was again pilloried by the press, but the chances are the settlement saved Curtis at least $2 million.

However, this second defeat must have further diminished the *Post*'s reputation with advertisers and agencies.

It was about this time—the spring of 1964—that my first friction with Cary Bok developed. It came about in an unexpected, curious manner. Almost from the day I arrived on the scene, Curtis had received offers to sell, or sell and lease back, the enormous Curtis Building at Sixth and Walnut streets, Philadelphia. Now, finally, the logic of the sale of the Curtis Building had become apparent to anyone simply walking through the building. Clifford had done his cost reduction work well—about 2,000 people had left the payroll and premises, and whole floors of the Curtis Building were vacant; in other office and manufacturing areas there was also unused space.

I reported a very good offer to the board from a bona fide prospect. Several days later, I received a memo from Cary Bok; Albert Linton also got a copy. The memo was astounding to me. It described the great hardship for the Curtis-Bok family if the Curtis Building were sold. For decades, the building had supplied heat and power to the Curtis-Bok family-owned Public Ledger Building, and it was Cary Bok's petulantly put plea that nothing be disturbed in that situation. I filed the memo, intending to get a legal opinion about conflict-of-interests. Then it occurred to me that I could hardly get such an opinion from Curtis corporate counsel because that firm was also counsel for the Curtis-Bok family. Obviously, an outside legal opinion would have to be sought at the first opportunity.

Not only did this problem with Cary Bok arise; my relationship with Albert Linton, which had never been warm, took a bad turn. I was respectful of him because of his age and position, but as the truth about his performance as a Curtis director between 1945 and 1962 dawned on me, I felt critical of this aspect of the man. However, I had avoided any conflict with him, and it was not until late in the spring that we had a serious disagreement. It came about in this way: At a board of directors meeting-luncheon, J. M. Clifford proudly announced that he was for Barry Goldwater—saying, "The country needs him." He offered to bet Goldwater would get the Republican nomination and win the Presidency, and I took his bet. Clifford, of course, was half right. I got the impression that Linton was strongly for Goldwater, and this was confirmed when the *Post*, for the first time since the days of

Lincoln, came out editorially for a Democrat, Lyndon Baines Johnson. I agreed with the stand taken by the *Post* editors on that matter, but I had not known that Blair detested Goldwater and his supporters so intensely. In the same editorial in which Johnson was supported, Blair attacked Goldwater savagely and his supporters only slightly less abrasively.

Clifford rushed this editorial to Linton in high glee. Linton promptly brought it up with me in a private meeting, and I told him I had approved the support of Johnson and would stand on it, but I did not agree with the tone and brutality of the Goldwater attack. A coolness developed between us thereafter, and this was maximized by Clifford in the finale of the following October.

Those were the forces that grew in February, March, and April, and changed the beautiful outlook for me and Curtis from what it had been in December. Later, I wrote a couplet that amused my friends:

> Hooray, hooray, the first of May,
> Culligan's assassination starts today.

Around that date, Blair and Kantor thought they could convince the Curtis board of directors to install Kantor as president. They were confused by Cary Bok, who agreed, in a telephone conversation with Strubing, to meet Kantor secretly. This was Strubing's service to Blair and Kantor that I described earlier.

That secret meeting had tragic overtones both for them and for Curtis. It was held in Cary Bok's apartment in the Public Ledger Building. The whole purpose of the meeting was to find out whether he would support Kantor for the presidency of Curtis. Kantor made a *verbal* presentation, describing the Curtis situation as he saw it; he gave me credit for what I had accomplished to date, but also reported the desperate state of morale of the editors because of the Clifford treatment. He talked about more cost reduction, about diversification opportunities and financial matters, in which he was quite well versed.

Bok listened courteously, but Kantor misread him somewhat. I had had several meetings with Bok; he would say very little in such a meeting, nodding pleasantly as points were made. One could get the impression, simply from his manner and lack of objection, that he was in full agreement. He was an indefinite type, hard to know, easy to misunderstand. Above average in height, around five feet eleven, he had a white-gray look about his skin, appearing unwell some of the time. Bok had partly withdrawn from business life, and from Philadelphia social life, somewhere around 1955. He moved to Camden, Maine, and married a nurse, and only infrequently came out of his seclusion.

I, too, misread Cary Bok. He became quite friendly during the two years in which my management and I saved Curtis and his fortune. I never heard a word of criticism from him directly, other than his complaint when I tried to sell the Curtis Building. This sale, great for the stockholders of Curtis, would have adversely affected the Curtis-Bok real estate holdings.

It is easy to understand how Kantor, caught up in a power grab, could also have been misled—head in the clouds, victim of "the wish being father to the thought." At any rate, he was somehow able to report to Blair that Bok would consider favorably their plan to have him (Kantor) made president, with me remaining as chairman of the board. What Kantor did not know, until I told him over eighteen months later, was that within minutes after he himself left, Cary Bok called Moreau Brown and had some most unflattering things to say.

Blair and Kantor also had several discussions with Semenenko's two young assistants, Peter Reed and Bill Thompson. They found Reed and Thompson courteous and attentive, for it was their job to listen, and to protect the bank, if anything they heard in criticism of me was valid. In one of these discussions Blair and Kantor hinted at their plan for Kantor to be made president. Reed and Thompson listened but made no reply. Once again, Kantor and Blair seem to have misread attitudes.

Next, Blair and Kantor came up with the idea of presenting their plan to the board of directors at the May board meeting, in the hope of getting a majority of the board to vote Marvin Kantor to the presidency, with myself as chairman of the board. Kantor told Albert Linton about the move to get the matter on the agenda. Linton advised me and other directors and we advised Serge Semenenko. A simple strategy was developed that was calculated to pull the teeth of the pair and possibly trigger their resignations. They were not to know that Semenenko had been told, or that he was sending a letter to Moreau D. Brown, chairman of the Finance Committee, exercising his "right of management approval." Serge's letter would state that "no change in the manage-ment of Curtis was acceptable to the banks." Their resolution would then be voted on and soundly defeated, eleven votes to two (Blair's and Kantor's). I anticipated, in the aftermath of such a rejection by the board, that they would resign.

Philip Strubing, of Pepper, Hamilton and Scheetz, inadver-tently wrecked the plan by telling Blair and Kantor *before the meeting* that the directors would vote No. He also told them about Semenenko's letter, and advised them that they would be fools to try such a force play under the circumstances. Blair and Kantor backed off. It soon became apparent that this rebuff had done nothing but prove to them they could not use traditional business methods in the Curtis situation to force their will on the Curtis board. They came to the conclusion then, or shortly thereafter, that only a major palace rebellion, properly timed and thoroughly organized, could dislodge me.

The planning began in deadly earnest in the summer of 1964.

8

I have had a difficult time trying to explain to friends why I failed to take action against Blair and Kantor after their unsuccessful move to force Kantor into the presidency in May 1964.

There were several reasons. Because of the advice from Philip Strubing, Blair and Kantor abandoned the plan to go to the Curtis board. Also, in their discussions with Cary Bok and with Thompson and Reed of the First National Bank, they did not attack me or indicate any desire to have me demoted—their plan was to have me continue as chairman of the board and chief executive officer. Blair and Kantor were also directors, and as directors of a public company, they had a right to their opinions. In fact, they had a duty as directors to demand an investigation of me at any time if they had evidence that I was not performing my duties properly as chairman and president.

There were other practical considerations. As editor, Blair was turning out a good—at times, very good—*Saturday Evening Post*. Even *Time* grudgingly admitted that. I had no replacement for him inside Curtis. Bill Emerson, managing editor, though a fine storyteller, was unimpressive to me. Inquiries outside Curtis were unsuccessful in uncovering anyone who might be able to replace Blair. There was also the fact that, as his superior, I was concerned about him. The Butts-Bryant defeat had changed him dramatically. It was about this time that he started to use an alarming phrase. Frequently, in attacks on an associate or a lawyer or director, he would say, "He is trying to destroy me." I had become used to the erratic behavior of many creative people over the years I had supervised them, but what I observed of Blair and what I heard about him from others led me to believe he was close to a crisis of some kind. He became baffling, infuriating, and incomprehensible—except in retrospect.

At this point, in far-off Timmins, Ontario, an event occurred that was to absorb virtually all my time for at least a month.

In the spring of 1964 Curtis was a bustling, frenetic, at times frantic, hive of activity. It was much like a hotel filled to capacity, with all the electric power in use, straining in every department to keep up with the problems cascading upon it. Consider the effect on such a hotel if a Whiskey Tasters' Convention were suddenly, without warning, dumped into the lobby. Pandemonium? That is the way the discovery of the biggest ore body in the history of the Western Hemisphere—300 feet from Curtis land—affected Curtis. It blew the fuse. I lost all doubt that I have an active guardian angel when, in retrospect, I reviewed the entire Canadian ore affair. I could so easily have made a $24 million mistake through inexperience.

The involvement of Curtis in Canadian mining came about entirely through its purchase of the New York & Penn paper company. The only reason New York & Penn was involved was its interest in timber. This wholly owned subsidiary of Curtis, through its Canadian and United States subsidiaries, the T. S. Woollings and Company Limited and the Armstrong Forest Company, had engaged desultorily in mineral exploration on its timberlands for more than fifteen years. A limited "joint-venture" mineral exploration had in fact been launched to the east of Kidd Township in 1954, in the general area of the fabulous Texas Gulf Sulphur strike ten years later. Approximately $50,000 was spent; five holes were drilled, but without success. Joint-venture deals were popular at the time because they kept the cash outlay for each landowner to the minimum. Over the years, exploration contracts had also been made on Curtis' Pennsylvania woodlands. Oil, coal, and natural gas had been discovered; New York & Penn actually used gas from wells drilled on the lands around the Johnsonburg paper mill.

In 1962, the mineral-rights situation in Canada was brought sharply to my attention when a major paper company offered to buy our Canadian woodlands. The offer came from an ultra-sophisticated paper company president, who told me with a shark-like grin that his "only interest" was to "help" me. He said he had been following the story of Curtis and noted that we seemed "cash poor." His company, he indicated, might pay $2 million for the 96,000 acres of woodlands owned by Curtis. To me this story did not have the ring of truth. I had some inquiries made through the head of New York & Penn, and he reported only that the Canadian Government had conducted a series of magnetometer (flying electronic sensor) tests. Nothing definite had been found, but the tests indicated "interesting anomalies." This was trade talk for electronic wave readings indicating that there was *something*, not necessarily valuable ore, under the ground.

Shortly after that offer was rejected in 1962, a sad, regrettable episode caused Bob MacNeal new embarrassment and brought his position as a director to a close. He had not said a word at the July and August board meetings. At the September meeting, however, he signaled to me, as chairman, that he had something to say. I listened, first with curiosity, then amazement, then shock, as he told the board that he had been approached by "a party who does not wish to be identified" who was keenly interested in buying the Canadian woodlands of Curtis. The shock came when he asked to be named "exclusive broker" for the deal. As broker, he would have made as much as 5 percent of the sale price. All the directors except Gould sat mute and embarrassed. Then Gould went after MacNeal—not too violently, to his credit. He expressed absolute opposition to the MacNeal proposal as being a "conflict of interest." There was no doubt in any director's mind that Gould was right. MacNeal seemed to shrink anew.

After the board meeting I talked with Linton and Fuller about MacNeal, and we concluded that his illness and the shock of his experience had clouded his judgment. We felt it would be a kindness to spare him further embarrassment. Walter Fuller, who had made MacNeal president, seemed the logical choice to suggest his resignation from the board. This Fuller did. MacNeal acquiesced. I was never to see him again. His health failed completely, and he died in 1966.

My instincts told me that somebody knew something about Curtis' Canadian properties that he was not telling, so I decided not to sell the Curtis woodlands *with* mineral rights. All buyer interest disappeared. I was to ask myself often (after the ore discovery): What if Curtis, during my presidency, *had* sold the Canadian woodlands for a paltry few million? I would have been the clown of the decade!

Discussions with the Canadian Nickel Company about exploration of Curtis land started well before 1959. Texas Gulf Sulphur Company entered the picture in 1959. These discussions advanced to negotiations in late 1963; it was Curtis practice to secure competitive bids from two companies. The skill and daring of Texas Gulf Sulphur management won that company the biggest ore body in the Western Hemisphere. The exploration contract they accepted included terms Canadian Nickel had turned down because they were too severe and would set a bad precedent for exploration in Canada. The Curtis agreement with Texas Gulf was for only 46,354 acres of our total holdings of about 98,000 acres. The remaining acreage was not committed. Under the agreement, Texas Gulf Sulphur would return to Curtis one-third of this acreage at the end of twelve months from the signing of the contract, another one-third at the end of twenty-four months, and all but 1,920 acres at the end of thirty-six months from the signing of the contract. Mining rights on the 1,920 acres would then remain with Texas Gulf Sulphur if they exercised their rights under the agreement, and Curtis would be compensated as follows for the exploration and mining rights:

(1) 25 cents per acre for the first year,
(2) 50 cents per acre for the second year,
(3) $1.00 per acre for the third year,
(4) $100 per acre for the surface rights of 1,920 acres, and
(5) $50,000 for the mineral interests plus 10 percent of the net profits after Texas Gulf Sulphur got back its basic cost (other than the cost of the plant and mill).

On April 16, 1964, the storm broke. The influential mining magazine, *The Northern Miner*, published a story that Texas Gulf Sulphur had made a major discovery in an area in which Curtis owned about a third of the land. I had every reason to respect Texas Gulf Sulphur—as soon as information was available, they supplied it to me. I called Claude Stephens, president of TGS, and told him I'd appreciate meeting him and getting "quickly educated," to protect myself. A most impressive chief executive, Stephens received me with great grace and warmth, and introduced me to Charles Fogarty, executive vice-president, also a fine, friendly man. I asked as many questions as I dared, and they evaded none. If the information was not immediately at hand, they would promise to send it, and did so, often by the next mail.

They told me that over a hundred holes had been dug on over sixty prospects in the general area of Kidd Township in Timmins, Ontario. Each hole had cost $5,000, plus other substantial costs, before the discovery hole was drilled. For the first time I realized fully what a risky business mining was. The discovery hole was on

TGS-leased land, at a spot just 300 feet from Curtis-owned land. The first drillings set the ore body as at least 300 feet wide, 800 feet long, and 800 feet deep, but that was only the beginning, they said. The ore body could be several times that size. In parting, they warned me to be supercautious in my release of information.

Milton Gould performed good service to Curtis and me during the hectic period immediately following the rumor of the Texas Gulf strike and its confirmation. TGS stock soared and Curtis stock jumped dramatically. He gave the alarm about possible problems with the Securities and Exchange Commission. I made a quick decision to take his advice, and also to handle matters personally. On April 17, 1964, I issued this press release:

> Numerous inquiries have been received about the Curtis Publishing Company timberlands in Ontario, apparently as a result of the announcement by the Texas Gulf Sulphur Company of a significant copper and silver ore discovery in that area. Mr. Culligan, chairman and president of Curtis, stated that the company has an agreement with Texas Gulf for mineral exploration of a portion of Curtis' holdings in Ontario. Under this agreement Curtis would participate in profits from successful exploitation of any mineral discoveries under its woodlands. While the reported Texas Gulf discovery appears to be adjacent to the approximately 40,000 acres in the area owned by Curtis, Mr. Culligan said that nothing more is known about the situation at this time. As soon as additional information becomes available, it will be made public. Curtis holdings in the area were acquired as a timber reserve for its papermaking operations.

Clay Blair overreacted. He burst into my office, bug-eyed, demanding information. I told him the release gave all the information I had.

On the same day I issued an internal bulletin:

> No statements of any kind are to be made by any employee of Curtis relative to our Canadian woodlands situation. This matter, which is of the utmost sensitivity, will be handled by my office and our legal counsel.

This enraged Blair, who did not know "slurry" from "overburden" (and neither did I); and he raced up to Timmins, Ontario, to see for himself. There was, of course, nothing to see. Texas Gulf

Sulphur protected itself with all legal safeguards. Blair demanded information from the local Texas Gulf people, but they would tell him nothing. TGS would permit no one on the discovery site. Blair could see only sinisterness in their actions. He stated his conviction that there was *no ore* in Timmins.

Blair also started making statements about a fancied stock promotion, even outside Curtis. He made one such statement to the best-informed mining expert in Canada. As a kindness, this expert wrote a letter, copy to me, showing his great concern over Blair's fantastic fiction and his other grossly unfair statements. I must protect this gentleman's identity, but given here are parts of Mr. X's letter, either paraphrased or quoted directly:

> Pursuant to our telephone conversation of this morning, I feel again that your thinking is clouded by a lack of understanding of the problem involved in the type of regional exploration program conducted by Texas Gulf Sulphur.
>
> I must, at the outset, say that I have nothing but the highest estimate of these people—their relations with myself have been first-class, and, at the least, I consider them gentlemen. But, on top of that, I feel they are of the highest professional calibre—their discovery was a really brilliant piece of exploration work, and it was also backed up with a serious sum of dollar bills and a great deal of intestinal fortitude.
>
> Texas Gulf is an American company which has put a lot of money into our country. They have done it with intelligence and a complete lack of flamboyance.

This capable and literate man went on to explain that TGS actually had a *system of exploration* that was far in advance of its competitors'. He said flatly that the particular program leading to the Timmins discovery had taken five years of expensive disappointment; and he described Dr. Holyk, the chief TGS geologist, as being "without peer in his field." To educate Blair further, he went on:

> And here is a point to consider carefully—if you had, as I have, visited the discovery site, you would be amazed at the fact that anyone could pinpoint an ore body in such a desolate spot. The country for miles around is just about completely overburdened, there being less than 5% rock outcrop. TGS, in having narrowed the regional structure, combined their geological work with geophysical work done by air-

borne equipment, with this work indicating a number of anomalies in the area.

His good manners showed up in the following statement, which, as he later told me, he hoped would make Blair see that his notion about any wrongdoing by TGS was preposterous.

It simply amazes me that so many people are critical of TGS. They have done a remarkable job, and scored a remarkable success. In your case, I have checked out (on the basis of the scanty information you have given me) similar deals with other people involving other companies in other parts of the country, and I can say that your terms would appear to be quite favorable. In essence, for example, Curtis held nothing but timbered-out swampland—the effect of Texas Gulf's efforts has been to establish an interesting but certainly not guaranteed mineral potential, and they seem to be prepared to spend a huge sum of money for evaluation, with Curtis getting a free ride for the capital commitment.

Mr. X was an estimable gentleman whom I now count as a friend.

As the Securities and Exchange Commission became hostile to Texas Gulf Sulphur, I raced around Curtis to see if we were in any way vulnerable. The enormous increase in the price of the TGS common stock brought the top SEC investigator into the picture. His name was Ed Jaegerman; his partner was a huge bear-like Irishman named Tim Callahan. They dove into the Timmins strike situation with dire results to my two respected friends, Claude Stephens and Charles Fogarty. Charges were filed. (A court proceeding followed, at which Stephens and Fogarty were absolved of any wrongdoing. But later the Government appealed, the lower court decision was overturned, and more appeals are now under way.)

Gould repeated his warning that I be supercautious and warn all Curtis people to be the same. He was particularly concerned that Curtis, lacking experience in mining, might have made a poor deal that could be attacked by shareholders.

The "strike lawyers" who exist on nuisance suits against public companies started needling Curtis about the "small percentage" it was to get from TGS. So I asked for the files on the Canadian timberlands competitive bidding, and found, with some relief, the following letter from H. F. Zubrigg, vice-president of Canadian Nickel, declining to accept the compensation terms Curtis had asked for exploration on its land.

CANADIAN NICKEL COMPANY LIMITED
55 Yonge Street
Toronto 1, Ontario
Canada

March 26, 1964

Mr. A. L. Bennett
President
T. S. Woollings and Company Limited
Johnsonburg, Pennsylvania

Dear Mr. Bennett:

Since your phone call of last week we have given further careful consideration to the proposed Woollings-Canico agreement that accompanied your letter of March 6, and I have now to confirm that it is not acceptable to Canico because of its departures from the accepted standards for Canadian agreements of this kind. We regret that the efforts expended by both Woollings and ourselves to reach agreement have not been fruitful, and we assure you that we would be happy at any time to consider resumption of negotiations based on the terms originally proposed by Canico.

We would, of course, offer different terms in the case of a known mineral deposit which on the basis of examination proved to be of interest to us. If there are any such deposits on the Woollings properties we would like very much to have representative samples for analysis.

Yours sincerely,

(*Signed*) H. F. Zubrigg
Vice-President

The letter proved that we had put the exploration out to competitive bids, and also that this great company had felt our demands were too tough for them and would set a dangerous precedent in Canada. This and other evidence of careful, traditional, businesslike handling by Curtis prevented any "strike lawyer" from stimulating stockholder actions against us. However, I became alarmed enough at the prospects of trouble to search for and find a giant figure in mining who agreed to become my personal consultant. His name was Allan Anderson. He had had an astonishing career as a miner and manager of mining operations. Now retired, he still loved mining so much that he stayed on the perimeter of the industry and took an occasional assignment as a consultant. He not only helped me and protected me and Curtis, but we also became fast friends.

Anderson sent me copies, with detailed analyses, of *The Northern Miner*, which was unusually accurate in its predictions. All the key stories carried the byline of Graham Ackerly, editorial assistant. I invited him to a meeting and he accepted. Blair and Sanford Brown, the business editor of the *Post*, met Ackerly in Toronto in late April 1964 to discuss the Timmins strike with him. He was astonished by their attitude and suspicions. Though Ackerly helped Sanford Brown get a better understanding of the superb achievement of Texas Gulf Sulphur, Blair persisted in the curious belief that there was no ore in Timmins.

The silver fever, however, was not restricted to Blair and the *Post* editors. I started getting inquiries and offers from all sources. One of the first came from Milton Gould, at that time legal counsel also to the Canadian Javelin Company, Ltd., an organization whose president, a freebooting Irishman named Doyle, was under investigation by the same SEC investigators, Ed Jaegerman and Tim Callahan, who were probing TGS and Curtis. Gould gave me a letter from Canadian Javelin, with loud protestations that he was not recommending anything; that he was simply "a messenger boy." It said, in part:

> We are prepared to negotiate for the acquisition of all of your right, title and interest in and to the aforesaid acreage, subject to your reservation of certain of the mineral rights as herein set out on the following basis:
>
> A purchase price of $3,500,000.00, payable on terms and at times to be negotiated.

The reservation to the vendor of one-sixth (1/6) of the mineral rights in the properties; provided, however, that Javelin shall have the right to dispose of 100% of the mineral rights, subject only to its obligation to account for one-sixth (1/6) of the consideration received from the sale of same.

Payment to Curtis and/or Woollings of ten percent (10%) of the net profits as defined under the Canadian Income Tax Act, realized in exploiting the minerals in said lands. Such profit will be after depreciation, depletion, and all other charges, save and except taxes on income.

If the terms of negotiation are acceptable to you, will you please advise.

Very truly yours,
J. J. DeSantis

My hackles started rising as such offers flooded in from all sources. Once again I was over my head in multimillion-dollar affairs completely foreign to me. To protect myself and Curtis, I formed a "Timmins Task Force" consisting of J. M. Clifford, my consultant, Allan Anderson, John O'Hara of Price Waterhouse, Milton Gould, and Peter Coogan, a lawyer from Ropes & Gray, the legal counsel to the First National Bank of Boston. He represented Serge Semenenko's interest in Curtis.

I rushed a conference report to the Curtis board. A digest of it follows:

DATE: June 4, 1964

TO: Board of Directors

FROM: M. J. Culligan

RE: Mineral Rights of T. S. Woollings & Company

A conference was held June 1, 1964, attended by J. M. Clifford; John O'Hara and several associates of Price Waterhouse; Allan Anderson, our mining consultant; Milton Gould of Gallop, Climenko & Gould, and Peter Coogan of Ropes & Gray, counsel for First National Bank of Boston.

Purpose of the meeting was definition of Curtis goals relative to the ore discovery by Texas Gulf Sulphur. To gain these objectives the following decisions were made:

(1) Appointment of J. M. Clifford as head of Task Force to coordinate all future activities in mineral exploitation.

(2) P. W. to study implication of liquidation of Woollings to enable Curtis to use tax loss against potential income from mining.

(3) Request of TGS denial of rumors that discovery hole was drilled on October '63. Also denial that holes were drilled on Woollings property before exploration contract was signed.

(4) The following companies who have approached us may be invited to present proposals on 52,000 uncommitted acres, not necessarily restricted to usual exploration deals. Could involve joint-venture approaches:

> Texas Gulf Sulphur
> Jowsey Mines
> Duval Mining (United Gas)
> Anaconda Copper
> Dome Mines
> Placer Development
> Canadian Nickel
> Conwest Exploration
> Probex

There was a kind of deathwatch at Curtis between the first of June and June 22. TGS stock had gone wild; Curtis stock had doubled in value, but it was not yet certain that any of the ore body was actually in the Curtis land. If not, the Curtis stock would plummet and Curtis would again be the "loser of the year." The psychological effect, both internally and externally, of a negative result might well have led to a severe increase in the Curtis loss for 1964.

I had anxious moments thinking about how Clay Blair would react to a "no ore on Curtis land" report, for I was starting to get a "playback" from one member of his staff whom Blair considered a trusted ally. According to my informant, Blair was attacking those who were close to me, and occasionally loosing a barb in my direction. Blair would be in a perfect "I told you so" position if TGS failed to find ore under Curtis land.

Fortunately, on June 23, the following letter arrived from Charles Fogarty, executive vice-president of Texas Gulf Sulphur. There *was* ore under the Curtis land.

CONFIDENTIAL

Mr. Matthew J. Culligan, Pres.
The Curtis Publishing Company
666 Fifth Avenue
New York, N.Y. 10019

Dear Mr. Culligan:

This is to advise that, in the normal course of evaluative drilling of our ore body in Kidd Township, two holes commenced on our property have now crossed underground into the south half of Lot Four, Concession Five, which lot is optioned to us by T. S. Woollings and Company Ltd.

Only one of these two holes has thus far reached the ore horizon. Visual estimates of cores from the holes indicate zinc and copper sulphide ore of good quality.

We also are drilling a hole in approximately the center of Lot Four. This work is to check on an anomaly unrelated to that of our discovery and to give data useful for determining the best location of our plant site.

Yours very truly,

C. F. Fogarty

CFF/mh

An upsurge was felt immediately, and Terry Robards, a young reporter from the New York *Herald Tribune*, wrote an excellent story, which appeared on June 23. The measure of his ability is in the fact that he obviously wrote the story before I got the letter from TGS, so he had a beat on Curtis as well as on the other newspapers. His story was headlined, "Ore Under Curtis Timberland."

We did not know how much ore there was, or how rich or how profitable it might be, but, even so, in early July some of the "fallout" from the Timmins discovery landed in the mining community. On July 6 the Windfall Oil & Mines Company announced that, in drilling a hole in Prosser Township, near Kidd Township, they had struck "interesting sulphides" (inside talk for copper, zinc, and silver core samples). Curtis owned land all around this particular drilling site. Windfall stock went from 56 cents a share on Friday of that week to $1.98 a share by noon Monday.

Once again a shiver went through Curtis. The Curtis stock had gone from $8.00 a share to $19.00 on the strength of the TGS discovery. If Curtis had another ore body in the Windfall strike, there was no telling how high its stock would go. I found the entire matter dizzying, since every point rise in Curtis stock meant a "paper profit" to me of $70,000 (my stock options).

Unfortunately, there was no ore in this area. Windfall was investigated, and its two principals were tried and convicted of fraud. A lot of speculators and suckers lost considerable money on this fictional ore strike.

The first definitive report on the Timmins strike by TGS came from Allan Anderson in a July 21 letter to me. These are the significant facts from his letter:

> On July 16th I visited the above noted property in company with Mr. Arthur Bennett, president, and Mr. Lloyd Netherton, general manager of the T. S. Woollings Company. We were received by Mr. R. H. Clayton, project manager, and Mr. Brian Hester, geologist, Texas Gulf Sulphur Company.

> They indicated that the ore body to the north did have widths up to 500 feet and the overall shape was somewhat oval, then narrowing down as it extended south toward the Curtis lot. As the body narrowed the mineralization became more concentrated and therefore higher grade. I consider my estimates to be conservative as the ore is quite massive and obviously high grade throughout the six intersections.

By September 1, Allan Anderson was willing to estimate that there were 5.6 million tons of ore under Curtis land. There was considerable elation at Curtis, except for Clay Blair, who brooded and seemed morose.

In August I had had my first experience with the SEC investigators, who wanted to investigate people and procedures. I received a call from the chief investigator, Ed Jaegerman, asking for a date. I gave him one, feeling that my procedures had been proper—I had bought no stock in Curtis or TGS. I also had warned all Curtis employees about security and personal deportment. I did not tell Gould or anyone else about the date given the investigators. It was a good decision. Jaegerman had been an adversary of

Milton Gould in at least one major case—the previously mentioned Canadian Javelin episode. Jaegerman told me later he was astonished to find me alone, open, and frank. For a short while, he admitted, he wondered if I were being deliberately ingenuous to disarm him and his partner, Tim Callahan. But I had the letters and releases of Curtis and TGS and New York & Penn, and I neither hid nor embellished anything. Jaegerman and Callahan were satisfied that I was completely beyond suspicion.

Jaegerman also called Marvin Kantor and asked for an appointment. Under normal circumstances such a call would be reported to the president, but Kantor did not report the Jaegerman call to me. He met with Jaegerman and invited Blair to attend. During the course of the meeting Kantor told Jaegerman that Clifford had recently sold a large block of RCA stock worth about $400,000. Kantor knew about it because Clifford had told him of his plan to sell. This was of great interest to Jaegerman, who was hot on the trail of a large purchase of TGS stock—a transaction that cost around $400,000.

When Jaegerman asked me about the sale, I told him to ask Clifford directly. He did, and was satisfied with Clifford's answer— to the effect that the proceeds of the sale of RCA stock were used to buy tax-free municipal bonds. However, the destructiveness of Kantor and Blair was painfully evident—first, in not telling me they were meeting with Jaegerman; then, in directing suspicion at Clifford.

All the executives of Curtis, including myself, got full clearance from the SEC of any impropriety.

Each big problem at Curtis seemed to have repercussions in more than one area. I thought we had all the problems one company could conceivably attract. I was wrong. The Timmins ore discovery triggered a curious by-product. In the spring while the pot was still boiling from the heat of the discovery, Milton Gould had come to my office for a visit. He spoke about the ore strike and its potential value to Curtis. Then he said he had done some arithmetic and had concluded that my stock options, at that date, were worth about $420,000 on a capital gain basis; all the other Curtis executives had substantial potential gains as well. What gave me a severe jolt was his warning that some stockholder might bring suit against Curtis because of the stock option plan participated in by key Curtis executives. He used the word "bonanza." Alarmed, I asked him to explain further. He told me there would be some question about the validity of the Curtis options if the directors and I had known about the ore in Canada when the options were granted. Then, quite casually, he shocked me with a remark speculating on the benefit of having a suit from some *friendly* stockholder.

On April 22, shortly after Gould had made that remark, a suit was filed by a stockholder, Miriam Wolf. Her legal counsel was the firm of Wolf, Popper, Ross, Wolf & Jones. The complaint stated:

> Please take notice that this is a derivative action seeking to cancel, revoke or reform stock options granted to certain officers, directors and employees, and for an accounting, damages and injunction against the exercise of said options.

Clifford was the first to respond. He was clear, concise, and direct—he wanted none of Milton Gould "as his legal representative." He said, "I do not propose to have Gallop, Climenko & Gould represent me." And also: "As a lawyer, it strikes me that the most ethical position for Milton to take would be for his firm to disqualify itself as counsel in this matter."

I told Gould about Clifford's objection in late June. Gould was irate. He wrote on June 26:

> The principal problem raised by certain directors seems to be that there are "conflicts of interest" or divergent interests in this case (to which, I assume, I am thought to be blind), so that not all of the defendants can be represented by the same counsel.

He was also offended:

> If there is any such reservation on the part of any of the directors as to my sensitivity in areas of this kind, perhaps there should be some change in the composition of the Board's committee which deals with this very subject. I am offended that anyone would suggest that I am not conscious of these problems.

And indignant:

> What I do not seem able to convey adequately is that there is no point in dealing with these divergences until we know that we must deal with them.

He was frugal:

> I thought that I had made it perfectly clear, that it was desirable to delay the designation of counsel in the various categories until I had exhausted what I thought was a reasonable opportunity to dispose of the case without committing the Company to substantial expense.

Also resentful:

> I resent the imputations that I am trying to arrogate the control of this case to myself or my firm. My only purpose thus far has been to try to save the Company's money, a purpose which I think is obligatory upon me as a director and as an attorney for the Company.

He was mindful of his prerogatives:

> The designation of a group of law firms in New York from which counsel is to be picked, without discussion with me, is offensive and I will discuss it on my return to New York.

And, finally, he was regretful but stern:

> I regret the necessity for this letter. The criticism of both my professional abilities and professional ethics implied by the action of the Executive Committee is not to be taken lightly, and I request that the subject be placed on the agenda of the Meeting of the Board of Directors following the July meeting, which I will be unable to attend.

Now, almost everyone was mad at someone else. Bad feelings and harsh words were routine.

The Wolf case started assuming major proportions after Milton Gould indicated his displeasure at the way it was being handled by Curtis and the other law firms involved. Her counsel broadened his allegations, attacking my board-approved bonus for 1963. Different law firms were hired by the various groups involved. Clifford and I, as director-optionees, employed Cahill, Gordon, Reindel & Moore. Larry McKay was given the assignment, and he was a pleasure to work with—tough, smart, decisive, and mercifully brief.

Pepper, Hamilton and Scheetz, hanging on to its prerogatives, responded to a request by Albert Linton for "clarification." A dull sixteen-page report from them arrived on June 23, 1964, describing the Curtis problems stemming from the Wolf suit. Briefly, there were six main contentions. The first was that the stock option plan (including the newly authorized stock to make it work) was not lawfully authorized. The Wolf suit demanded that the Culligan-Clifford employment contracts be nullified because the "existence of minerals was known, or should have been known" by the directors. The second contention was that the plan and option grants constituted a "waste of assets and fraud on the company and its shareholders." Contentions numbers three and four—that the Culligan and Clifford bonuses and salary increases constituted a waste and a fraud on the company and its stockholders. Contention number five—that the options granted to Marvin Kantor were illegal. The sixth contention was that the directors were charged with "gross negligence, imprudence and fraud, gross mismanagement, failure to exercise reasonable and ordinary skill, care and diligence."

As remedies, Wolf demanded cancellation of the stock option plan, employment contracts, and my salary increase and bonus. Another demand was that the directors be held liable for the damage sustained, and (here is why such suits are popular) the company be required to pay reasonable costs, attorneys' and accountants' fees, and other lawful expenses.

A matter of this magnitude and significance would probably have been considered a major crisis in any normal corporation. At Curtis, it was just one more added to the long list of major problems. But it did have a special overtone. One reason for my taking the Curtis job, to make a million dollars or so, was now in jeopardy. If I lost my stock options, my bonus, and the salary increase, the move to Curtis, the work, worry, travel, the firing of almost 2,000 people, would have been a disastrous mistake. One court has upheld Curtis against Wolf.

The Blair-Kantor attempt to force Kantor into the presidency was pushed out of focus, into the background, by the Timmins ore strike and continuing serial of developments. The good news was a palliative that, to a degree, eased the pain of the Butts-Bryant fiasco (by now called the Bare-Butts case within the company) and the scaling down of the favorable forecasts for financial results of the second half of 1964.

But the tide had turned against me. I was the bullfighter no longer. Criticism was starting to swell about the libel suits, the Texas Gulf Sulphur arrangement, the advertising lull in the *Post*, the newsstand returns of the *Journal*. Press reports and Madison Avenue rumor turned dark and ugly again, particularly in the case of Gallagher. Though initially his comments about me in his report had been quite favorable, he changed violently in the spring of 1964. At the time, I had no way of knowing why he changed, but a retrospective view by Milton Gould of certain correspondence led him to his own conclusions. The correspondence from Gallagher had started, innocently enough, a long time previously with this letter:

September 25, 1962

Mr. Matthew J. Culligan
President
Curtis Publishing Company
380 Madison Avenue
New York, N.Y.

Dear Joe:

One of these days you are going to slow down long enough to have lunch with me again. I'm looking forward to it.

Meanwhile, I would like you to consider a suggestion and let me know what you can arrange. As you know, besides publishing The Gallagher Report and acting as a negotiator of communications properties, I own and operate World Wide Publications, Inc., described in the enclosed brochure.

We have over four hundred full-time field-selling agents throughout the United States and Canada. They sell to top management executives and professional men and women at their places of business. Subscriptions are bought either for reception rooms or for the executive's personal use.

I'm sure you agree this influential type of circulation is particularly fitting for American Home, The Saturday Evening Post, The Ladies' Home Journal, Holiday and Jack & Jill. It would be to the mutual advantage of Curtis and World Wide Publications, if you would arrange to give us a 10% remitting rate on these magazines.

If this is not feasible at present, I would appreciate your

extending us a courtesy remittance rate of 15% or 20% on "demand" orders.

Thanks for giving this your attention.

Cordially,

(*Signed*) Barney
Bernard P. Gallagher
President

Later, his assistant, Jim Mann, had called me about having Gallagher's subscription company sell subscriptions to a Curtis magazine, *Jack and Jill*. He asked for a special remittance rate— that is, a commission on the sales higher than that for the rest of Curtis' subscription operations. When I said I could not oblige him, he replied, "Barney won't like this."

In February 1963, C. L. MacNelly, publisher of the *Post*, had come to me puzzled and a bit concerned by a letter from Gallagher asking for a consultancy fee:

February 15, 1963

Mr. C. L. MacNelly
Publisher
Saturday Evening Post
380 Madison Avenue
New York, New York

Dear Bud:

I shall be happy to work with you in recruiting a sales promotion director. I can be of help to you on either of the following bases:

1) You can retain me as the exclusive recruiting agent, with the customary fee equal to 20% of the first year's salary, and the understanding that I will be paid $50 an hour for interviewing and consultation time, not to exceed 100 hours and deductible from the 20% fee.

2) Or you can merely ask me to counsel you and interview applicants you refer to me, on a straight $50-an-hour consultation fee.

Please let me know which arrangement you prefer, and

whether I can be of service to you.

Best regards.

Cordially,

(Signed) Barney
Bernard P. Gallagher

I had told MacNelly to ignore it.

The third request for me to put Gallagher on the Curtis payroll had arrived June 9, 1963. It said:

June 7, 1963

Mr. Matthew J. Culligan
President & Chairman
Curtis Publishing
380 Madison Avenue
New York, New York

Dear Joe:

In relation to our telephone conversation, I really think I am in a position to do something for you. The right kind of acquisitions could be of considerable value to Curtis and I'm confident that you'd know what to do with them.

I think you know how I operate when I'm wearing my negotiator's hat. I work on a finder's fee equal to 5% of the final purchase price, plus $50 an hour, deductible from the finder's fee when the transaction is successfully completed.

With my present schedule, you don't have to worry about my abusing the $50-an-hour time charge.

If you want me to get to work, drop me a line authorizing me to look for one or more properties for Curtis.

Best regards.

Cordially,

(Signed) Barney
Bernard P. Gallagher

After that, I started some serious thinking about Gallagher, for a definite pattern seemed to be emerging. He handled some publishing companies with great tenderness, or stayed away from them almost entirely. I suspected, after getting two broad invitations to put him on the Curtis payroll, that I might see another side of him if I kept refusing. There was no question about accepting, regardless of the consequences.

Gallagher turned on me in early 1964 and started an assault that is now in its fifth year. After a particularly bad dig at me, he would call and invite me to lunch. I would refuse. He would run another whole series of attacks, then call again for lunch. I refused his telephone calls and ignored his letters.

By May 1964, and thereafter, Gallagher's attacks were intense. He had me "kicked upstairs"—"on the shelf"—with "Serge Semenenko running the show." I had previously made the decision to ignore him, and now I issued instructions to all Curtis employees that subscriptions to *The Gallagher Report* would not be considered a legitimate business expense. His attacks became even more intense. I did some investigating and visited District Attorney Frank Hogan to ask his opinion. He advised me not to take legal action, for a wide variety of reasons. I learned from an acquaintance that there had been some court testimony, during a state liquor authority hearing, that Gallagher was a "shadow" part-owner of The Harwyn Club, a spin-off from the Stork Club.It was an advertising man's hangout.

Gallagher then included Marvin Kantor in his attacks, and Kantor insisted on striking back. I advised against it, but agreed to let Milton Gould take a whack at Gallagher. Gould did, in a letter reprinted here in its entirety:

Mr. Bernard A. Gallagher
"The Gallagher Report"
500 Fifth Avenue
New York, N.Y.

Dear Mr. Gallagher:

Your "Reports" of March 18 and March 25, 1964 (Vol. XII, Nos. 11 and 12), have been referred to me by the Curtis Publishing Company. I am asked by the Company to recommend a manner of dealing with an apparently deliberate and malicious effort to depict a situation at Curtis which simply does not exist, except, perhaps, in your imagination or in the minds of those who are feeding you so-called "information."

Normally, I would recommend to the Company that this sort of irresponsible, psuedo-sensational, gossip-mongering should be ignored. The cliché is right—to answer it is to dignify it. But I feel that many loyal and devoted people in the Curtis management are entitled to be informed that the wild rumors stimulated by your reports are false. They have been so informed. Next, when your "Reports" contain statements obviously intended to injure Curtis, it becomes necessary to put you on notice that such conduct is actionable. You are so informed.

Lastly, it becomes appropriate that those who read your "Reports" should be informed not only that they are replete with falsehoods, but that there is an apparent motive for the transformation in your attitude toward Curtis. Your readers will recall that not long ago you boasted of your contribution to the management of Curtis and you were loud and eloquent in trumpeting the progress being made. They will, perhaps, be puzzled by your change in temper. They are entitled to be informed that on February 15, 1963, you wrote to C. L. MacNelly, Publisher of the "Saturday Evening Post," offering your services to him in "recruiting a sales promotion director" at $50 per hour or "the customary fee equal to 20% of the first year's salary" (a copy of your said letter is attached; that on June 7, 1963, you solicited Mr. Culligan to employ you in obtaining "acquisitions" for Curtis at "a finder's fee equal to 5% of the final purchase price, plus $50 per hour" (copy of letter attached); that as early as September 25, 1962, you solicited Mr. Culligan for a "courtesy remittance rate of 15% or 20% on 'demand orders'" for your World-Wide Publications, Inc. (copy of your letter attached).

Your readers should know these things so that they can appraise the fairness and objectivity with which you report on events at Curtis and determine for themselves how much is honest reporting and how much is pique and pressure.

I am recommending to Curtis that under no circumstances are you to be employed as a consultant or in any other capacity; that you are not to get any special "courtesy remittance rate." This may result in continued abuse and vilification, but all parties will now know where they stand.

Very truly yours,

(*Signed*) Milton Gould

Gould sent a copy of his letter to *The New York Times*, which did a brief report on it. Gallagher blustered and threatened, demanded a retraction. Curtis ignored him. His bluff called, Gallagher retreated. He kept up his attacks, but they faded to insignificance in contrast to what was to come, far more painfully and with more enduring destructiveness, in *The New York Times* and *Time*.

9

There was a lull of sorts at Curtis in July and August. The dog days held sway. Vacations and sheer exhaustion of an overworked staff brought an uneasy calm. What energy remained was used up in the move of Curtis' New York staff into "our own" shiny new building at 641 Lexington Avenue, New York City, a change representing a good piece of work by several Curtis executives, including Marvin Kantor.

Robert Farrand, a Curtis veteran of fifteen years, was actually the originator of the plan. Deploring the waste and inefficiency of maintaining seven different locations in New York with duplicate facilities in each one, I had directed Farrand to study out and recommend a consolidation program. He came up with the plan to get all our facilities together in one building, and he and Marvin Kantor found the spot, a new Rudin building on Lexington Avenue, which had got off to a slow start. Kantor made a good deal with Lewis Rudin, a splendid young operator. Curtis was able to move all its New York components into what was called the Curtis Publishing Building in the summer and early fall of 1964.

By September 15, however, the Blair-Kantor drive to gain control of Curtis was renewed in earnest. I was about to say that the stage was set—but what was performed was a circus, not a play. It would be more accurate to say the rings were set.

The center ring was the old, anachronistic, enormous, half-empty Curtis Publishing Company Building at Sixth and Walnut streets in Philadelphia. Most of the final action took place there, in my huge office, that of Clifford, and the paneled, high-ceilinged, tradition-laden boardroom on the eighth floor, directly below my office.

The ring on the left was the spanking new Curtis Publishing Building at 641 Lexington, the northeast corner of 54th Street. Most of the Blair-Kantor-Ballew-Emerson strategy meetings were held there. One meeting, perhaps the single most important one, was held in a thoroughly unlikely place, Manero's Steak House on Steamboat Road in Greenwich, Connecticut. This accented the Alice-in-Wonderland quality of the whole fiasco.

156

The ring on the right was the sumptuous, exquisitely appointed apartment and office of Serge Semenenko at the Pierre Hotel in New York City. Not far from the Pierre, in the Regency Hotel, was my command post, a two-room suite that I maintained, as most company presidents do for late nights in town (too many, considering my wife and four children in Rye, New York) and confidential acquisition merger meetings. During the period when Blair was convinced his office telephones were being bugged, he used this facility. (The first time he came into the Regency suite, he rushed around testing every telephone; he unscrewed every mouthpiece and looked inside for a "bug.")

The places and dates are quite easy to reconstruct and describe. The motivation of the cast of characters is much more obscure. *Clay Blair wanted power.* He wanted desperately to be president of Curtis. He told that to Milton Gould. He told it to Robert Sherrod. Here is Sherrod's own description to me of Blair's personal drive for the presidency of Curtis.

> Earlier in June 1962, managing editor Blair had asked permission to prowl around the building to learn something about manufacturing, paper, circulation and advertising.
> Some of the things Blair learned were shocking. By talking to the number two or number three man in a department, he could learn just how inefficient operations had become. He uncovered a lot of personal patronage.
> While the directors were looking for a new man, Blair came to me and said, "I know a lot about this company now. May I have your permission to try for president myself?"
> The idea was bemusing. The company was floating toward the drain anyway. As you have said, we were sixty days from bankruptcy. Blair said he wasn't interested in editorial; he had only praise for the things I had accomplished in such a short time on the *Post.* The editor of the *Post* would have the complete freedom to which he had been accustomed. So I said, "Go ahead, Clay, and good luck to you."

At this point Milton Gould made a baffling recommendation to the Executive Committee: that Clay Blair, then the managing editor of the *Post,* be elevated to vice-president, Editorial, as well. This would mean that he was, at the same time, both subordinate to Robert Sherrod and superior to him. When asked about the idea, Sherrod agreed. But Clay Blair wanted power badly enough to undermine his benefactor at Curtis, Robert Sherrod. Here is Sherrod's description:

> I should have said I wouldn't stand for it [Blair being both a boss and subordinate]. But I had Blair's word that he was not interested in editorial, and would not interfere with editorial operations. So I said I would go along. The implications didn't sink in, possibly because I was so eager to restore the *Post* to vitality—and I had only three months.
>
> Less than two weeks later, as you know well, Joe, you were elected president. On July 13 it was announced that you had appointed Blair "director of editorial development," a new title. Blair assured me that it had to do with long-range planning, and that he had no intention of concerning himself with the operation of the magazines.

The envelopment of Robert Sherrod and the sapping operation to undermine him started almost immediately—within a matter of days. Sherrod sadly recalled the Davis Thomas gambit:

> One day in July Dave Thomas met me in New York to pursue some of the details concerning the move. He came to the apartment where I was staying and said, "I want to be your managing editor. I swear to you all the loyalty I have given Clay as assistant managing editor." [Blair had hired Thomas for the Washington office from the Los Angeles office of *Life*.] Blair urged me to appoint Thomas, saying we were in danger of losing him to television. Thomas had a certain amount of talent. I made him managing editor, for reasons not unlike those which persuaded you to make Kantor an executive.

Sherrod's reward for making Dave Thomas managing editor:

> The result, as I was to find out, was that I soon had two knives in my back instead of one.

Blair spent August and early September of 1962 putting the skids under Sherrod. He kept telling me that the young editors were getting very restive and dismayed under Sherrod's leadership. But Blair seriously overestimated his strength, and had Sherrod been a vindictive man, Blair should have been fired, or completely isolated from the *Post* for one episode alone. I was then in California.

Sherrod again reported:

> On September 5, two days before the New York move was scheduled, Blair struck and in doing so he violated every pledge he had made to me for more than two months. Presumably because he would have been ashamed to look me in the eye, he said nothing to my face. He placed a mimeographed announcement on the bulletin board at the sixth floor elevator, which is where I read it with astonishment and dismay:

> "Upon completion of the work of the Study Group on September 15, Clay Blair, Jr., will direct his attention to the task *to which he was assigned on July 9* [italics mine], namely, that of Vice President and Editorial Director."

Most arrogant and objectionable was Blair's claim:

> ". . . His responsibility includes the editorial content of the magazines, the operational staffing of the magazines, and the public acceptance of the magazines."

Robert Sherrod, a mild, almost courtly gentleman, hit the ceiling when he read the Blair announcement. He called me in California, read it to me, and then said, "Joe, I quit."

Assuring Sherrod that Blair, taking advantage of my absence, had completely overstepped himself, and that he had no support from me for that double cross, I asked Sherrod to do nothing until I could get to Blair and straighten the matter out. Sherrod agreed. I called Blair, blasted him, and suggested he make amends to Sherrod and "stop acting like an ass."

Blair was most contrite the next day, as Sherrod reported to me: "I called a staff conference, and Blair told them that the release was a mistake; he didn't intend it that way."

Sherrod continued:

> Within two weeks Blair was in my office at 666 Fifth Avenue, pleading for a place to sit. He had not moved from Philadelphia because he had no office. He didn't want to get involved with the Post, but he did want temporary quarters

until the other half of the third floor was ready. Then he would move over with the other vice-presidents.

I had one senior editor's spot that had not been filled. I told Blair he could occupy that office until I needed it. I hope you don't mind my repeating a quote of yours, "How naïve can you get?"

Now Sherrod's goose was cooked. Over him he had Blair as V.P.–Editorial; under him, Blair's three closest confidants, friends, and recipients of his benefactions: Emerson, Thomas, and Schanche. Sherrod's final remark:

Of course, Blair and a few of his fellow conspirators were soon busier than termites. From the day I let him into that office I never had a chance.

Unfortunately, the *Post* was at that time an improving, but still poor, editorial package. Sherrod was short of time, money, and experienced personnel, though he did wonders with what he had. However, Curtis and the *Post* needed dramatic action. Blair, using Thomas, Emerson, and Schanche as his stalking horses, told me that they and several other young *Post* editors had "had it" with Sherrod—they were seeking new jobs. Their loss would have been crippling. Blair recommended that he go back to the *Post* as editor and make Sherrod editor-at-large. I accepted his recommendation. In the short term, this was a good decision. In the long term, a fateful, fatal mistake.

Marvin Kantor wanted power. He seemed preoccupied with it. He sought it initially as a "corporate raider" via stock ownership and voting control and psychological pressure. When I brought him into Curtis, he switched to the more traditional method of gaining power through title and position. Kantor's favorite expression on the subject was "Power is what Power says it is." Milton Gould had an opinion about Kantor's need for power. As he described it, "Kantor has delusions of grandeur."

The ore strike apparently had a profound effect on Kantor. I now believe that he, unlike Blair, accepted the fact that there was a considerable ore body in the strike area, that Curtis would own some of it, and that Curtis was on its way to becoming an industrial giant. His old yearning for control emerged again, and from that point on, Kantor moved toward one objective—the presidency of Curtis.

Milton Gould wanted power as a puppeteer, and money, and a judgeship. He had had a heaping taste of power in mid-1962, when he forced the Curtis board to fire Bob MacNeal by delivering an ultimatum. He got power again when I was attacked by Blair and Kantor, and the Curtis board was again in panic. Gould got the money, too—fees in 1964 of almost $102,000. As for the judgeship—who knows!

Clifford wanted a return to power. He had power, but I took it away from him when he alienated and enraged the Curtis editors. Clifford wanted it badly enough to undermine me with the old Philadelphia directors of Curtis and with Cary Bok. He wanted it badly enough to sit back and wait for his opportunity for revenge.

Serge Semenenko wanted success for Curtis. With his retirement from the First National Bank already programmed, Serge wanted no stain on his escutcheon, no break in his proud record of "never having a loan go sour in thirty-five years."

The Curtis Philadelphia directors wanted peace and quiet and the avoidance of publicity, particularly about the ten years from 1952 to 1962. I was their unwelcome conscience, the youngish marketing and advertising specialist who had arrived when Curtis was at the abyss, and had done the painful things they themselves, as directors, should have insisted on: editorial improvement, marketing improvement, massive cost reduction, and reorganization.

Jesse Ballew, Bill Emerson, Don Schanche, Dave Thomas, the minor figures, all wanted the security, promotions, and raises they thought would accrue to those on the winning side of a coup d'état. They chose as champions Clay Blair, Jr., and Marvin Kantor—interesting evidence of their judgment.

Allison Page and Philip Strubing of Pepper, Hamilton and

Scheetz wanted continuance of Curtis' corporate business and fees, a not unusual passion for corporate lawyers.

I wanted what I had—power, as given to me legally by the directors and shareholders. I wanted the honors, the wealth, the satisfaction that would have come had I survived the Blair-Kantor, Ballew-Emerson attack.

So much for settings and motivations; on to the opening scenes of the final drive to wrest control of Curtis from me.

As described earlier, Blair and Kantor were defeated in their attempt to install Kantor as president in May of 1964, but the defeat taught them an invaluable lesson: They could not move the Curtis directors by themselves. They needed a mass movement of editors and publishers. That apparently became their first objective—to recruit as many supporters as possible. Blair's initial step was the selection of an aid-de-camp. He picked Mike Mooney, a senior editor of the *Post*, and tried to give him the assignment of marshaling strength for his drive with Kantor for control. Blair did not tell Mooney about his plan to ruin me.

Mooney was not enthusiastic. He hesitated, then demanded more information. There was one hilarious episode. After Blair had tried to enlist Mooney, explaining that only he, Blair, with Kantor as his aide, could save Curtis, Mooney, a delightful, irreverent Irishman, asked, "Clay, what makes you think you're the one for this role as savior?"

According to Mooney, Blair flew into a small rage over the question, but when Mooney insisted on an answer, he stormed off saying he would tell Mooney the next day. The following morning Blair and Mooney met. Blair had a note before him on which seemed to be written a list of the reasons for his role as savior. First on the list, as Blair intoned it, was, "Because God had told me so."

After Mooney regained his composure, he said, "You're too late, Clay. God has already picked Henry Luce for publishing." Mooney refused to go along with the assignment. Blair almost fired him, but met too much resistance from the rest of the *Post* staff.

Next, Blair turned to Norman Ritter, who was an editorial assistant. Ritter, an impressionable young man, was awed by Blair.

He jumped at the chance to do his work, and tried very hard to succeed. Toward the end of 1964, Ritter was to do something at Blair's direction that very nearly wrecked Curtis for all time. His assignment was the same one Mooney had refused, plus trying to gather evidence of mismanagement that Blair and Kantor could use in recruiting editors and publishers for the putsch. Blair worked on the editors, those he had hired.

Kantor worked on three of the five publishers, using Jesse Ballew as his "front man." Ballew had been promoted to publisher of the *Post* by Kantor, and his loyalty to his benefactor was assured. I found the participation of Jesse Ballew more irritating than that of anyone else because I had saved his employment at Curtis when I arrived, had traveled with him on sales calls, and even helped him get into my country club in Rye. Ballew was very active in, of all things, the Boy Scouts. He and Mike Mooney actually squared off for a few wild blows at each other at a large meeting when Mooney characterized Ballew derisively as a "Boy Scout." Ballew, a complete square, bounced up and demanded, "Don't you like the Boy Scouts?" Mooney's retort was eloquent but inelegant:"——the Boy Scouts." Ballew swung at Mooney and Mooney lashed back. They were separated undamaged.

I took no steps against Ballew because of his lovely wife and fine youngsters. My belief that "you generally get what you deserve" was confirmed in Ballew's case. His nickname on Madison Avenue and at the Apawamis Club is quite unflattering. That is punishment enough, it seems to me.

The Blair-Kantor, Emerson-Ballew character-assassination technique was thoroughly effective over the short term. Blair knew his editors well. He appealed to each of them on whatever basis had the most to do with his particular personality and vulnerability. Don Schanche, Blair's closest friend, wanted the editorship of *Holiday*. Blair promised it to him. That was, indeed, a rare plum. *Holiday*, built slowly and soundly by Ted Patrick, was among the most prestigious magazines in the English-speaking world and in Europe. Blair was premature. Nothing could have persuaded me to remove Patrick as long as he lived. His magazine —and *Holiday* was uniquely his—grew in circulation, influence, advertising, and profits during his stewardship. His personal area of influence also was extensive.

Ted Patrick undoubtedly had as many friends and admirers as

any editor in current history. He sampled as many good wines as any sommelier. His palate was legendary—he was a true gourmet, eating often and well, but with sufficient discretion and discipline to retain a slim, erect figure, kept that way by regular sessions of tennis. Ted was not at his best when we became colleagues at Curtis. He had lost his wife, his famous dog, and much of his zest for life. I believe Blair envied Ted's enormous prestige and resented Ted's icy indifference to him. Blair came to me, time after time, asking, pleading, demanding that I fire Patrick and install Schanche as editor. I refused and kept refusing until Ted Patrick died, prematurely, after a brief illness.

One touching episode illuminates the genuine affection and regard in which Patrick was held by most of the *Holiday* people and the influential, creative heads of the major advertising agencies in New York. The Blair attempt to undermine Patrick became known to Jim White, then publisher of *Holiday*, and White decided to take no chances. He engineered a tribute to Ted Patrick that was heartwarming, getting David Ogilvy of Ogilvy, Benson and Mather, an outstanding advertising agency, to write a full-page newspaper advertisement in which a eulogy to Ted Patrick was endorsed by the top creative people in the advertising world. Blair took this as a personal affront and shouted, "Jim White is trying to destroy me."

Ted was an enriching kind of man, completely constructive. He, like Pat Weaver, knew the essentiality of developing and preserving an atmosphere in which creative people could expand, be at ease, and do their best work. *Holiday* was the favorite port of call for writers, photographers, and artists. One very well-known photographer, Slim Arons, would regularly drop in to see me just to tell me what a pleasure it was to work for Ted Patrick and his editorial team.

I got some delicious side benefits because of Ted. The *Holiday* award was the United States equivalent of maximum stars in the famed *Michelin* guides of France and parts of Europe. Any American restaurant that gained the award was "made." I was getting a lot of personal publicity, including pictures. Whenever I went to a good restaurant, the management would recognize me and would respond—I had some of the finest meals imaginable all over the country. There was some surprise when I invariably demanded a check.

Holiday declined dramatically after the death of Ted Patrick. Blair recommended the appointment of Schanche, and Schanche alienated the *Holiday* staff, which could have carried him for years. Another showdown occurred, and Clifford backed Schanche—a serious error. The staff, which had with Patrick built *Holiday*, exited. So Schanche was finally fired and Caskie Stinnett, then an editor on the *Journal,* became editor. It is too early to tell, of course, whether *Holiday* will struggle back to the eminence it enjoyed under Patrick. He was the best in his field.

Blair distorted a not unusual situation that came about because of my passion for golf. I had been invited by a prominent local attorney to play in an Invitational Golf Tournament in the Southwest. After the main tournament was over, my host invited me to play at a new club in the same city. This club had been built over an underground river in a fertile valley. While there, I met the manager, a youngish man I shall call Al. My host had done some legal work for Al in establishing the golf club and the surrounding facilities. The overall development plan for the club was classic. Building sites were sold around the golf course, and with the sites went membership in the club. When Al learned I was president of Curtis, he tried to get me to buy a building site. He made no bones about his reasoning, frankly admitting that the sites were not moving very fast and that there was a good deal of competition from surrounding promotions of the same type. My purchase of a site, he said, would help him attract and convince other prospects. I told him I had neither the money nor the time.

Al came to New York a month later, and phoned to ask if he could see me at the office. I agreed. He arrived with a set of site plans and again asked me to invest. I declined. Then he asked for an introduction to someone at *Holiday* so that he could promote the possibility of editorial coverage for his operation, when it merited it. I asked Schanche to come to my office to meet my caller. When Schanche arrived, the land site plans were strewn over my desk. After I made the introduction, Al gathered up his plans and went off with Schanche to his office. I promptly forgot the entire incident.

Later, I learned that Schanche had gone to Blair's office as soon as Al left, to tell Blair what he had seen in my office and about my introduction of Al and Al's pitch for a *Holiday* editorial. Blair's mind clicked into high gear. He suggested to Schanche that

I owned land and was trying to improve its value by getting free publicity for it in *Holiday*. He said that he would investigate. Blair made no true investigation, but he sold Schanche on that idea.

Something about Al's last name struck a responsive chord with Blair. He dug into the copious *Post* files and found that there was a family of the same name in the Midwest. Blair assigned a Chicago stringer to a study of the family head, found that he had a son, that the son was the manager of the golf club, and that the father seemed to have some questionable associates in the Midwest. By the time Blair had finished constructing an incredible fiction, he had me, as the imagined owner of land in the club, linked with the questionable people in the Midwest. He then encouraged Schanche to spread *this* story to some of the other editors. Coming from Schanche, the story was believed. Kantor also used the story with the three publishers he was recruiting.

Both Blair and Kantor had a strange ambivalence about publicity and public relations. Blair had asked me to let him hire a public relations firm to handle him, and I agreed because it was good business. But Blair had little regard for public relations people who worked for anyone else. He also did not seem to understand the public relations function, but considered personal publicity and product plugs its full extent. In fact, though Blair and Kantor themselves sought personal publicity, they seemed to me to resent the favorable amount of it that a public relations firm got for me. Blair circulated a charge among the editors relating to public relations people and me that I cannot repeat without damage to innocent people. I learned about it from my contact within the Blair camp, who, shortly thereafter, cut himself out of the group in sheer disgust.

Two other innocent, routine incidents were seized upon by Blair and enlarged by Ritter to seduce the handful of editors Blair was able to gather around him to support his power play. One involved an old friend of mine named Eddie Sutherland. Eddie came to me one day with what he thought were legitimate stories. The first concerned the sole surviving member of the Romanov family. There had been rumor that Anastasia, one of the daughters of the Czar, had escaped execution. The other story was a personal account by the purported assassin of Count Bernadotte of Sweden. Eddie Sutherland had been hired by the agent for the lady and the alleged assassin, and he came and offered me the stories for the *Post*. As in all such matters, I sent him to see Clay Blair.

The name *Sutherland* registered with Blair, and when *Eddie* Sutherland left, Blair studied my biography and found that I had been employed by Sutherland Productions, a motion picture company, many years before. So he decided that I had once worked for *Eddie* Sutherland, and was now paying off an old friend and employer by promoting him to the editorial department with a bogus story. The Sutherland I worked for was *John* Sutherland, no relation to Eddie.

I don't want to make all the editors seem completely gullible, but by this time a few were pretty well brainwashed. These few considered Blair their hero, a conviction he generated in clever ways and, about which I was to learn later. For example, after Blair had been fired and I was in limbo, Bill Emerson busily courted favor with Clifford and the directors. He told the board members that Blair, before he would leave for Philadelphia to attend the regular monthly board meetings, called his key editors together for "crisis" meetings. He would announce that he expected to be attacked in the coming board meeting about a specific story in the *Post,* and would invite the editors to tell him how best he could defend them against the attacks of the directors. There was not a single instance in any board of directors meeting of an attack on the editors of the *Post* for the stories they had written. But Blair gave the editors the impression that the Curtis board, archconservative, was constantly heckling him and trying to influence him on *Post* editorial policy. He was their champion and defender.

Blair was successful in recruiting a few of the editors into his cabal. Out of a total of around seventy editors at Curtis, he was able to get eight. But he would not have attempted the power play with so few. He also had to have support from the advertising side. In the Curtis system, the publishers were actually glorified advertising salesmen. Marvin Kantor was indispensable in this plan. The directors might not be overly impressed by an editors' rebellion, but that, plus a publishers' rebellion, would be a major crisis. Kantor had a much easier time in his recruitment than Blair. Kantor got the support of Jesse Ballew with a title and raise—he made Ballew publisher of the *Post.* Ballew recruited Mike Hadley, the ambitious publisher of the *Journal.* Ballew seized on two joint-venture programs, one with Admiral, one with Longines, as evidence of more than mismanagement—he and Kantor distorted them into "advertising kickbacks."

The Admiral situation developed this way: The Chicago advertising manager, Jim Hagen, sent an urgent message to me to call on Ross Siragusa, president of the Admiral Corporation. Hagen had a good plan calculated to appeal to Siragusa. It involved the purchase by Curtis of the names of Admiral customers who had warranties on expensive merchandise, if Admiral would purchase over $2 million in advertising space in Curtis magazines. Hagen's suggestion came shortly after I joined Curtis, when the company was in desperate need of advertising, and so I naturally agreed to make the trip and the presentation. I had the plan sent to Maurice Poppei, treasurer, and Allison Page, legal counsel, for advance approval. Both gave an OK, and I made the presentation. Siragusa bought the idea on the first call. I came back from Chicago in high spirits, with an order for over $2 million in space in all four magazines. The effect of this sale to a famous, tough merchant like Siragusa was magical. The staff applauded, the board was jubilant, the trade press impressed.

The arrangement with Admiral provided that Curtis would pay Admiral for the names it had as a result of the warranties given on the high-priced merchandise it sold. For example, every time Admiral sold a color television set, the buyer was given a warranty for the replacement of defective parts and workmanship for a certain minimum period. Television set buyers at that time were a very desirable socio-economic group in the United States, and their names and addresses were extremely valuable to people in the direct mail business. Such lists of names were salable at rates of up to seventy-five dollars per thousand. Admiral bought advertising from Curtis and paid for it. Curtis bought names from Admiral and paid for them at a prearranged rate. A similar kind of deal was also made with the Longines-Wittnauer Watch Company.

Kantor and Ballew tried to use these joint-venture arrangements as evidence of "advertising kickbacks." The Admiral arrangement as interpreted by Ballew, Kantor, and Blair was the most serious charge made by the Blair-Kantor group. The term "kickback" was well known to everyone in the business world; even the public was well aware of it as a result of the "payola scandal" in the radio and television business. A typical kickback consists of a buyer issuing a purchase order at a published rate, then getting a payoff from the seller. A kickback charge is heavy with connotation of personal gain. These and other such charges were presented in an inventory assembled for Blair and Kantor by Norman Ritter.

There were two distinct phases of the Blair-Kantor, Ballew-Emerson attack on me. The first was the verbal smear campaign with the objective of recruiting editors and publishers for an official attack. It worked, and its success enabled the four leaders to mount the final assault. This second phase was synthesized in the letter composed by Blair, Kantor, and Schanche, and signed by them. Never before seen by anyone other than the Curtis Executive Committee, here is that letter:

PERSONAL AND CONFIDENTIAL

September 29, 1964

Mr. M. Albert Linton, Chairman
The Executive Committee
The Curtis Publishing Company
4601 Market Street
Philadelphia, Pennsylvania 19139

Dear Mr. Linton:

The undersigned, as you may know, constitute the effective operating management of the Curtis magazines. All of us have devoted years to our profession and years to the Curtis Publishing Company, which we now see in jeopardy as the direct result of mismanagement and questionable behavior on the part of Mr. Culligan.

We are, quite frankly, in a state of revolt on the simple moral premise that we cannot, in good conscience, continue to contribute our skills and our reputations to what we view as an immoral deception of our fellow employees, our readers, our loyal advertisers, the directors and the stockholders of Curtis.

We fear that the Board of Directors has been deluded by Mr. Culligan and is unaware of the many instances of questionable and perhaps even illegal conduct of the company management. There have been shocking instances of advertising kickbacks, which we understand may be illegal under the Robinson-Patman Act. There have been consistent misrepresentations to us and to the public of the truth about the company's extremely bleak financial position. There has been consistent frivolous waste of the company's funds by

Mr. Culligan and a coterie of men around him—and this in the face of a certainly disastrous profit and loss statement. Most recently, Mr. Culligan offered to "buy off" two dedicated company officers, Mr. Blair and Mr. Kantor, with a settlement involving sums in the hundreds of thousands of dollars in exchange for their agreement to leave the company quietly. We believe this is unethical.

We know of numerous incidents of similarly questionable conduct and plain mismanagement. We feel it is our duty to inform you, as Chairman of the Executive Committee of the Board of Directors, of these incidents and of our moral revulsion. We are confident that the board, once informed, will act to impose a responsible and ethical management on the company.

In our view, outward evidence of a management explosion in Curtis at this point could very well be fatal to the company. Therefore, we suggest that Mr. Culligan be quietly stripped of his executive power, but left nominally in charge for the sake of appearances only, at least until an internal investigation of the legality of some of his more questionable actions has been completed. In his place we suggest an executive committee be formed headed by yourself and including Mr. Blair, Mr. Kantor and Mr. Poppei. We feel that this committee, if appointed by the Board, should act immediately to implement a plan to save the corporation, a plan which exists and to which Mr. Culligan has paid only lip service. In our judgment, these magazines and the company can be saved if all of us, working with the plan and under an ethical management, continue to devote to them the energy and dedication we have demonstrated in the past.

On the other hand we are convinced that the company and the magazines face ruin in the very near future if such steps are not taken immediately.

Individually we are determined to bring this to your attention in a last effort to correct the situation. If nothing is done to correct it, none of us, as a matter of individual conscience, feels that he can continue to participate in what he knows to be deceitful and wrong. In each case, we are determined to terminate our employment with the company if the status quo is maintained.

We do this with full awareness that our action will undoubtedly cause sufficient loss of reader and advertiser confidence to kill the Curtis publications and thus kill the company. Obviously, we hope that this will be unnecessary. But we prefer to see these great institutions die with honor than expire, as they are now doing, under a corrupt leadership.

Marvin D. Kantor
Chairman, Magazine Division

Clay Blair, Jr.
Editor-in-Chief
Editor, *The Saturday
Evening Post*

Norman R. Ritter
Assistant Managing Editor,
The Saturday Evening Post

Hank Walker
Assistant Managing Editor,
The Saturday Evening Post

Charles Davis Thomas
Editor, *Ladies'
Home Journal*

Caskie Stinnett
Executive Editor,
Ladies' Home Journal

Don A. Schanche
Editor, *Holiday*

Hubbard H. Cobb
Editor, *American
Home*

William A. Emerson
Managing Editor, *The
Saturday Evening Post*

Otto Friedrich
Assistant Managing Editor,
The Saturday Evening Post

Jesse L. Ballew, Jr.
Publisher, *The Saturday
Evening Post*

John Connors
General Sales Manager, *The
Saturday Evening Post*

Garth Hite
Advertising Director,
Holiday

J. Michael Hadley
Publisher, *Ladies'
Home Journal*

John L. Collins
Publisher,
American Home

The condition of Blair's imagination at this juncture is clearly etched by an episode that is backed by incontrovertible physical evidence. The member of Blair's staff who split with the Blair cabal when he detected their design to ruin me slipped quietly into the Curtis Building early one morning, knowing that I would be the only living soul in the office before 8:00 A.M. He spread out on my desk a most interesting List of Contents page of an upcoming issue of the *Post*. He played his little game, neither saying anything nor pointing out anything unusual. I scanned the page, which looked normal. Then I did a double take at the upper left-hand column. For almost three years it had shown the Curtis management team with my name first, then that of Kantor as chairman of the Magazine Division, then Blair's name as editor.

This particular page bore—in solitary splendor—just one name: *Clay Blair, Jr., Editor.* Blair, biting on an unripe victory, had actually set up a new masthead without my name in a secret foundry, and had the masthead plated, ready to go in the very first issue after my downfall. If ever there was a monument to the fantasy in which Blair drifted, it is this masthead, which I have in my file.

The letter to the Executive Committee was drafted just prior to and during the secret meeting called by Blair over the weekend of September 26 at Manero's Steak House in Greenwich, Connecticut. A participant later shamefacedly described that meeting to me. Blair had arranged for a private room; drinks were served liberally. After dinner, Blair chaired the meeting and introduced Schanche to tell the story of the Southwest land deal. Dave Thomas was introduced to describe the Sutherland incident. Jesse Ballew added the "advertising kickback" story of Admiral and Longines-Wittnauer. Blair himself aired the story about the public relations matter briefly referred to earlier, but not described here in detail—to avoid injury to innocent people.

Then a draft of the letter was read, reworked, and generally agreed upon. Monday, September 28, it was typed and signed by Blair, Kantor, Emerson, Schanche, Walker, Ritter, and Ballew. Ballew got his assistant, Jack Connors, to sign. These were the easy signatures to get. Next to sign were Otto Friedrich and Hubbard Cobb. Caskie Stinnett, a *Journal* editor, and John Collins were the last holdouts, but they finally signed. Friedrich later admitted to me in writing that he had not read the letter.

Marvin Kantor then called Albert Linton, chairman of the Executive Committee, and demanded to see him on a "matter of the greatest importance." He told Linton he had a letter to discuss. Linton refused to meet him and said, "Send me the letter." Kantor had it hand-delivered by Norman Ritter. Linton, shocked when he read it, called the other members of the Executive Committee. Among them, they came to a decision to tell only Cary Bok and me. Kantor and Blair had timed the delivery to be shortly before the regular Curtis board meeting, which took place the first Thursday of each month—in this case, October 1.

An Executive Committee meeting was hurriedly called on September 30, *before* the board meeting. Albert Linton, as chairman, conducted the meeting. As soon as it was officially called to order, he held up the letter and said, "This was hand-delivered to me this morning—it is most serious." He then read it.

As the horrifying words rolled out, I felt as though a giant hand had seized my chest—I could scarcely breathe. "Advertising kickbacks" hit me hard; "corrupt and immoral conduct" was like a hot knife in my ribs; "illegal actions" seemed mild.

I demanded an immediate investigation of the Executive Committee. They agreed to recommend one to the full board, and then adjourned.

The next day the full board meeting was called to order by me, as chairman. The letter was described, not read. I asked Blair and Kantor if they realized the import of their charges of "corrupt, immoral and illegal" conduct. I asked particularly about advertising kickbacks. They seemed shocked that the letter had gotten to the board, and *they admitted to the board that they did not really mean what the letter said about "advertising kickbacks, corrupt and immoral conduct."* Blair said the language was strong because they wanted to attract attention to their demands.

I then offered a resolution calling for a full investigation of the charges. The board voted unanimously in favor of it. An "Investigating Committee" was formed with Albert Linton as chairman; M. D. Brown was the only other member. I realized later that I should have asked for a larger committee, with one or two practical general businessmen such as H. C. Mills and Curtis Barkes. Linton asked for legal assistance, and the board, including me, assigned Allison Page of Pepper, Hamilton and Scheetz to assist the committee. Since Page had approved the deals for which I was criticized, I agreed. Milton Gould *volunteered* his assistance, loudly. It was accepted.

As chairman, I made an impassioned plea to all the directors to remain silent until the investigation was completed. With unanimous agreement, including that of Blair and Kantor, all of them vowed silence. The board then directed Blair and Kantor to deliver documentation of their charges. They promised to do so "immediately," implying that the documentation was all prepared. Delivery was promised for the next day, Friday, October 2. But no documentation appeared. It was then promised for Monday, October 5.

On Saturday morning, October 3, I received a telephone call at home from Marvin Kantor. He asked me to meet him that evening at seven-thirty for an attempt to work out a peaceful solution. I agreed, expecting to meet Kantor alone, but when I arrived at the meeting place, the elegant Four Seasons restaurant in the Seagram Building, Blair was with Kantor. I decided to remember details and statements and to make notes immediately after the confrontation. My greeting was cool and there was no handshaking. We followed the captain to a table in the Fountain Room. Drinks were ordered quickly.

I said to Kantor, "You asked to meet about a peaceful solution. What could we possibly have to talk about?"

Kantor replied, "We never meant you any harm. We'll withdraw the charges, and you stay as president and chief executive officer. Name me the executive vice-president, and get rid of Clifford."

"Withdraw the charges?" I asked. "You must be insane—this is a publicly held company. You've unleashed something no one can stop."

Lifting up his water glass, Kantor said, "This can be described as half empty or half full. We'll take care of the directors."

"I won't make any deal of any kind with you," I said, and I got up and left the restaurant—and the check for the drinks.

On my way home, after making notes, I realized that I had let my temper get the best of me. I should have agreed to think it over, then gone to the Investigating Committee and told them of the offer. I could have convinced them, I think, to go along with a plan to have Blair and Kantor withdraw the charges and advise the others of the unconscionable deal they had made. The almost-certain result would have been the breakup of the group. After that, without publicity, I could have fired Blair and Kantor with restraints sufficient to keep them from destructive actions with the press. The situation could then have been resolved within the confines of the Curtis boardroom or executive offices, since the charges were false. But the die was cast—I simply could not make a deal with them—and the gut-rending drama had to be played out.

The documentation of the charges was not delivered on Monday. I called Linton and demanded that he get the documentation, and he had Gould call Kantor. Gould did, and warned Kantor that the delay in delivery of the documentation was making a bad impression on the officially established, special Investigating Committee of the board of directors. Kantor delivered the documentation—one set to Linton, one set to me—on Tuesday, October 6. I told my secretary not to disturb me under any circumstances, locked my door, and started reading what Blair and Kantor had billed as documentation of charges of mismanagement. A sense of disbelief swept over me, then something akin to pure joy. The pile of papers consisted of memos about acquisition and merger opportunities. There were literally scores of them, which had cascaded on the office of the president of Curtis, as would be the case with any president of an equivalent-sized company. There were dozens of memos on joint-venture arrangements of a routine nature, most of which had never come to my personal attention. Under a heading, "frivolous waste," were such things as the company airplane, the ancient twin Beech that was used long before I got to Curtis, to carry Curtis and New York & Penn executives to and from the remote locations of the paper mills. The plane was also used by Cary Bok to get him out of Camden, Maine, into Philadelphia. I used it for business when it was available. I almost laughed at the charges that I had overestimated and overpublicized the Canadian ore strike, having heard confidentially that there were at least 6.5 million tons under the Curtis land. So absurd was the situation that I felt sure the whole mess would be thrown out.

That same day I rushed my set to William Coogan, my friend and lawyer, and started a series of consultations with him to prepare my rebuttal. Linton, Brown, and Page went into almost continuous sessions investigating the charges and analyzing the evidence. Someone close to Linton called and warned me that Gould had taken charge and—after dismissing all the other accusations as "junk" and decrying the attack letter as "monstrous"—spotlighted only one allegation as serious, dangerous, and pivotal. This was the charge that the Admiral and Longines joint-venture arrangements were possibly in violation of the Robinson-Patman Act.

Linton and Brown were terrified. However, there was no Robinson-Patman violation involved because Curtis was at all times prepared to offer the same arrangements to any advertiser who had something of equivalent value to offer to Curtis. Both Jesse Ballew and his assistant, Jack Connors, knew this because I went with Connors to General Electric to offer them a deal similar to the one offered to Admiral. General Electric declined it. Allison Page, the corporate legal counsel who had approved the Admiral and Longines deals *in advance* of my approval, knew it full well, too. The attack letter, which Blair and Kantor admitted they really did not mean, and the pile of documentation they offered in support put me on the rack for four years because of the lamentable habit of newspapers, even good ones, of making banner headlines out of *charges*. My *vindication* was routinely reported deep in the recesses of the *Times*. Never in *Time* or *The Gallagher Report*.

On Wednesday of that week, October 7, while the Investigating Committee of the board of directors (Albert Linton and Moreau Brown) was evaluating the documentation, Blair fired his best shot. He used his position as an editor to enlist the press in his battle against me. Despite his pledge of silence, he sent Norman Ritter to see Bob Bedingfield and his staff of *The New York Times* who had been following the Curtis story for several years. Bedingfield, the senior reporter in the financial section of the *Times*, a good, tough reporter and an intensely religious man, is truly incorruptible. Norman Ritter spent the late evening hours of Wednesday, October 7, in the offices of the financial department of *The New York Times* conferring with Bedingfield's staff. Although Ritter told them a great deal about the attack, he did not actually show them the letter of attack, but merely described it in general and stated who signed it.

Bedingfield called my home shortly before two o'clock the morning of October 9 and told my wife that he would be forced to run the story in the morning edition. He wanted to hear my side of it. I signaled my wife to say nothing. Unfortunately, I had given my word to the board that, in the interest of Curtis, I would say nothing about the crisis.

The New York Times story, which spread the attempted Blair-Kantor power grab all over the English-speaking world, was written during the late hours of the night of Thursday, October 8, and up to about 1:45 Friday morning. It ran, under the large headline "15 Accuse Culligan of Mismanagement," on the front page of the paper. There was a picture of me, flanked by two large subheadlines, "Editors and Production Men Join in the Charges" and "Special Directors Meeting Set for Week of October 19."

As I read the story, I felt that it had to have originated with Blair and Kantor, although I did not think they were foolish enough to have revealed the information personally, having taken a solemn oath as directors to remain silent. I recalled the tip I had received from an editor at Time Inc. (not *Time*), that Blair had visited him and hinted that he might be interested in supplying a "bombshell" story about Curtis to *Time*. We learned shortly thereafter how the story had got to the *Times*. This story caused Curtis and me untold grief, and at least $11 million in advertising was lost by the *Post* and other Curtis magazines partly because of the damage to advertiser and agency confidence in Curtis.

As I read the story, I had a rush of cold dread to the heart, seeing twenty years of hard work collapsing in ashes. I knew all too well the effect of such a story in a prestigious paper like the *Times*, and *my lips were sealed*. The story was totally one-sided, as could be expected, considering the assistance Bedingfield and his staff got from Norman Ritter.

One statement was particularly irritating:

When the charges were aired at the October 2 board meeting, Milton Gould, a director and a New York lawyer, said he would call for Mr. Culligan's resignation if the charges were proved.

Gould made no such statement at the board meeting.

One portion of the story showed the advantage of getting there "fustest with the mostest." Bedingfield wrote, "It is known that Blair and Kantor renewed their attack on the basis of the company's continuing losses."

The grossly unfair aspect of this was that the "continuing losses" were caused by failures in the two departments run by Blair and Kantor—Editorial and Sales. All other departments of Curtis were doing well. Another inaccurate statement reported by Bedingfield was: "Blair and Kantor favored a wholesale cost-cutting program to tide the company over...."

Bedingfield knew when he wrote the story, or should have known, that one of my major contributions in 1963 was a personnel reduction of almost 2,000 people, which yielded a saving of over $13 million. In fact, Bedingfield had cited my extraordinary cost-reduction program as one of the reasons why the *Times* had honored me as "one of a gallery of men who left a strong imprint on 1963." No "wholesale cost-cutting" was possible.

For sixteen days, the Curtis story was on either the front page of the *Times* or the front page of the business section. The coverage was absolutely unprecedented. I later had occasion to compare *The New York Times* coverage of the Curtis story with its tender handling of the demise of three New York newspapers. The difference was and still is striking.

Within ten days after the attack letter had been sent to Linton, I submitted my reply and full rebuttal. Here, for the first time, this document is exposed to public view. It was prepared with the help of William Coogan, of the law firm with the improbable name of Sullivan, Donovan, Hanrahan, McGovern & Lane. Fortunately, for me, I had employed this law firm when the disagreements between Gould and Pepper, Hamilton and Scheetz became so serious that I could no longer cope with them. I wired Albert Linton that I was now employing this counsel to assist me in resolving the present difficulties.

The highlights of my rebuttal were accompanied by a covering memo which, in part, read:

"The inventory of complaints instigated and authored by Clay Blair—and Marvin Kantor—is beneath contempt.

"The Board has had several opportunities to see and hear Mr. Blair in some of his almost unbelievable performances.

"I have been attacked by a curious man who is capable of the following statements:

> "TO THE BOARD: 'He [pointing to J. M. Clifford] is a psychotic, who is determined to destroy me.'
>
> "TO ME: 'MacNelly is trying to destroy me.'
>
> "TO THE BOARD: 'I think the figures [Maurice Poppei's financial statements] are rigged.'
>
> "TO ME: 'Jim White is trying to destroy me.'
>
> "TO THE BOARD: 'Everybody is trying to destroy me.'
>
> "TO ME: 'You are trying to destroy me.'
>
> "TO THE BOARD: 'The whole Westchester Meeting [Budget Meeting] was designed to destroy me.'
>
> "TO ME: 'Veronis is trying to destroy me.' ''

My rebuttal read, in part:

To the Board of Directors of Curtis Publishing Company:
Gentlemen:

On September 29, 1964, a letter was sent to Mr. Linton which was signed by fifteen of the editorial and publishing personnel of this company. This letter makes certain extreme allegations in general terms against me and, among other things, charges unethical and "perhaps even illegal" conduct, frivolous waste of company's funds, and advertising kickbacks. At that time the board asked that detailed specifications of these charges be furnished in order that I may have a chance to reply to them. A rambling, disorganized mass of data was presented. Certain specifications have been made, and while I consider most of them contemptible and almost too absurd for comment, I will nevertheless attempt to answer each and every specific allegation made.

Items 1, 2, 3, 4, 5, 6, 9, 10, 11, 12, 13, 16, 17, 18, and 20 involve discussions by me of acquisitions or mergers or sales of this company to or with other companies or of acquisitions by this company. I consider it one of management's duties to discuss such matters and if they are advantageous so to report to the board. The board will remember that I put all mergers and acquisitions in the hands of the executive vice-president, Mr. Clifford. I was generally familiar with the activities and approve of the actions taken by him.

Item 8 states that I exaggerated the Timmins situation to a "ridiculous" degree to public groups. This is totally false. It has since been substantiated that there has been a great deal of ore involved in this transaction and I frankly am at a loss to say in what way I exaggerated Timmins. The SEC has commended me for our conservatism in public announcements. You know that I have reported to you all data supplied by Texas Gulf Sulphur. Also, in order to avoid personal involvement I put all "Timmins" matters under J. M. Clifford. I was generally familiar with the activities and approve of the actions taken by him.

Item 14 criticizes the fact that the company purchased two large offset presses at a cost of $3 million. This is actually a "no-cost" transaction. These presses were bought on a chattel mortgage basis on a recommendation of J. M. Clifford and Leon Marks whereby we would acquire title to the presses after completing payment of rentals over a certain period of time. These presses were bought against contracts I knew we could get, and, in fact, did get. This matter was submitted to the board and approved by them. Our loan agreement called for bank approval, which was granted.

Item 15 relates to the creation of a Legal Department at

Curtis. This was recommended to me by the executive vice-president in the interest of efficiency and economy, and while we have not completed a cost analysis for it, we will do so shortly and I will submit it to you.

Item 19 criticizes me for appearing before financial and other groups to give misleading statements about the company's 1964 earnings. No evidence is supplied to show that such statements were misleading and, in fact, at present the facts will bear me out that my statements were not misleading. I did predict the first quarter of 1964 would be in the black and it was.

Item 2 claims that club dues paid by the company for various individuals are excessive. It states that a list is attached, but I see no such list. Despite the lack of such a list, I maintain that dues paid are not excessive and are comparable to or less than those paid by other businesses similar to Curtis.

Item 3 criticizes the maintenance of a suite in the Regency Hotel. The use of this suite was initiated during the Butts-Bryant case. Mr. Blair and Mr. Kantor have met with me there on numerous occasions. It has been used in other situations (Mr. Gould) and by other executives and clients.

Item 7 criticizes the employment of the Taplinger public relations firm. This firm has replaced the enormous Public Relations and Publicity Department Curtis once had and at a fraction of the former cost. One of their functions is, of course, to aid the corporation's image, both in the advertising community and the public. Their advice, contacts, and know-how have been invaluable.

Item 8 relates to the Book Division. The head of the Book Division, William Buckley, was hired by me on the recommendation of Mr. Blair. [Author's Note: *The Audubon Nature Encyclopedia*, its first venture, was immediately successful and made a profit in its first full year of over $400,000.]

Item 9. It has been charged that I have indiscriminately used employment contracts. Details are not given, so I cannot answer except in a general manner. I have used employment contracts during the darkest hours of this company as a method of attracting necessary personnel away from other companies. This was a necessary and certainly not an unusual procedure. Incidentally, both Mr. Blair and Mr. Kantor have contracts, and Mr. Blair recently recommended three of the personnel under him for contracts.

Item 11 complains of a *Post* reader research study which was authorized by Mr. Clifford purportedly without the knowledge or consent of Mr. Blair. It further states that the study was designed to furnish an indictment of the editorial operation. I am not quite sure what is meant by this unless

this is meant to be an admission by Mr. Blair that he is
deficient in his operations. Such studies are, of course, not
the least bit unusual in this business. The study is available to
the board for study.

In addition to the memoranda, the so-called evidence
and specifications submitted by Messrs. Blair and Kantor
mention other advertising contracts entered into by Curtis.
These involve Admiral Sales Corporation, and the Longines-
Wittnauer Watch Company. These contracts are apparently
the ones referred to in the letter to Mr. Linton of September
29 where they state, "There have been shocking instances of
advertising kickbacks." *Mr. Kantor and Mr. Blair admitted to
the Board that this language was inaccurate and unfair.*

The Admiral deal involved a minimum of $2 million
worth of advertising in Curtis magazines exclusively at a 26
percent discount, and are standard network discounts. Additionally, a rider was attached to this contract whereby Curtis
employed Admiral services for twelve months at the rate of
$19,833 per month for a total of $238,000. Curtis is to
receive:
(a) The right to use Admiral's customer list containing not
    less than a million names.
(b) Admiral will conduct a national survey of magazines in-
    cluding ours and make the results of each survey available
    to us.
(c) Admiral will distribute direct mail subscription cards for
    Curtis magazines with the Admiral warranty cards in no
    less than 2 million of Admiral's products, and
(d) Admiral will provide Curtis space at its trade show and
    industry convention booths.

The Longines contract involves a $400,000 credit
against base charges in return for Longines':
(a) Hiring a consultant to develop different mailing subscrip-
    tion offers to be tested for Curtis magazines,
(b) Sending out a minimum 400,000 test mailings.
(c) Including the inserts or tie-ins and up to 10 million addi-
    tional Longines mailings during 1964, and
(d) Providing Curtis with the detailed market analysis show-
    ing full results of the tests as requested by Curtis.
(e) Longines surrendered exclusive rights to Curtis lists.

The Longines and Admiral contracts were admittedly
out of the ordinary, but extraordinary measures were needed
to meet extraordinary conditions. These arrangements were
entered into in good faith by both parties.

Any claims that have been made that these contracts
were secret are, of course, false. I did not personally negotiate any contracts but gave general approval to those recommended to me by task forces which I appointed, while I was
going about the country seeking to obtain contracts from the

200 largest advertisers throughout the United States.

Mr. Poppei should be asked about his participation in these contracts. Pepper, Hamilton and Scheetz should also be asked.

The other matters brought up in these specifications relate to a Mr. Eddie Sutherland, a Mr. Brinsmade and a Mr. Al. Mr. Blair claims that I was an employee of Mr. Eddie Sutherland. That is false. Mr. Sutherland approached me with a story relating to the assassin of Count Bernadotte. I referred, as I always do, to the Editorial Department. It turned out that the story was dropped after being checked out by the Editorial Department. Mr. Harold Martin should be asked about this story. [Author's Note: It took a lie-detector test to convince the editors not to accept the story.]

I met Mr. Al while in the Southwest at the invitation of a prominent local attorney. While there, this attorney took me to a new golf club. It was there that I met Mr. Al. I know nothing of his background. Mr. Al tried to interest me in investing in the country club. I gave him courteous attention but nothing more. He later called on me in New York, this time with maps and pictures of the country club development. I showed only a courteous interest in it. He then asked if he could talk to the *Holiday* people about a possible story, and that is when I introduced him to Mr. Schanche. I have never invested in this development.

Despite Mr. Blair's statement about my ideas, it is a matter of record that I originated *NBC News on the Hour*, rescued the *Today Show*, reprogrammed *Monitor* and originated *Emphasis*, on NBC television and radio. My ideas have made profits now countable in the millions. Mr. Blair's coolness to ideas other than his own is a primary weakness.

I met with Serge Semenenko regularly during this period. He was sympathetic and helpful. He had a very good source at the *Times* with whom he spoke regularly, and he was able to get some facts to the *Times* that kept it from doing even greater damage to Curtis.

I also took action to keep the *Post* editorial staff functioning in case Blair, Emerson, and Friedrich made good their threat to quit if their demands were not met. I called in Bob Sherrod, Stewart Alsop, head of the *Post* Washington office, and Harold Martin of Atlanta, the dean of magazine writers. They agreed to step into the breach and put out as many issues of the *Post* as necessary. The other magazines were not a problem. The *Holiday* staff editors did not join the cabal, nor did the staff editors of *American Home* or *Jack and Jill.* In any case, *Holiday* and *American Home* were monthly magazines with at least two issues already locked up.

We had a final tension-packed afternoon at the crux of the crisis. Semenenko, Sherrod, Martin, and Alsop met in my suite at the Regency. I told them what I needed and expected of them. They agreed. Semenenko made a suggestion that Sherrod call the *Post* staff editors, including Emerson and Friedrich, and try to get them to withdraw their threat. Sherrod tracked Emerson down at the apartment of a sales manager of the *Post,* Richard King, who let Blair and Kantor use his apartment for strategy meetings. Sherrod, not disclosing that he was with me, told Emerson that he, Alsop, and Martin wanted to see him and the *Post* staff. Emerson refused to come and meet them but invited the three to King's apartment to meet the whole group of attackers, Blair and Kantor included. Serge Semenenko and I waited for their return. We chatted about everything but Curtis for a while, I'm sure by his design—he may have thought the pressure was getting to me. He described the problems of other businesses he had helped: paper, motion pictures, Mexican industry. I asked him if he had ever experienced anything as bad as the publishing business—the attacks on Curtis by *Time,* the scathing stories in *The New York Times,* the character assassination attempted on me, and the formal attack. His answer was a classic, so typical that I had my first laugh since the attack. Here he was, in the middle of a potential calamity, with his reputation at stake. He knew that a score of blocks away an absolutely pivotal meeting was taking place. Everyone else was using such words as "disaster," "tragedy," "incredible sabotage."

Serge said, "No, Joe, my dear, this is unprecedented." Hero worship was strange for a forty-seven-year-old like me, but at that moment I had some of it for Serge Semenenko.

In about ninety minutes Sherrod, Alsop, and Martin reappeared, visibly upset. Martin, particularly, seemed shaken. They told a strange tale. When they got to King's apartment and entered his living room, heavy with smoke and liquor fumes and tension, they tried to calm down the group and failed. Several of the clique were drunk and loud. Bill Emerson shouted insults at them about me and about Semenenko. It was, according to Sherrod, an ungovernable mob, out for a "lynch party"; he reported sadly the situation was hopeless. Sherrod, Alsop, and Martin assured Semenenko and me that they could put out the *Post* "for as long as necessary." We closed that day with some sense of uplift—at least the *Post* would appear on time.

Blair and Kantor's confidants—Bill Emerson, Don Schanche, Dave Thomas, Hank Walker, Norman Ritter, and Jesse Ballew—were variegated personalities from different backgrounds, but they had several characteristics in common. For one thing, they accepted Blair's characterizations of me without proper research or investigation or simple reasoning. The others—Caskie Stinnett, Hadley, Connors, Friedrich, Collins, Cobb, Hite—were too easily led. However, the names on the attack letter, whether prime activators or "sheep," had a very powerful cumulative effect on the recipient, Albert Linton.

Linton was no friend or fan of mine, although I was always cordial and respectful because of his age and position. Our relationship, even before the attack letter, had become strained because of three abrasive developments. First, in late 1963, I had tried to have the Executive Committee, of which Linton was chairman (the other members were Franklin, Fuller, and Brown), combined with the highly effective Finance Committee. My plan was to make Linton honorary chairman and Moreau Brown chairman. Linton resented this and objected to it. I withdrew the plan. Then Linton, courted by Clifford, suggested that Clifford be reinstated as head of Operations, the post he had held and abused by infuriating all the top Curtis editors. I refused. Finally, as described previously, Linton resented the editorial attack on Goldwater and seemed to blame me for it.

I indicated earlier that the death of Linton freed me from one of the many restraints about the writing of this book. Linton was a poor director of Curtis for fifteen years, but he was a fine man, a high-principled one, a pillar of Philadelphia society, a Quaker, an outstanding leader of the insurance industry, and a dedicated husband and father. His fairness and objectivity are indicated in the memorandum he wrote for the board, for the banks, and—most importantly—for the record. I have condensed some material written by others in this book, but so important is Linton's memo to the whole story that I present it here in its entirety as he wrote it:

The current crisis in Curtis started with a letter to the chairman of the Executive Committee dated September 29, 1964, and signed by Messrs. Clay Blair, Jr., and Marvin D. Kantor, two members of the Curtis board holding positions of senior vice-presidents of Curtis. Joining Blair and Kantor in signing the letter were thirteen editors and publishers in the Magazine Division. This letter charged the president, Mr. Culligan, with mismanagement and even wrongdoing. It stated that Mr. Culligan should be downgraded to an unimportant status and the management be entrusted to a committee of four of which Blair and Kantor would be members.

The extremely serious consequences that might result from this letter if it were made public were immediately recognized. A very limited number of copies were made. It was considered by the Executive Committee on September 30 and reported to the board the next day; but copies were not distributed to the members of the board. The board appointed a committee of two to evaluate the charges made in the letter. Blair and Kantor were directed to supply the evaluating committee with documentations of their charges. These would be transmitted to Mr. Culligan, who was directed to prepare documented answers. The results of the evaluation were to be reported to a special meeting of the board, now scheduled for October 19. It was hoped that the crisis could be resolved within Curtis without public discussions. It was recognized that the letter and its charges were like a bomb with a fuse, which if lighted by someone could cause immense damage. How Messrs. Blair and Kantor could have apparently been so bereft of business judgment and imagination in choosing the method they did is almost unbelievable. They had much safer methods of proceeding. For example, all they had to do was to address a letter to the chairman of the Executive Committee signed by themselves alone, stating that they had documented evidence of what they believed to be mismanagement and wrongdoing on the part of the president and asking that I receive such evidence if given to me. Upon receipt of that letter it would have been my duty to answer in the affirmative and I would have done so. In that way the matter could have been handled quietly within the Curtis board. Instead the signatures of Blair and Kantor on the letter were joined by those of thirteen important members of the editors and publishers, all of whose positions were largely dependent upon Blair and Kantor. By using this method, as already mentioned, a bomb was created which if the fuse were lighted would explode with extremely serious consequences. Well, someone lighted the fuse and the

bomb exploded on October 9. The responsibility must rest
upon Blair and Kantor since they set up the bomb in the first
place. We may someday know who was responsible for lighting the fuse, but that is much less important than the fact
that Blair and Kantor were the creators of the bomb.

With the publication of the *Times* story on October 9
and its dissemination throughout the country, the bomb exploded and the picture changed instantly. The image of
Curtis as seen by the readers of its magazines was that
of a great corporation challenged publicly by two directors
who demanded that the president be demoted with the
strong implication that they be given a prominent, if not a
dominant position, in the future management. All this, of
course, before the charge made in a previous letter had been
evaluated.

On Friday, after giving the subject the most careful consideration, it became clear to the Executive Committee that
the proper course was to relieve Messrs. Blair and Kantor of
their duties as employees of Curtis until the matter could be
considered and acted upon by the board on October 19. Only
in that way could it be demonstrated to all concerned that
the Curtis board was master in its own house and would not
be coerced by threats or by unjustified publicity in the press.
The board will act promptly, and when that has been done I
believe Curtis will emerge with a strong executive management—a management which will command the respect and
loyalty of the various branches of the Curtis organization so
that all can pull together to accomplish great things for Curtis. It has a staff of loyal dedicated individuals who can do
wonders if properly led. Once the image of the Curtis Publishing Company in the eyes of its readers, advertisers, and
the public generally is truly set forth, the company will be on
its way to profitable operations.

In Albert Linton's memo, I underlined the sentence stating,
"We may someday know who was responsible for lighting the
fuse"; at that time we had not yet learned that Norman Ritter had
been responsible for the leak to Bedingfield of *The New York
Times*. But we knew who had planted the bomb—Blair and
Kantor. A special meeting of the Executive Committee was called
by Albert Linton on Friday, October 10. It was attended by
Moreau Brown, Linton, and me. We decided to suspend Blair and
Kantor; we could not fire them until the investigation of their
charges was completed. October 10 was filled with charges and
countercharges about just who leaked the story to the *Times*.

Semenenko, Linton, and the Executive Committee and I now knew beyond question that Norman Ritter, Blair's aide, was the man, "who lit the fuse" with such devastating results.

Blair and Kantor were now in a perilous position. Although both had contracts, they knew they could be summarily fired for breaking their word as directors, and could even be sued by Curtis for the damage done to the company. Several attempts were made to cover the scene with a smoke screen of false rumor, charges, and countercharges. As a last desperation move, Blair convinced his cabal that Serge Semenenko had leaked the story to the *Times.* This was an absurd idea, for it threatened the $10 million bank loan to Curtis—and Semenenko's most prized abstract possession, his reputation that in thirty-five years he "never had a loan go sour."

Blair and Kantor called another meeting of their dwindling band, but found for the first time that some of the group had defected. Caskie Stinnett, editor of *Holiday,* Hubbard Cobb, editor of *American Home,* and John Collins, publisher of *American Home,* flatly refused further participation.

The final convulsive gasp of the group came the night of October 11. A Western Union telegram was composed and sent to Albert Linton. These are its significant portions:

1051P EDT OCT 11 64 PA 130
A706 S Y NA873 NL PD 30 Extra New York N.Y. 11
ALBERT LINTON, PHONE AND MAIL
315 EAST OAK ST MOORESTOWN NJER
  THE MOST RECENT ACTION OF THE EXECUTIVE COMMITTEE IN SUS-
PENDING CLAY BLAIR AND MARVIN KANTOR FROM THEIR DUTIES AT
CURTIS HAS PRECIPITATED A FLOOD OF BAD REACTION AMONG ADVER-
TISERS IN THE CURTIS MAGAZINES.
  WE BELIEVE THAT THE EXECUTIVE COMMITTEE HAS ACTED ON THE
BASIS OF MISINFORMATION IN THIS MATTER, AN ACTION WHICH WE ARE
INFORMED WAS TAKEN UNDER PRESSURE FROM MR. SEMENENKO. SINCE
THIS ACTION APPARENTLY WAS BASED ON CHARGES THAT MESSRS
BLAIR AND KANTOR WERE RESPONSIBLE FOR THE LEAK OF INFORMA-
TION ABOUT THE CURTIS MANAGEMENT CRISIS TO THE NEW YORK
TIMES, WE URGENTLY WANT THE EXECUTIVE COMMITTEE TO BE AWARE
OF THE FOLLOWING:
  WE HAVE POSITIVE PROOF, BACKED UP BY THE NEW YORK TIMES
REPORTER WHO INTERVIEWED HIM, THAT THE ORIGINAL LEAK OF IN-
FORMATION TO THE NEWSPAPER CAME FROM MR. SEMENENKO HIMSELF.
THE NEW YORK TIMES REPORTER CONCERNED HAS ATTEMPTED TO
CONTACT YOU TODAY TO CONFIRM THIS FACT.
  IN VIEW OF THE ACTION OF THE EXECUTIVE COMMITTEE IN THE

SUSPENSION OF THESE TWO MEN, OUR CONFIDENCE IN THE EXECUTIVE COMMITTEE AS EXPRESSED IN OUR LETTER OF SEPTEMBER 29 HAS BEEN SHAKEN.

WE MUST INSIST THAT MESSRS BLAIR AND KANTOR BE REINSTATED IMMEDIATELY. WE ALSO WISH TO AMEND OUR ORIGINAL RESOLUTION AGAINST MR. CULLIGAN. WE INSIST THAT HE BE REMOVED ENTIRELY FROM THE CURTIS PUBLISHING COMPANY.

THESE TWO ACTIONS ARE A CONDITION OF OUR CONTINUED EMPLOYMENT. H G WALKER   OTTO FRIEDRICH   J S CONNORS   WILLIAM A EMERSON JR   JESS L BALLEW   RICHARD M KING   CHARLES D THOMAS JOSEPH R WELTY   DON A SCHANCHE   J M HADLEY   NORMAN R RITTER

Missing, for obvious reasons, were the names of Blair and Kantor. Two new names appeared for the first time, two lower-echelon associates of Jesse Ballew—Joseph Welty and Richard King, host for the meetings in New York City. I do not believe there is any better evidence of the unreality of the whole situation than that telegram. A group of adults charged that a banker, who had a great deal to lose by the disruption of Curtis, was responsible for the leak. The group delivered a public ultimatum given by them to the press simultaneously. Only from a bedlam could such gibberish come.

Much of the thrust of the plot to take over frittered away from October 11 on. Two editors, Stinnett and Cobb, and one publisher, Collins, defected. Blair and Kantor were suspended. Some elements of the press—*The Wall Street Journal, Advertising Age, The World Telegram and Sun* (now defunct), and others—came through, but not enough to repair the damage. I was badly hurt, and I knew it.

10

Suddenly, like entering the eye of the hurricane, I had a period of enforced review and introspection. My rebuttal was delivered on October 9. The board meeting at which the Investigating Committee was to make its report was scheduled for October 19. Though I was still chairman of the board, president, and chief executive officer, my position during those ten days was extremely odd. For the first time in twenty-five years I had little to do.

Kantor and Blair, suspended and not permitted into their offices, set up a command post nearby and held daily strategy meetings with their co-conspirators. However, the dream of conquest was over; in retrospect, several of the group had developed guilt feelings and defected—Stinnett, Cobb, Collins, Friedrich, Emerson. Schanche cut loose from Blair, burrowed into the *Holiday* setting, and almost survived.

The Investigating Committee went into action and "held court" in Philadelphia, calling in all the signatories of the letter to grill them about their knowledge of the charges. They were astonished to learn that most signers did not remember the full contents of the attack letter they signed, nor had they seen the "supporting evidence."

(Otto Friedrich, articles editor of the *Post,* wrote me April 9, 1969: "Most of the accusations . . . involve charges I've never heard of." Even so, he had signed the attack letter.)

One of the last signers told the committee that he had made "a terrible mistake" in signing the letter, and offered his resignation on the spot to make amends. This was John Collins, publisher of *American Home.*

As reports came back to me, it seemed the situation was shaping up as a solid victory for me. Soon, all the charges were dismissed, save the question of "several joint ventures," which Milton Gould insisted was the whole crux of the matter.

But something was wrong in the equation. I learned that Maurice Poppei, "Clifford's man," was sitting with Albert Linton during the discussions of these joint-venture deals, and he was fogging up the matter of his own advance approvals of the deals before I had approved them.

Then I got a tip that Allison Page, of the law firm, who also approved them in advance, had said, "If I knew then what I know now, I might not have approved them." I recall a cold shiver when I heard the Page comment.

Something else was wrong, too. Not a single director stepped strongly forward in my defense in the interim. I had a lot of time to think during those ten days in October—and out of the deep recesses of my memory came the moving memory of my meeting with Bob MacNeal when I tried to console him the day I was made president. Suddenly I thought, "My God, this is the same board that knuckled under to Gould's ultimatum on MacNeal."

I did live in a fool's paradise at times during that period, reasoning that the effective directors were working quietly on my behalf in the background—even imagining that the Curtis-Bok family might come to my aid in gratitude for my saving them about $40 million in common and preferred stock values. I kidded myself into believing that the $78 million in advertising I had sold, the cost saving of $13 million a year, the six months' profit by March 1964, and—most of all—the $38 million refinancing plan that I alone engineered, would weigh heavily on the scale. These hopes dwindled, then disappeared, and a sense of helplessness developed as I saw my future at Curtis in the hands of Albert Linton and Moreau D. Brown—now infiltrated and surrounded by Poppei, Page, and Gould (Kantor's friend and lawyer).

The reports from Madison Avenue were depressing. Many of the faithful supporters of the *Post* and Curtis were finally conceding that Curtis had reached the end of the road as the fateful day of the board meeting, October 19, approached. I was close to admitting that I was finished as the effective head of Curtis, no matter what the Investigating Committee reported, but I felt that I had to do something, anything, to stem the advertising tide. So I made a series of advertising agency calls, saying, "The public doesn't care about Blair, Kantor, or Culligan. Curtis magazines are still a great value. Please don't let the internecine warfare affect your media judgment." They had some effect. I got quite a few letters and vocal comments somewhat along the lines expressed by Archibald McG. Foster, now president of the Ted Bates Agency.

He wrote:

> I do recollect your coming before us at the height of the
> crisis and speaking to us in a most frank and modest way of
> the future of Curtis and your hopes for it, at the very
> moment when you yourself were being shown the door. That
> was a magnificent display of loyalty, wisdom, and your fine
> human qualities.
>
> Sincerely yours,

As the board meeting neared, I visited Semenenko again and
told him of my belief that I had outlived my usefulness at Curtis—
as president, at least. Releasing him from any last-ditch fight on
my behalf, I reminded him of my introduction of Ed Miller,
publisher of *McCall's*, to him. Six weeks earlier, I had sent Miller
to see Serge as a replacement for Kantor, whom I had been determined to fire after the fall selling season was over. Now, I gave
Miller the strongest possible recommendation as my replacement
as president. Semenenko asked me to see Raymond McGranahan
of the Times-Mirror organization in Los Angeles, whom he had
been evaluating as a new top executive for another of his companies. I saw McGranahan and liked him, but told Semenenko that
Miller would be far superior, taking into account the awful problems of Curtis in the *Post* war (Blair-Kantor *vs.* Culligan) period. I
also told Semenenko I would stay on as chairman as long as I
could be useful. This was not charity or plaster saintliness on my
part. I wanted to protect my deferred income and stock options.

In one other self-evaluating session, I asked, "Why did Blair
and Kantor do it the *way* they did?" A single word flashed out—
"Kamikaze!" I thought, "It *was* a suicide attack. They couldn't
win. They had to be killed. But they took me with them."

On October 18, the day before my judgment by the board, I
got a call from my friend John Burns, for whom I had worked at
NBC. He was president of RCA at the time. Like Pat Weaver (who
did so much for NBC for so little reward), John Burns had picked
up the management reins at RCA when it was in a state of great
disarray, having had several product failures in too short a time.
Burns did a remarkable job of setting RCA on the course that gave
it huge growth and profit. He made millionaires of some subordinates who later criticized him. Burns and General Sarnoff
differed on an issue on which no difference was possible, and

Burns left RCA; to this date he has not received the acclaim he deserved.

Burns asked me to his office where we chatted briefly about families and golf. Then, with great friendship and compassion, he said, "Joe, you'd better get yourself psychologically set for your first major defeat."

I guess I gulped, maybe stammered. He went on. "There has been too much press, too much rumor, too much bitterness, for you to survive at Curtis. The board must take the easy way out."

I can't remember my reply, but I will never forget his next words: "Joe, success is wonderful, but it doesn't build character. You'll come out of this a better man."

I realized later, as I made the long two-hour trip to Philadelphia that afternoon, October 18, that John had synthesized what my instincts had been telling me: I was finished at Curtis; it was just a matter of time.

I had been asked the day before by Cary Bok to attend an informal meeting of "some directors," as he put it, in his apartment the night before the board meeting, around eight o'clock. After I had checked into the Warwick Hotel, I called him and said cheerily, "Hello, Cary, what time do you want me at your place?"

His chilling answer: "Joe, a group of us have been meeting for some time. The meeting is about over. Really no need for you to come."

"That sounds ominous, Cary."

He said, "Joe, we think it would be better all around if you resigned as president tomorrow."

"Thanks, Cary," I said. "I'll think about it."

I got to my office at Curtis early on the morning of the board meeting, for I needed answers to a few questions before making the final decision to resign. Albert Linton and I had always met for a few minutes before each board meeting for a briefing. This time I made notes of our conversation.

"Joe," Linton said, "because of the nature of this meeting, I'd suggest you do not act as chairman, for obvious reasons. We'd like Curtis Barkes to chair this meeting. It would make a better public record."

I agreed. The handwriting was getting larger. I asked Linton about his report of the investigation.

"All the charges are without any foundation," he replied. "But you'll get a mild rebuke for some joint-venture deals. That's all I can tell you now."

"Will Curtis honor my contract in all respects if I resign as president?"

"Yes. The Executive Committee will make it official—in writing."

"And I'll continue as chairman of the board?" I asked.

Linton answered, "Yes. That will also be put in writing."

"What about Blair and Kantor?"

"They will be fired as soon as the meeting opens," Linton said.

"In that case, Albert," I told him, "I will resign as president before the meeting ends."

We shook hands, then walked down one flight to the board-room.

The meeting went like clockwork. Linton read the report of the Investigating Committee. It was lengthy, but the essence was put forth by Linton and Brown later in the official letter to me closing out the investigation. This letter is reproduced here in its entirety.

LETTER FROM INVESTIGATING COMMITTEE

Mr. Matthew J. Culligan:

We, the undersigned, were appointed by the Board of the Curtis Publishing Company as a Special Committee to examine charges made against you in a letter signed by Clay Blair, Jr., and Marvin D. Kantor and by a number of their key subordinates.

The examination revealed no irregularity on your part (as could be inferred from the wording of the letter) nor any profiting by you personally from Curtis business transactions. It did reveal a very few joint-venture cases which, although they had been cleared with counsel, involved what the Committee felt were errors of business judgment. However, the Committee does not feel that the errors were such as to warrant your dismissal from the Office of President as demanded in the letter nor to justify the vituperative language used in the letter.

Your voluntary resignation as President was to expedite the appointment of a successor to that office in line with your prior recommendation that someone be found to furnish the Company with additional administrative personnel.

> *(Signed)* Moreau D. Brown
> M. Albert Linton
>
> Members of the Investigating
> Committee of the Board of
> Directors, Curtis Publishing Co.

Then a motion was made by Cary Bok that Messrs. Blair and Kantor be separated from the company for "gross insubordination and an attempt, through coercion to seize control of the company." The board voted "Aye," Blair and Kantor said "Nay." They sat there— Blair with a stunned, glazed look; Kantor, intense, with an eye-blink rate many times normal, white and drained.

After they were fired, I offered my resignation as president and chief executive officer, remaining as chairman of the board. The meeting ended. I walked up to Blair and said, "Clay, I hear you are going to write a book about this. Make it good—it will be my annuity," and walked away. That was the last time I saw Blair.

True to his word, Linton drafted a statement signed by the Executive Committee, continuing me as board chairman and stating that my contract would be "honored without exception."

In any rational situation, this should have been the end of the Curtis-Culligan story. The president of a public corporation had been accused of mismanagement by two directors, who were also employees. They were supported in their charges by a few subordinates who depended on them for promotions and raises, a not unanticipated development. The accused president had demanded an investigation by his peers. The investigation was made and completed, and the Investigating Committee reported in writing that the charges were without foundation. The insurgents who had "created the bomb" were fired when the bomb exploded. The president, realizing his mistakes and his liability, resigned to make way for a successor, willing to be kicked upstairs if useful. *Finis?*

Not at Curtis—there was still hell to pay.

It was fully expected that Ed Miller, publisher of *McCall's*, or Raymond MacGranahan of the Los Angeles Times-Mirror Company would accept the presidency as soon as I resigned. Semenenko regarded Miller now as a top prospect, and other directors had been impressed. In a brilliant stroke, Semenenko paired Miller with the exceptionally talented Newton Minow, lawyer, former head of the Federal Communications Commission. This one-two punch was just what Curtis needed for recovery and revitalization.

Only one small problem: *Miller wouldn't take the job.* He turned down a salary of $150,000, options on at least 50,000 shares of stock, and carte blanche as far as authority was concerned. I believe, though Ed Miller never told me this, that he knew what kind of a job I had done, and did not want to get overly exposed with the sort of people he judged the Curtis board to be, on the basis of their abandonment of me when the chips were down. Minow also refused to join Curtis in any full-time capacity, but did become a director. As a stockholder, I breathed a deep sigh of relief, knowing Minow would be on the Curtis board.

Then MacGranahan, who had seemed eager for the job, dropped out of the running for the presidency and settled for a directorship. The Curtis board and Serge Semenenko came to the horrendous conclusion that *no one* remotely qualified for the job would touch Curtis as president. In utter frustration and desperation, the Executive Committee (of which I was still a member) concluded that Curtis would come unglued unless a president were named immediately. Irony of ironies—the only man around who knew anything about Curtis overall, the man who caused the original editors' rebellion, the cause of the editorial manifesto, J. M. "Mac-the-Knife" Clifford, was named president and chief executive officer, with me as chairman of the board.

That arrangement might have worked—but Clifford would have none of it. Despite a written agreement with the Executive Committee that my contract be honored to the letter and that I would remain as chairman of the board, Clifford told the board, in my absence—and these are his actual words—"Culligan will stay as chairman over my dead body."

I did not at this point in time know why Clifford had to get me out of Curtis.

Over the next few weeks, there were various harassments too petty to discuss here. I mentioned them to Serge Semenenko. He advised me, as a friend, to spare myself further indignities. He was right. I resigned as chairman of the board on January 17, 1965, with the resignation taking effect officially on January 17, 1966, because of my contract provision of one-year prior written notice.

I left Curtis with no real regrets, quite relieved to sever connections with Linton, Franklin, Fuller, Cary Bok, Clifford, and Poppei. But I had not lost my fondness for M. D. Brown, though I was saddened by his failure to leap to my defense when I was attacked. Brown was smarter, more practical, more experienced in business than the other Philadelphia directors, and he knew better than any of them, the dire condition of Curtis when I came in. He kept a scorecard on personnel and dollar reductions at every board meeting. He was with me when I persuaded the banks to renew the $22 million loan and add another $4 million; and he knew that I had engineered an incredible tour de force by single-handedly getting Serge Semenenko interested in refinancing Curtis. Understandably, his failure to stand up for me was a great disappointment.

However, I still had my health, and my family was progressing well. Curtis owed me $500,000 on the day I resigned as chairman; I also had options on 70,000 shares of Curtis stock. I had not broken my word about silence during the abrasive press treatment stimulated by Blair and Kantor. Nor had I whined or blamed others for my mistakes. So I felt I could look forward to a whole new career.

But Curtis wouldn't go away! It took almost a year after my resignation on January 17, 1965, for me to find out how Clifford and Poppei had successfully undermined me. Clifford cannily had chosen the night of October 18, 1964, for his move. The occasion was the meeting in Cary Bok's apartment, described earlier, the meeting from which I was deliberately excluded. I never would have found out if it had not been for the poor manners of Clifford. In a display of pettiness, he refused to pay a small legal bill, which was coincident with the attack on me by Blair and Kantor and my defense against the attack. The Curtis bylaws provided that any director would be indemnified for expenses incurred as a director unless he was found guilty of some misconduct.

When Blair and Kantor attacked me, I had used Bill Coogan of Sullivan, Donovan, Hanrahan, McGovern & Lane to defend me. (As already mentioned, I had brought Coogan into the Curtis situation earlier because of the mess in the Gould-Strubing feud.) Coogan handled the assembling of the material for my defense against the charges, and he billed Curtis for his work. When I decided to resign also as chairman of the board, Coogan handled the negotiations with Curtis for my orderly withdrawal, and again submitted a bill to Curtis for his services. Clifford refused to pay the legal bill for the second part of Coogan's assignment, contending that the lawyer's work from that point on had been purely for my personal benefit.

Deciding to teach Clifford a lesson, I instructed Coogan to take the matter to compulsory arbitration, as provided by my contract. This decision proved of great value to me, since it is doubtful that I would in any other way ever have learned why some of the Curtis directors deserted me after I had been officially cleared on the Blair-Kantor charges.

The arbitrator, Mr. Manuel Maxwell, was a very high type of lawyer. The arbitration proceeding was held in his own law office conference room, and he set the mood for the meeting with a charming, skillful introduction, but left no doubt that he was and would be in full control of the situation at all times.

Bill Coogan presented my side of the case, putting in evidence the letter from Albert Linton and Moreau Brown saying that the charges of mismanagement were without foundation. This letter also stated that I had resigned to expedite the selection of a new president. The premise was clear, therefore, that the legal bills for the services that followed were simply a continuation of my defense and a direct result of the Blair-Kantor attack.

Allison Page, of Pepper, Hamilton and Scheetz, represented Curtis during the arbitration. He felt he had to destroy my claim that the charges were adjudged to be without foundation; and to do this he mentioned the rump meeting October 18 at the apartment of Cary Bok. Page tried to introduce a small portion of this meeting to discredit me. He told the arbitrator that after Albert Linton had read his report and advised the group, his Committee had found the charges to be without foundation; "several directors" expressed the opinion that even though the Blair-Kantor charges were false, it had been discovered during the investigation that I had "lost control of the management of Curtis."

I felt a surge of excitement. My instincts signaled that this was the whole crux of the matter, and I had a quick caucus with my lawyer. I told him we must find out how such a conclusion could have been promoted and by whom. Here was the first inkling of what had really gone on during the investigation and at the meeting at Cary Bok's apartment! I started to burn, then calmed down when I realized the cul-de-sac into which Page had led himself.

Pulling a copy of the Curtis organization chart out of my briefcase, I suggested to Coogan that he show it to Page and the arbitrator, point to each division, then ask specifically, "Did any directors say Mr. Culligan had lost control of *this* division?" Coogan went through the entire organization chart, mentioning each division—Circulation, Manufacturing, Distribution, Paper Company, Special Projects—and repeating the same question. Page, more flustered at each question, had to say "No"; that I had not lost control. Under oath, he painted himself into a corner, and was forced to admit that only Clifford and Poppei, whose loyalty should have been to me, the man they reported to, gave their partisan view of the situation to the, on the whole, flocculent group of frightened, old Philadelphia directors assembled in Bok's apartment.

Coogan then demanded that Page describe the rest of the meeting in Bok's apartment. Page tried to decline. Manuel Maxwell said, "Mr. Page, you brought the matter up. Please answer the questions."

Coogan tried to pin Page down on the exact identity of the Philadelphia directors to whom Clifford and Poppei had made their derogatory statements. Page could not remember exactly. Finally, bit by bit, Coogan dragged the story out of him. Clifford and Poppei had, during the investigation, continued to criticize me to some of the directors, and at the critical point had delivered an ultimatum. It was not as brazenly stated as the Blair-Kantor ultimatum, but it was more effective. Under oath, Page stated that Clifford and Poppei had said, "We cannot continue to do our jobs if Culligan remains as president and chief executive officer."

Coogan made Allison Page repeat the comment several times. As he said it the third time, a remembrance of poor Bob MacNeal flashed through my mind. Some of the same Philadelphia directors who had bowed to the ultimatum of Milton Gould in that instance had in my case let themselves be influenced by Clifford and Poppei, the very ones who had been the original cause of the editors' anger. Moreau Brown later told me *he* did not hear Clifford and Poppei make the above remark. I believed him.

The thing that disgusted me most, however, was my exclusion from the meeting at which my fate was decided. Though I had been invited, at some time between 4:00 P.M., the time I left

New York, and 7:00 P.M., when I called Cary Bok, the die was cast. The meeting had obviously been called early, and the Clifford-Poppei pressure exerted, while I was known to be on the way by car from New York.

The arbitration proceeding concluded with an excellent summation by Coogan, who stated with good effect: "So here was the chief executive officer, invited to take over Curtis when it was ninety days from bankruptcy, cleared of the management charges, given a mild rebuke for business deals approved in advance by legal and financial counsel, undermined by the very men, Clifford and Poppei, who caused the major problem—two men who used the ultimatum to gain their ends."

Mr. Manuel Maxwell, the arbitrator, took about five days to reply. His decision came in this form:

AMERICAN ARBITRATION ASSOCIATION, Administrator
Commercial Arbitration Tribunal

AWARD OF ARBITRATOR

In the Matter of the Arbitration Between
MATTHEW J. CULLIGAN
            AND
THE CURTIS PUBLISHING COMPANY
Case Number: 1310-0352-66

I, THE UNDERSIGNED ARBITRATOR, having been designated in accordance with the Arbitration Agreement entered into by the above-named Parties, and dated July 9, 1962 as amended, and having been duly sworn and having duly heard the proofs and allegations of the parties, AWARD, as follows:

1. THE CURTIS PUBLISHING COMPANY, hereinafter referred to as CURTIS, shall pay to MATTHEW J. CULLIGAN, hereinafter referred to as CULLIGAN, the sum of FIVE THOUSAND FORTY-ONE DOLLARS AND TWENTY CENTS ($5,041.20), without interest.

2. The administrative fees of the American Arbitration Association totaling TWO HUNDRED FIFTY-ONE DOLLARS AND TWENTY-FOUR CENTS ($251.24) shall be borne by CURTIS. Therefore, CURTIS shall pay to CULLIGAN the additional sum of ONE HUNDRED FIFTY-ONE DOLLARS AND TWENTY-FOUR CENTS ($151.24) for its

share of said fees previously advanced by CULLIGAN to the Association, and CURTIS shall pay the American Arbitration Association the sum of ONE HUNDRED DOLLARS ($100.00) for the balance of said fees still due to the Association.

3. This Award is in full settlement of all claims submitted to this Arbitration.

MANUEL MAXWELL

The amount of money was *de minimus,* as lawyers like to say, meaning "insignificant," compared to the revelation that Clifford and Poppei, aided by Allison Page, "drove a blade into my back" while I was facing the other enemies—Blair, Kantor, Emerson, Ballew, et al.

In an effort to confirm the fact that the chief financial officer of Curtis, Maurice Poppei, had approved the Admiral and Longines joint-venture programs *before* I accepted them, I asked Albert Linton to confront Poppei specifically on this issue. Linton did, and reported to me in a letter of March 21, 1966, as follows:

We [meaning himself and Moreau D. Brown] never had any doubt that Mr. Poppei had informed you that he had approved the Longines and Admiral programs. You would not have entered into them if you had not been assured that they would produce a net return for Curtis.

I will never know if Linton and Brown had twinges of conscience about the mild rebuke they issued, when they realized that corporate legal counsel and the chief financial officer had approved those programs in advance.

Final incontrovertible evidence of the sponginess of will of the Philadelphia directors was to come in 1968 and 1969. They had bowed to Gould in 1962, acquiesced to Clifford and Poppei in 1964, and they surrendered totally to Martin Ackerman in 1968-1969.

11

Curtis was chaotic when I took it over in 1962. There was a division between New York and Philadelphia, between Editorial and Marketing, between Editorial and Manufacturing, between Manufacturing and Circulation, between Manufacturing and Papermaking, between Editorial and Circulation, between the Philadelphia directors and the "outside directors," between the treasurer and the comptroller, between the treasurer and the lending banks, between Robert MacNeal and Cary Bok, and between Robert MacNeal and Milton Gould. They did not understand one another, and the will to understand was lacking.

However, past and current history proves that a common enemy can make even the bitterest partisans work and fight together *for a time*. The common enemy of all the factions at Curtis in May, June, and July of 1962 was bankruptcy. The Paul Revere of that hour was Milton Gould, the fast-thinking, fast-talking master of the quid pro quo.

The victors were the Curtis stockholders and Curtis employees. The losers, who did not fight very hard or well because they had no heart for a fight, were Robert MacNeal and his key aides in Curtis management.

Milton Gould, with the common enemy closing in, roused the Curtis directors to the consideration of action. Then he drove them to action by the oldest technique of unarmed conflict—the ultimatum. Of course ultimatums usually work only when the opposition is in an indefensible position. But the Curtis directors were in an indefensible position and knew it. Gould held the common enemy off for about five weeks, then brought me forward as the field commander to rout it.

Time, text, and talk have obscured the fact that I was brought into Curtis to save it from bankruptcy and dismemberment. And that I did, despite some mistakes made under pressure-cooker conditions. I rallied the dissident groups both inside and outside Curtis and got the Curtis staff to work as a team for over eighteen months. I found and secured a powerful ally, Serge

Semenenko, and by December 1964, had led Curtis to a position in which every victory over bankruptcy was assured and a victory over dismemberment a strong possibility. I did not have the wisdom or power to complete the job, or save myself within Curtis. I often have wondered if anyone under sixty would have been that wise.

Serge Semenenko put it best. After I had resigned as president and was debating resigning as board chairman, Serge said, "The tragic fact is, my dear Joe, that *right now* you are the best equipped executive in the country to run Curtis."

The Curtis experience was an accelerated-use test of a human being. I became wiser because of it. Writing this book has made me wiser still, I think, and more tolerant. Also more tranquil. The story is now out of my system and, hopefully, no longer an internal irritant. I can report to my doctor on the therapeutic value of his prescription. It has seemed to me that chagrin and an inclination to self-pity have drained away through my fingertips, as I have written and rewritten this narrative. My golf swing, always a faultless barometer of my inner feelings, has improved greatly, though I am still too preoccupied with thoughts other than golf ever to score very well again. I intend not to look back at Curtis, except for guidance, particularly for guidance in not repeating any of the major mistakes I made there.

A potentially valuable conviction has intruded on me more and more during the work on this book. Curtis almost failed. In such a disaster, everyone connected with Curtis would have been blamed indiscriminately. This would have been unfair. Coherent criticism can now be leveled at one area—Curtis' top management and the Philadelphia directors. The editors did not fail (except Fuoss and Blair with the "New *Post*.") The printers, circulators, and papermakers did not fail; they were simply badly led.

It has become alarmingly obvious that magazines, newspapers, radio, and television should be directed by editorialists and marketeers, *backed up* by financiers and administrators. The latter are at least one step removed from, and often insensitive to, changes in public taste. They should never be in command. Curtis, like Time Inc., NBC, CBS, Cowles, *The New York Times,* Scripps-Howard, *The New Yorker,* and *Reader's Digest,* was built by great editors and marketeers. Tragically, it came under the total domination of financial experts and administrators when Walter Fuller became president. The deadening hand of bureaucracy held the throttle.

Three superior men built Curtis: Cyrus Curtis, George Horace Lorimer, and Edward Bok. Curtis was a marketeer; Lorimer and Bok, editors. Four of their successors almost ruined it—Walter Fuller, former president; Robert MacNeal, former president; Cary Bok, senior executive vice-president—absentee; and Albert Linton, senior director.

Fuller's contribution to the decline of Curtis was the compulsion to integrate and become independent of the outside world. In an age of rapidly advancing technology, this could have had only one result: the loss of the ability to compete with other publishers who could take full advantage of the intense competition in the paper and printing industries. Fuller also erred heroically in refusing to get Curtis into television when construction permits were being urged on the company. Like most of his associates, he believed, "If you can't read it, it's no good."

MacNeal's sins were mostly of omission. He adhered fanatically to the pattern of Fuller. He too missed many opportunities to get into television and encouraged an astounding bureaucracy. And he boarded up the windows of his mind, let his editors encyst, and then seemed to watch, hypnotized, as Curtis slipped— first almost imperceptibly, then with noticeable speed, and finally with sickening momentum—to the brink of bankruptcy.

Albert Linton did not function adequately as the protector of the rights of stockholders during his two decades on the Curtis Board. He failed to learn anything about the publishing or advertising businesses in that time. He had no influence on MacNeal, who confused and confounded him with statistics. When the fissures appeared in the walls, and the foundations started to crumble, Linton could do little but attend board meetings, bewail the worsening financial picture, and snap at the financial officer. I now pity the old Philadelphia directors, though earlier, I did not.

Cary Bok, whom I admit I understand the least, permitted a fatal power vacuum to develop. Nature, we're told, abhors vacuums, and there were scores of predators sniffing around Curtis who knew about power vacuums and how to exploit them. If, as I have heard, Cary Bok deserted Curtis for reasons of health, then he should have had tough pragmatic nominees on the Curtis board to protect the family interests. His failure to do this is a dark monument to his lack of intelligence or concern.

These four permitted Curtis to be led to the brink of bankruptcy by the early summer of 1962.

Then, with time running out and the liquidators about to run in, three new, oddly matched men saved Curtis from bankruptcy—the first time in mid-1962. They were, in order of appearance though not necessarily of importance, Milton Gould, Matthew J. Culligan, and John M. Clifford. Fourteen months later I saved Curtis from another bankruptcy threat by finding, persuading, and securing a powerful ally, the banker extraordinaire, Serge Semenenko. Gould, Clifford, Semenenko, and I saved Curtis by exercising some very special skills each of us developed over a varying number of years.

Gould's specialty was corporate law, strategy, and tactics; Clifford's was unusual talent for cost reduction and control. Serge Semenenko's critical skill was banking. My contribution was leadership, organization, recruiting, editorial and marketing supervision, and personal selling and public relations. I like to think that my part of the equation was special, for in addition to what I did personally, I brought Semenenko and Clifford into Curtis. I batted 100 percent with Semenenko, but only 50 percent with Clifford. He did a superb job in the role for which I hired him—cost reduction and control. However, he did mortal damage to me and himself and Curtis by his personality and his inability to comprehend creative people and the creative function.

If aspiring young leaders will take just one lesson from this book, it will be worth the purchase price and reading time spent: *There are problems in business so serious that the necessary radical solutions create other problems that only a very wise man can anticipate.* I simply did not have that wisdom. I do now, I think.

I now know that the Curtis adventure, though I was president less than four years, will continue to affect me for the rest of my life. The initial, intermediate, and continuing interest of the press and the business, banking, and legal fields have seen and will see to that. I also realize now that any man who gets into a leadership position ultimately becomes three people: the one he is, the one circumstances force him to be, and the one the press and his friends and enemies make him appear to be. My trial by press is not over. One book, a dreary piece by an author named Joseph

Golden, has already quickly passed through the book market un-
acclaimed. It abounded in snide rumor and inaccuracy.

The press treatment of my final resignation was less abrasive
than the coverage during the controversy, though only *The Wall
Street Journal* paid any attention to my accomplishments. *The
Journal* listed many of the advances made by Curtis under my
direction. Toward the end, some elements of the press turned on
Blair and Kantor. One, in particular, charged them with "an
incredible act of sabotage."

Blair and I had only one thing in common, a disdain for
Time. His probably started when he left that magazine. My dislike
began when a financial executive of *Time* convinced a friend in the
upper echelons of the First National City Bank of New York that
Curtis would fail, a deliberately selfish and destructive act calculated to force Curtis into bankruptcy. His motive was to reduce
competition for *Life* and acquire pieces of Curtis on the auction
block. My dislike grew when the *Time* system made me look like
an idiot by using my picture and the unrelated, out-of-context
quotation described earlier. It became white hot when, in November 1965, eleven months after I left Curtis, *Time* said, for no
discernible journalistic reason: "The Culligan-Blair regime was a
textbook example of mismanagement."

I boiled at that statement. But I thought of Jim Linen, for
whom I had a lot of respect, and Andrew Heiskell, for whom I had
respect and affection, and calmed down long enough to write a
letter to Linen. In it, I complained about the senseless, needless
cruelty of the *Time* statement, and its incompleteness and inaccuracy. I received no answer, no telephone call—nothing—from
Linen in answer to my letter, but it was so unlike him to be other
than a thoughtful gentleman that I waited, then wrote another
letter January 31:

Mr. James Linen
Time Inc.
Time & Life Building
Avenue of Americas at 50th St.
New York, N.Y.

Dear Jim:

Supplementing my letter of December 8th, I have learned
from excellent, non-Curtis sources that Curtis may shortly

announce a modest profit for the 4th Quarter of 1965. A profit for the entire year of 1966 is also possible.

This condition has been brought by the efficient and dedicated labors of the management which, without exception, was either promoted from within by me or brought to Curtis by me, with the help of the banks, auditors, and management consultants employed by me.

Also, all the programs of development, innovation, and reduction of facilities which brought about these results were originated, researched, and launched during my stewardship.

These facts, plus those enumerated in my letter of December 8th, make grossly unfair, libelous, and malicious the *Time* Magazine's charge of a "textbook example of mismanagement" leveled against me in the November 26th issue.

Is not a retraction in order?

Sincerely,
Matthew J. Culligan

Linen answered, explaining the delay in his reply—he had been in Europe. Not at all soothing, however, was his final sentence responding to my demand for a retraction. He wrote, "The editors stand by their story."

I wrote back immediately asking Linen to have the editors tell me that in person. Bernie Auer, then publisher of *Time,* sent me a note inviting me to meet the editors in question. The meeting was held in the last week of May, in 1966, in his office. Otto Fuerbringer, managing editor of *Time* was there, and several editors from the business and press departments. I wasted no time. I told them I had had experience with editors before in such meetings, and was quite familiar with the game usually played when the visitor had made his speech and left. Invariably, some editor would say, "Very interesting—but what did he say?" Then everyone would laugh and go back to his private world. I said I did not want that to happen.

Then I handed each one a copy of a memo prepared specially for the meeting. For extra emphasis, I read it to them while they followed in their copies:

TO: Mr. Bernhard M. Auer
    Mr. Otto Fuerbringer

FROM: Matthew J. Culligan

Gentlemen:

In the November 26, 1965, issue of *Time* was the statement—
"The Culligan-Blair regime was a textbook example of mismanagement."

This statement was false and libelous. Coming almost a year
after the Curtis controversy, it was also unnecessary and brutal. I
asked Mr. James Linen for a retraction. Mr. Linen advised that
"the Editors stand by their story."

The statement "The Culligan-Blair regime was a textbook
example of mismanagement" is false for these reasons:

1. There was no "Culligan-Blair regime." Blair was promoted
to VP Editorial of all Curtis magazines by the Curtis Board at
the same meeting at which Mr. MacNeal was removed. Blair
remained in that job. I appointed him also editor of the *Post*.
He had no operating responsibility or authority outside Editorial. J. M. Clifford, brought to Curtis from RCA by me, was
executive vice-president, and first in line of succession, as
provided by the Curtis bylaws. If any label were indicated, it
would be the "Culligan-Clifford regime."

2. Time Inc. editors cannot cite libel suits as an example of
mismanagement without self-incrimination.

3. *Time* editors cannot cite the impropriety, or irresponsibili-
ty, of one editor as an example of mismanagement without
hypocrisy in the light of the Joseph Purtel case.

4. As president of Curtis, I operated within the limits of the
bylaws of Curtis and operating procedures established by the
board of directors. The Curtis board approved every resolution offered by me in more than thirty monthly board
meetings. Not one resolution submitted by me was refused
by the board.

5. The Curtis bylaws dictated that all capital expenditures be
approved, in advance, by the board of directors. This rule was
never violated.

6. I employed the following organizations as consultants in

special areas, and invariably accepted their recommendations:

Price Waterhouse . . . . Public Accountants
Fenton B. Turck & Company, Inc. . . . . . Paper Operations,
                          Printing, Cost Reduction
Booz, Allen & Hamilton . . . . Executive Search,
                    Marketing Study—Paper Company
Loeb, Rhoades & Co. . . . . Sale of Paper Company
Blyth & Company . . . . Sale of Paper Company
Allan Anderson, Toronto, Canada . . . . . Mining Consultant
Pepper, Hamilton and Scheetz . . . . Libel & General
                                     Corporate Counsel
Shea, Gallop, Climenko & Gould . . . . . Legal Counsel—N.Y.
Cahill Gordon . . . . Legal Counsel—Special
Dewey, Ballantine, Bushby,
Palmer & Wood . . . . Legal Counsel—Special
Georgeson & Company . . . . Proxy Solicitation

7. With the signing of the $38 million bank loan in December
1963, every decision of any consequence had to be approved
in advance by the banks via The First National Bank of
Boston, the agent bank. This rule was never violated.

8. I organized and personally directed the proxy drive to
permit recapitalization of Curtis. Management won an unprecedented shareholder vote.

9. A Finance Committee of the board of directors was recommended by me and established to guide me in all financial
matters. On this committee were: Curtis Barkes of United Air
Lines, M. D. Brown of Brown Bros. Harriman, and J. M.
Clifford. Every significant decision in financial affairs was
approved by this committee and by the full board of directors.

10. Negotiations for the sale of the New York & Penn paper
company were started by me with Mr. Donald Leslie, chairman of the Hammermill Paper Company. This sale was completed in the fall of 1965, and opened the way for the biweekly frequency of the *Post*.

11. Acting on the advice of Allan Anderson (mining consultant) and corporate legal counsel, Curtis management avoided
entanglement in the many problems brought about by the
discovery of ore in Canada. The trial of the eleven employees
of TGS is a case in point.

12. Negotiations for the sale of Canadian ore and timber were

opened by me with the principals of TGS. These negotiations were successfully completed in the spring of 1966. The state and federal courts approved this sale as "fair and equitable." The reduction in the bank debt of Curtis is partly responsible for the restoration of confidence in Curtis.

13. The Curtis Circulation Company was reorganized by me in the fall of 1962. Its president, G. B. McCombs, was appointed by me, with advance approval of the board. The record of accomplishment of this division under McCombs speaks eloquently for itself.

14. The Curtis Book Division was formed by me under the direction of Bill Buckley. It was profitable in 1965.

15. The entire present Curtis management was either promoted from within or recruited by me, with the single exception of John Mack Carter. However,

16. I brought Mr. Edward Miller into the Curtis situation. His recommendation of John Mack Carter as editor of the *Ladies' Home Journal* was a major contribution.

17. The need for more administrative management was reported by me to the board of directors and the banks months before the Kantor-Blair controversy. Boyden Associates was employed by me with approval of the board and Serge Semenenko—to locate a new president. I planned to move to chairman of the board.

18. The Blair-Kantor charges of mismanagement were investigated by a special committee of the board. The letter to me from Messrs. Albert Linton and Moreau D. Brown regarding their findings is reproduced here in its entirety:

> We, the undersigned, were appointed by the Board of the Curtis Publishing Company as a Special Committee to examine charges made against you in a letter signed by Clay Blair, Jr., and Marvin D. Kantor and by a number of their key subordinates.

> The examination revealed no irregularity on your part (as could be inferred from the wording of the letter) nor any profiting by you personally from Curtis business transactions. It did reveal a very few joint-venture cases which, although they had been cleared with counsel, involved what the Committee felt were errors of business judgment.

However, the Committee does not feel that the errors were such as to warrant your dismissal from the Office of President as demanded in the letter nor to justify the vituperative language used in the letter.

Your voluntary resignation as President was to expedite the appointment of a successor to that office in line with your prior recommendation that someone be found to furnish the Company with additional administrative personnel.

19. During my stewardship a complete employee benefits program was introduced. It included life insurance, a stock option plan, and pension program improvements.

20. The inherited loss for 1962 was $18.9 million. The loss in my first full calendar year, 1963, was $3.4—a reduction of $15.5 million. A profit for six consecutive months was achieved for the October 1963 through March 1964 period. The Curtis Board voted me a substantial bonus and salary increase in December 1963.

21. I resigned as president when I became a liability to Curtis due to the public controversy.

22. The Curtis board of directors directed the new president to honor my contract without exception.

23. Curtis will achieve a profit in 1966 under the dedicated management of the executives I either recruited from without or promoted from within. All the present programs were developed and started during my term as president.

I looked at my audience often during the reading and noticed Fuerbringer's face setting grimly with suppressed rage, starting with my comment about Joseph Purtel, one of his editors. Purtel had been discharged in the wake of an SEC investigation.

After I finished reading the memo, I asked if there were any questions. There was only one—"Why didn't you tell your side of the story during the Blair attack?" When I explained I had given my word to the board that I would remain silent in the interest of Curtis, I seemed to detect in the eyes of the questioner a look of pity for my being such a fool.

There was no further comment from Fuerbringer or the others; they did not object to a single claim I made. I left feeling quite frustrated—as though I had been punching feather pillows. I realized I had simply wasted my time, except for one fact. My memo charging *Time* with libel and offering definitive evidence of their libel now stands on the record. Auer and Fuerbringer made no reply to me in person, nor did they reply later in writing.

For a brief period I thought of suing *Time* for libel, since a trial would enable me to get people under oath who had things to say that could only benefit me. I called a very famous lawyer with whom I had a most rewarding (for me, anyway) relationship, and asked his advice on the matter. He won my permanent gratitude by his warmth and graciousness in our discussion. Even more important, he had his senior law partners study the question in great depth. After they had made a detailed analysis of the situation, he sent me their report and his conclusions, from which the following is excerpted or paraphrased:

> Unhappily I am compelled to say that I have not changed the tentative views I expressed to you at lunch. The libel was a tiny portion of a total article which has been forgotten by practically everybody. A libel suit would remind everybody of this single sentence, and then the progress of the litigation would extend over weeks, months, and probably years, reminding them constantly. However false the statement, there is nothing that could compensate you for the grief which would inevitably follow this lawsuit. If you lost it—and all lawsuits of any kind are susceptible of being lost—it would be a blow from which it would be hard to recover.
>
> There are a whole lot of sayings in the language about letting sleeping dogs lie and the dead bury the past, etc. You are alive, happy, busily employed, prosperous, and well regarded. My advice is to forget the lawsuit.

The libel specialists' report was something like this:

> The article was published in the *Time* issue of November 26, 1965. The only language in the article on which any libel action could be founded is that which reads:

> "Curtis has also made a substantial recovery from the internal revolt that shook it last year. When Editor in Chief Clay Blair, Jr., whose policy of 'sophisticated muckraking' involved the *Post* in costly libel suits, tried to oust President

Matthew Culligan, Curtis dumped them both. But not before the entire organization had suffered. The Culligan-Blair regime was a textbook example of mismanagement."

We believe that this is libel per se; and therefore, it would not be necessary to allege or prove any "special damages."

Time would undoubtedly rely upon two standard defenses, namely: (1) truth and (2) fair comment.

The defense of truth, if they can prove it, is valid. As for "fair comment," there is a question. But it might be held to be available, and that defense will likewise present issues of fact for resolution at a trial.

The defense of "fair comment" can be defeated if it can be established that malice was involved on the part of the publisher. However, we doubt that a charge of malice could be sustained. As a whole, the statement concerning the Culligan-Blair regime does not have the earmarks of what is customarily regarded as malicious.

The defense of "fair comment" can defeat a libel action even though the defense of truth fails.

When it comes to the question of whether it would be advisable to prosecute a libel action, there are important practical considerations, despite the fact the charges are false, and we list below some of the factors that we believe should be carefully weighed.

It must be assumed that a jury trial will be involved, and that fact should be considered in light of the subject matter involved. The subject matter here involved is not simple. It does not deal with a charge about some specific act or some bad character trait. Rather, it deals with the whole complex area of what is involved in good management and mismanagement of a large publishing corporation, which includes financial, business, editorial, personnel, morale, public relations, and other matters.

This complexity makes it difficult to predict what a jury would do. No matter what the truth is as to who or what was responsible for the condition of the company, fingers can be pointed, even without justification, in one direction or another; and just how it will all add up in the jury's minds is hard to predict.

Moreover, the language "the Culligan-Blair regime" is adroit. That language lends itself to an explanation by *Time* that it was Mr. Blair who performed directly the acts of mismanagement and that Mr. Culligan is responsible in the sense of having been the president and not having taken steps to fire Mr. Blair. If this anticipated strategy on the part of *Time* is employed, Mr. Culligan might find himself in the position of having to defend Mr. Blair in order to defend himself; and we understand that Mr. Culligan would never want to find himself in that position.

Another factor to be considered is the harassment and the publicity that will be involved. *Time* can, and it must be assumed would, take extensive depositions and obtain extensive discoveries of records, correspondence, etc. Those discoveries would probably cover all of the directors of the company, especially those in office during the period involved, and also other key officers and employees. After all this, there will be, of course, the trial itself.

We believe that, as a general rule, the prosecution of a libel action with respect to business affairs will subject the person bringing the action to more harm than good.

At the same time, knowing that this well-known lawyer's firm traveled the highest road of ethical, responsible conduct, I got in touch with another lawyer known especially for his flexibility and aggressiveness, and asked him the same question: "Should I sue *Time* for libel?"

He almost immediately said No, and he gave me nine reasons, from memory. I made him repeat the litany while I made notes:

First: You take your whole life into the courtroom when you sue for libel.

Second: Intimidation and harassment will be employed to discourage you.

Third: No one can predict what a jury will do. They may find for *Time*—no matter what the evidence.

Fourth: Even if you win, they can hang you up for years with appeals.

Fifth: What will the "Establishment" think of you for suing, even if you win?

Sixth: Can you afford a long legal battle?

Seventh: What will be the effect on your business career?

Eighth: What is the attitude of your present employer?

Ninth: Can you get witnesses to testify?

This set of questions, plus the other opinion, settled the matter for me.

The character assassination Blair and Kantor attempted worried me considerably. Though the business mismanagement charges were serious, of course, personal attacks spread by rumor and innuendo could have been far deadlier. I could not take full-time employment at all during 1965 (that was my year of notice at Curtis), so I became a consultant to Sherman and Bruce Burns of the William J. Burns International Detective Agency. I developed a plan, stimulated by Sherman Burns, that laid out the change in security from the uniformed guard to servo-electro-mechanical techniques. My Burns connection helped me overcome some of the rumors because the Burns reputation for integrity, plus their research facility, aided me inferentially.

I took more direct action in early 1965. A good friend, Leonard Marks, was appointed head of the United States Information Agency. Knowing of the near impossibility of his job, I volunteered to be of any assistance possible. Marks asked me to become a Public Member of a State Department inspection team, and an ambassador, a top-level USIA careerist, and I went to Central America. Using Costa Rica as headquarters, we conducted a thorough survey of diplomatic, military, and economic aid, and cultural and intelligence activities. I traveled on an official passport, which required a complete FBI and CIA investigation. When the facts about my assignment became known, and also the FBI-CIA clearance, the last vestige of the Blair-Kantor-Emerson accusations was dispelled.

There were other rumors, distortions, and hatchet jobs, but I will not bother to go into them. The record speaks for me.

In September 1966, I acquired 10 percent of the stock of the Mutual Broadcasting Company and became president and chief executive officer. This was a useful temporary alliance for me, providing me an opportunity to learn whether I still had the comeback touch. I found it had not deserted me. To meet the payroll in March 1967, it was necessary to borrow $50,000—the Mutual Broadcasting System was broke. With the help of Jim Fuchs, whom I brought over from Curtis, I turned in a pretax profit of $715,000 for the year ending July 1968, the first large profit Mutual had earned in the post-television era.

During all this time I was keeping a close watch on Curtis and its people, for financial and emotional reasons. Of the original group I met in July 1962, Robert MacNeal, Walter Fuller, and Albert Linton are now dead. Clay Blair dropped completely out of sight for almost three years. His name reappeared later as the author of a book about James Earl Ray, the accused killer of Martin Luther King, and of the already mentioned book, *The Board Room.*

Only recently did I learn what probably happened to Marvin Kantor to change him from a cool, smart, financial entrepreneur into a plotter with Blair and a "forgotten man" in the business world. A long-term acquaintance of mine, Ted Lloyd, a television producer, phoned me one day and asked, "Who do you think called me this morning?" in his finest conspiratorial tone. Kantor had called Lloyd to ask him to get me to meet him (Kantor) for supper or lunch. I told Ted: "I wouldn't meet Kantor under any circumstances. He cost me a million dollars; he's no ――― good."

"Joe, you always told me to stay in touch with my enemies for my own protection," Lloyd replied. "Don't you think you should take your own advice?"

I thought it over, and finally decided that it might be to my advantage to see Kantor and to note well what was said. Perhaps I could learn something about the power drive that I did not know. The meeting was arranged by Lloyd for the Terrace Club of LaGuardia Airport. I went out early, en route to Washington, D.C. Kantor came in, approached me uncertainly and put out his hand as though he was not sure whether it would be shaken or shaken off. He said, "It's been a long time."

After some inconsequential talk, he finally said, "Joe, my only reason for wanting to see you was to tell you I made a terrible mistake and that I'm sorry."

"It takes a man to admit that, Marvin," I answered. "Thanks.

But I'll never understand how you could have been suckered into such a bonehead ploy."

Kantor pursed his lips and shook his head sadly, but did not answer.

I continued, "I knew virtually everything that was going on with Blair and a few of the editors. After all, he had hired them; they owed everything to him—raises, promotions, the works. His attack would have been laughable if you had not got the publishers involved."

"I know, I know," Kantor said. "There was a kind of madness in the air—I don't know what happened to me."

"Well, it was a good lesson to me," I said. "I thought I had protected myself fully. Semenenko was on my side. I knew that by this time the Curtis board was sure Blair was as unpredictable as a rockslide, and that you were untrustworthy. You just don't expect your opponents to commit suicide," I went on, "and that was my fatal misjudgment. I also didn't believe that you and Blair would take the story to the press."

All Kantor could do was shake his head and grimace. He talked briefly about his future plans, and then we parted.

Kantor's actions and words indicated sincere repentance, but I remembered other words and actions, particularly after I had hired him in the midst of his greatest personal crisis, the collapse of his company, Williston & Beane. I had to weigh the possibility that his performance now might be a coldly deliberate bit of acting, particularly when he ended our meeting with a remark about looking around for something to do in the publishing business again. He might have reasoned, rightly, that no one would hire him without a check of his previous jobs. If he sought a job of any importance, it would be virtually certain that I would be asked about him. I have since learned that he bought a small, technical book publishing company in Holland.

Jesse Ballew became connected with a controlled circulation women's magazine, which failed. Bill Emerson, who must have an outsize survival instinct, was editor of the *Post* until it failed. He was a good "undertaker."

Dave Thomas and Don Schanche, Blair's close friends, once editors of the *Journal* and *Holiday* respectively, have apparently fallen into obscurity.

Serge Semenenko, with whom I have maintained close ties, is now board chairman of the Chemway Corporation, and I am on his board of directors, as I explained in the Prologue. It is a delight to see Serge operate as the head of a company in a competitive business.

J. M. Clifford, after remaining president of Curtis for almost two years, was forced out of the company and has returned to his avocado farm in California. Maurice Poppei has retired, and Gloria Swett was fired.

The dismemberment of Curtis has been entirely completed under the direction of Martin Ackerman, a tough, skillful, well-financed, unemotional man who seems to have had a master plan for the dissolution of the company. Serious charges have been made against Ackerman by Cary Bok and representatives of the Curtis preferred shareholders and Curtis union employees.

For historical reasons, a few months after the attack letter, I wrote to some of the signatories of the letter suggesting they purge themselves:

THE CURTIS PUBLISHING COMPANY

MEMORANDUM   January 4, 1965

To: Messrs. Emerson, Schanche, Thomas, Stinnett, Hadley, Connors, Friedrich, Collins, Cobb, Hite

From: Mr. Culligan

The damage sustained by Curtis and by me personally cannot be undone, and I have no present intention to defend myself publicly any more than I have done in the past since I do not feel that public statements on my behalf with attendant publicity and speculation would constitute any discernible benefit to Curtis. However, Messrs. Kantor and Blair have indicated the probability of additional publicity because of their announced intention to publish a book involving the Curtis publications and possibly you and other top personnel. Since I have received very clear indications that you might have signed the letter of September 29, 1964, without mature consideration and under pressure from these two men, your superiors, you might well consider it appropriate, especially in view of the copy of the enclosed letter from Messrs. Linton and Brown, dated November 30, 1964, to mitigate the damages resulting from the September 29th letter by sending me a written explanation of, or more properly an apology for, your association with such a letter.

I have been advised that most of you signed the letter of September 29th under such circumstances that you do not have a copy of it presently available to you and that you might not presently recall some of the offensive language used therein. If this be the case, Mr. William H. Coogan of Sullivan, Donovan, Hanrahan, McGovern & Lane, 70 Pine Street, New York 5, N.Y., will, upon request, exhibit a copy of this letter to you or your attorney so that you may have a reasonable basis for whatever action you may deem appropriate to take.

In addition to several oral apologies, I have already received a copy of a letter in the above vein from one of the signatories, and I suggest that, particularly in view of the enclosed letter, a similar disassociation on your part from this ill-conceived venture might well be in your best interests. Failing to hear from you, I can only conclude that you stand by the outrageously libelous statements made in the letter of September 29th.

MJC:st

Hubbard Cobb, editor of *American Home*, and Caskie Stinnett replied. Stinnett wrote, in part:

January 19, 1965

Dear Joe:

It is now easier in retrospect to get a somewhat better view of what has gone on here in the past chaotic six months, and I would like to say that the part I played in the "editors' rebellion" has brought me no satisfaction of any kind. Although I spoke out in several meetings in favor of moderation and once refused to participate in a joint action, I still feel that I owe you a personal apology for the actions ultimately taken. . . .

In any event, I earnestly ask your forgiveness for the part I played in these events. I value your friendship and would like very much to have it restored.

Sincerely,

(*Signed*) Caskie Stinnett

But it was the reply of John Collins, publisher of *American Home*, that touched me most deeply. Less than two weeks after he signed the letter attacking me, he wrote:

October 15, 1964

Dear Joe:
    The full story of the events preceding the current embarrassing publicity for all of us, and most especially the company, may never be revealed.
    In any case, Joe, I want you to know that because of my involvement, no matter how brief, or what the circumstances, I have offered my resignation to the Executive Committee in case they, or you, wish to accept it.
    In addition, I offer you a deep and heartfelt apology for a misguided moment.

Most sincerely,

(*Signed*) John L. Collins

Apologies when one makes mistakes and injures another are admirable. Collins went further. He tried to make amends, a kind of penance, by offering his resignation, though he was a married man with young children and no independent means. The statistic is depressing—only one out of fourteen tried to make amends, but nevertheless, in an imperfect world in which all of us have "a misguided moment" or many, the Collins gesture was symbolic.
    Thus I conclude "The Curtis-Culligan Story"—one with no heroes and no villains.
    A group of intelligent, articulate, highly charged human beings were magnetized to a potentially explosive situation. Some were motivated by the avocative nature of communications—some by soaring ambition, some by hope of financial reward, some by a thirst for the power and influence that flows from public information media.
    The situation did explode.
    Blair, Emerson, Kantor, Clifford, Poppei, and Gould, the few who hurt me most deeply, all made major contributions to Curtis between 1961 and 1964. In all fairness, I have tried to record those contributions.
    Of the old Curtis board of directors, three have died; the others have slipped, unscathed, out of focus, having only their consciences to remind them of what they failed to do from 1945

to 1960, and of how they capitulated when threatened with ultimatums in 1962, 1964, and 1968.

For me, I know my "place shall never be with those cold and timid souls who know neither victory nor defeat."

Index

of people mentioned in the text